THE AMERICAN RENAISSANCE

THE AMERICAN RENAISSANCE
1876–1917

The Brooklyn Museum

Distributed by Pantheon Books, New York

Cover:
Interior of dome, reading room, The
Library of Congress, Washington, D.C.
Murals (1895–1896): *The Evolution of
Civilization* and (in the lantern) *Human
Understanding* by Edwin Blashfield
(1848–1936).
Oil on canvas.
PHOTO: Robert C. Lautman.

Frontispiece:
FIG. 1
Dressing room, John D. Rockefeller
house, New York City, *circa* 1880.
COLLECTION: Museum of the City of
New York.
PHOTO: Scott Hyde.

Published for the exhibition
The American Renaissance: 1876–1917

The Brooklyn Museum, New York
October 13–December 30, 1979

National Collection of Fine Arts,
Smithsonian Institution, Washington, D.C.
February 22–April 20, 1980

The Fine Arts Museums of San Francisco, California
M.H. de Young Memorial Museum
May 31–August 10, 1980

The Denver Art Museum, Colorado
September 24–November 30, 1980

Library of Congress Cataloging in Publication Data

Brooklyn Institute of Arts and Sciences.   Museum.
   The American renaissance, 1876-1917.

"Published for the exhibition the American
renaissance, 1876-1917."
   Bibliography: p.
   Includes index.
   1. Art, American—Exhibitions.   2. Art, Modern—
19th century—United States—Exhibitions.   3. Art,
Modern—20th Century—United States—Exhibitions.
I. Title.
N6510.B75 1979   709'.73'074014723   79-13325
ISBN 0-394-50807-6 (Pantheon)
ISBN 0-87273-075-1 (Brooklyn Museum) pbk.

Designed and published by The Brooklyn
Museum, Division of Publications and
Marketing Services, Eastern Parkway,
Brooklyn, New York 11238. Printed in the USA
by the Falcon Press, Philadelphia.

© 1979 The Brooklyn Museum, a department of
the Brooklyn Institute of Arts and Sciences.

This exhibition was made possible with the aid of a grant from the National
Endowment for the Humanities in Washington, D.C., a Federal agency.

Contents

Foreword

FIG. 2
The Museum of the Brooklyn Institute
of Arts and Sciences, 1893. McKim,
Mead and White, architects. Rendering
by Francis L. V. Hoppin (1867–1941).
Gouache and ink on paper;
62.9 x 166.4 cm. (24¾ x 65½ in.)
COLLECTION: The Brooklyn Museum,
New York.

Standing on the grounds of the World's Columbian Exposition in Chicago in 1893, Henry Adams, the illustrious intellectual chronicler of the period, was astounded by the accomplishment of the American artistic community as expressed by the achievement of the Fair. In consideration of their having forged a new intellectual order reversing a five hundred–year trend, Adams suggested that in the future people would "talk about Hunt and Richardson, La Farge and St. Gaudens, Burnham and McKim and Stanford White when their politicians and millionaires were otherwise forgotten." Well, their politicians ranged from Boss Tweed to Teddy Roosevelt, and among their millionaires were the Astors, Whitneys, Morgans, Fricks, and McCormicks—and we have certainly not forgotten them. Regrettably, we have not remembered the artists, sculptors, architects, designers, and draughtsmen quite as well.

Michael Botwinick

DIRECTOR, THE BROOKLYN MUSEUM

We have long since recognized the social and political figures of the age and understood the excitement and vibrancy of the course of the nation from 1876 to 1917. It was a period in which consolidation gave perhaps as much satisfaction to citizens as expansion had to the preceding generation. During this period America acquired the sophistication to use the extraordinary resources unleashed by the twin engines of Westward Expansion and the Industrial Revolution.

It has been harder to recognize that the painters, sculptors, architects, designers, and draughtsmen were very much an integral part of the life of the period. They were not passive recorders of change. On the contrary, they represented the leading edge of the sense of confidence and intellectual prowess that characterized America's coming of age.

It was the artistic community that elevated the sights of the period, that informed the young culture that it was not some rough frontier society, rich in natural resources, but primitive in other respects. The artistic community announced that America was the unique synthesis. It proclaimed that a new society based on science, industry, commerce, rational order, democracy, and the great energy of the people had been forged and was the legitimate heir to the concept of the Renaissance.

As nineteenth-century historians rediscovered the Renaissance and drew endless parallels between it and the American civilization that emerged after the Civil War, the most cogent expressions of the latest "new Athens" came from its artists. What is potentially different and most exciting about their role is the notion that it was this artistic community itself that actually helped forge the new vision. We are accustomed to seeing the artist as an inevitable reflection of his time. But as we re-examine the late nineteenth century, the sense of the artist as a participant is most striking. And while every age has been directly stimulated by its artists, we more often see the literary artist at the core of intellectual ferment, while the visual artist has been seen as somewhat diffident, objective.

Maybe Henry Adams's musing is more convincing now. Recently the artist has appeared to be more deeply involved in the social, aesthetic, and philosophical issues of our time. This is not meant in the sense of "activist" involvement; rather, today artistic vision is again an essential intellectual ingredient in the evolution of contemporary thinking. Perhaps this has made it easier for us to see the artist of the American Renaissance.

If we can simultaneously shed our ambivalence about American Victorian style on the one hand and our ambivalence about America's growth into a world power on the other, we may see the artists of this time with more insight. They were not apologists or celebrants of the politics of a new order, but were fundamental believers in the process in which they were intimately involved. They did not believe that they were taking on a role reserved for them by some divine right. The vision of a great civilization was founded on their perception of the possibility of drawing together all of the fundamental elements present in America. They must have believed that they were indeed the new bearers of the torch of Western civilization.

In 1976 Richard Guy Wilson, Professor of Architectural History at The University of Virginia, and Dianne H. Pilgrim, Curator of Decorative Arts at The Brooklyn Museum, met at a Society of Architectural Historians meeting in Philadelphia. Professor Wilson broached the idea of an exhibition in honor of the one hundredth anniversary of the architectural firm of McKim, Mead and White. It seemed particularly appropriate to present the exhibition at The Brooklyn Museum, an institution so much affected by the energy of the nineteenth century and one that is housed in a Charles McKim building. As their notion of the exhibition expanded, it seemed an ideal time to reassess the art of the late nineteenth and early twentieth centuries. With the addition of Richard N. Murray, then Assistant to the Director at the National Collection of Fine Arts, now Director of the Birmingham Museum of Art, we had a team that could sift through literally thousands of objects to find those that best expressed the period. In the end, the scope and quantity of the material was so great that it could not be accommodated entirely by the exhibition, and the publication in hand stretches far beyond the show. It represents a successful attempt to create a comprehensive notion of the American Renaissance period. For this and for the exhibition they have created, we are much in debt to our authors.

We are grateful to the many collectors and institutions who have graciously lent to this show. Our requests often presented them with complicated situations, and in this regard, we give special thanks to John K. Howat of The Metropolitan Museum of Art. His commitment to this project was great enough for him to recommend lending generously despite conflicts with the opening of the Metropolitan's new American wing. Our gratitude goes to Brendan Gill for his constant support and encouragement. We also give special thanks to Dr. Joshua C. Taylor, Director of the National Collection of Fine Arts, for his early support and for his institution's involvement in the evolution of this project. Additionally, we are grateful to Thomas N. Maytham, Director of The Denver Art Museum, and Ian McKibbin White, Director of The Fine Arts Museums of San Francisco, and their staffs for making the tour of the exhibition possible.

PART I THE GREAT CIVILIZATION

Richard Guy Wilson

CHAPTER

1

Expressions of Identity

Hᵒw men perceive themselves influences what they see and how they create their surroundings. A people or a nation may identify or locate themselves in a variety of conceptual molds: particular religious or philosophical dogmas, the natural landscape, the existential here and now, or an epoch of the historic past. For Americans, the preoccupation with national identity has produced a varied body of commentary, literature, and art containing both superficial and profound statements on the nature of American culture. Typically, periods of intense physical and social change have led to alternating visions of the American experience. And while many periods can be pointed to, the era of the later nineteenth and early twentieth centuries has produced some of the more diverse expressions of American art. Here, within the same space-time continuum, exist the low-slung Prairie houses of Frank Lloyd Wright and the Renaissance palazzos of McKim, Mead and White; the futuristic compositions of Joseph Stella and the tradition-laden paintings of Kenyon Cox; the simplified oak furniture of Gustav Stickley and the Colonial Revival highbacks of A.H. Davenport. The visual and philosophical differences in these works have been viewed as representing on one side a nativistic, modern-oriented spirit, and on the other side, a conservative-academic viewpoint tied to stultified Old World traditions. Later generations have easily grasped the modern work, while the conservative work has been viewed as an anachronism caught in the web of the past and having little if any relation to American civilization and identity.

Yet the conservative, largely European-oriented art had an impact in its time; overwhelmingly popular, the art projected an image of culture and civilization that many people approved of. Partaking of the air of genteel idealism and higher service, the art also gave a sense of release from the stuffy confines of Victorianism. An art and architecture of superb craftsmanship was produced, one of wealth with tinges of exoticism that delighted in ornamental richness for its own sake. Investigation of the art and the surrounding corpus of literature and activity indicates that many people felt it implied a special connection with the grand traditions of history representing what they identified as the "American Renaissance."[1]

The term "American Renaissance" concerns the identification by many Americans—painters, sculptors, architects, craftsmen, scholars, collectors, politicians, financeers, and industrialists—with the period of the European Renaissance and the feeling that the Renaissance spirit had been captured again in the United States. Concurrently, the Italian Renaissance (1420–1580) came into focus through the work of scholars and provided initial identification for many Americans. This was the Renaissance with a capital R. In time, other Renaissance manifestations were admired and seen as providing important models: France and England of the sixteenth through the eighteenth centuries, America in the formative years of the late seventeenth and eighteenth centuries, and other countries, including the original sources for the Renaissance, Greece and Rome.

FIG. 3 *Facing page:*
Infant Bacchus, circa 1880.
John La Farge (1835–1910).
Stained glass window; 226.5 x 114.0 cm.
(89⅛ x 44⅞ in.).
From the Kidder house, Beverly, Massachusetts.
COLLECTION: Museum of Fine Arts, Boston, Massachusetts, Gift of W. B. Thomas.

1   The term "American Renaissance," as will be explained below, came into usage in 1880. Historians have continued to use the term but not exclusively. See Ralph Henry Gabriel, ed., *The Pageant of America*, vol. 13,"The American Spirit in Architecture," Talbot F. Hamlin (New Haven, 1926), p. 165; Oliver W. Larkin, *Art and Life in America*, rev. ed. (New York, 1960), p. 293; and Howard Mumford Jones, "The Renaissance and American Origins," *Ideas in America* (Cam- bridge, Mass., 1945), pp. 140–151. This last is an especially important study to which this essay owes a great debt. An alternative usage of the term appears in F.O. Matthiessen, *American Renaissance: Art and Expression in the Age of Emerson and Whitman* (New York, 1941), which obviously covers a very different period.

Analogies with the Renaissance were obvious. The American robber baron had been preceded by the Italian and French merchant princes.[2] Artists found an affinity with the Renaissance, identifying each other in terms such as "Old Master" or with personalities such as Bramante and Benvenuto Cellini.[3] Many aspired to the Renaissance example: Stanford White designed buildings, magazine covers, jewelry, furniture, and picture frames; John La Farge painted, wrote art criticism and history, and designed stained-glass windows (Fig. 3) and interiors; Charles Adams Platt was an architect, landscape architect, painter, and etcher. The collaboration between architects, painters, sculptors, decorators, and landscape architects in world's fairs, public buildings, and city plans received confirmation by the example of the artistic unity in High Renaissance Rome. To some, the periods were comparable. Augustus Saint-Gaudens exclaimed after the initial planning session of the World's Columbian Exposition: "This is the greatest meeting of artists since the fifteenth century!"[4] The painter Theodore Robinson claimed that many of his comrades "persuaded themselves for a year or so that the days of the Italian Renaissance were revived on Manhattan Island."[5] The past spoke to today claimed Bernard Berenson, a Boston-educated boy soon to become the world authority on Renaissance art, who wrote in his first book: "We ourselves, because of our faith in science and the power of work, are instinctively in sympathy with the Renaissance. . . . the spirit which animates us was anticipated by the spirit of the Renaissance, and more than anticipated. That spirit seems like the small rough model after which ours is being fashioned."[6]

According to the ideas of the American Renaissance, the art of the past could provide useful sources for the development of a national American art. While the reliance on sources or authority would be important, what would be produced would be a unique American art; it would be tied together not only by styles, but also by a unity of tradition and approach. Senator James McMillan, the "father" of the 1901–1902 Senate Parks Commission Plan for Washington, D.C., predicted the future of governmental architecture: "It is the general opinion that for monumental work, Greece and Rome furnish the styles of architecture best adapted to serve the manifold wants of today, not only as to beauty and dignity, but as to utility."[7] To this end the American Academy in Rome was founded. Charles F. McKim, one of the prime leaders of the school, felt that just as other countries had gone to Rome to learn "the splendid standards of Classic and Renaissance art," so must Americans, and he added, "I pity the artist who does not feel humbled before its splendid examples of art."[8] But ultimately a new art resulted, for, as John La Farge claimed in speaking about the Academy: "We are going to be established in Rome. . . . This is in itself a statement that we too are rivals of all that has been done, and intend to rival all that shall be done, and we can then feel that the old cycle is closed and that a new one has begun."[9]

The American Renaissance, by both definition and action, was intensely nationalistic. It appropriated images and symbols of past civilizations and used them to create a magnificent American pageant. America became the culmination of history for an age that believed in progress. Prime Minister William Gladstone of England noted: "Europe may already see in North

2   Harry W. Desmond and Herbert Croly, *Stately Homes in America* (New York, 1903), p. 251; and Harold D. Cater, *Henry Adams and His Friends* (Boston, 1947), p. 404.

3   John La Farge was referred to as "'old master'" in a letter, Charles L. Freer to Jaccaci, quoted in Susan Hobbs, "John La Farge and the Genteel Tradition in American Art: 1875 to 1910," (Ph.D. diss., Cornell University, 1974), p. 74. Charles McKim was known as Bramante and his partner Stanford White as Benvenuto Cellini;

see Charles Moore, *The Life and Times of Charles Follen McKim* (Boston, 1929), p. 57. Another expression of identification, "Burnham was a Roman of the Augustinian age," is found in Charles Moore, *Daniel H. Burnham, Architect, Planner of Cities*, vol. 1 (Boston, 1921), p. 67. Moore was a participant in a number of the significant planning schemes of the period such as the Washington Plan of 1901–1902, the Chicago Plan of 1906–1909, and finally as member, 1910–1915, and then chairman, 1915–1937, of the Commission of Fine Arts.

America an immediate successor in the march of civilization."[10] The civilization envisaged for America was a public life, one of the street, the park, the square, or the mall, of large monuments, memorials, and public buildings in the eternal style, adorned with murals and sculptures personifying heroes and symbolizing virtue and enterprise. Several commentators of the period claimed the United States needed a national *Valhalla*, and in a sense this was attempted with the great arch in Grand Army Plaza in Brooklyn (Fig. 4), the projected "Pantheon" of national heroes in Washington, D.C., or the Hall of Fame at New York University.[11] The projected vision could be caught in a variety of places—ascending the stairs at the new Library of Congress,

FIG. 4
Soldiers' and Sailors' Memorial Arch, Grand Army Plaza, Brooklyn, New York, 1889–1892. John H. Duncan (1855–1929), and McKim, Mead and White, architects. Sculpture: (top) *Quadriga*, 1898, (south pedestals) *Army* and *Navy*, 1901, by Frederick MacMonnies (1863–1937); Bas-reliefs: (inside arch) *Lincoln*, 1895, by Thomas Eakins (1844–1916); *Grant*, 1895, by William O'Donovan. COLLECTION/PHOTO: The Library of Congress, Washington, D.C.

4   Quoted in Moore, *Daniel H. Burnham 1*, p. 47.
5   Quoted in Will H. Low, *A Chronicle of Friendships* (New York, 1908), p. 285.
6   Bernard Berenson, *The Venetian Painters* (1894), reprinted in *The Italian Painters of the Renaissance* (Cleveland, 1957), p. iii.
7   Senator James McMillan, "The American Academy in Rome," *The North American Review* 174 (May 1902), p. 627.
8   Moore, *McKim*, p. 260.

9   "Mr. La Farge on Useless Art," *Architectural Record* XVII (April 1905), p. 347.
10   Quoted in Robert Kerr, "Supplement" to James Fergusson, *History of the Modern Styles of Architecture*, 3rd ed. (London, 1891), p. 373.
11   Edwin Blashfield, "A Word for Municipal Art," *Municipal Affairs* III (December 1899), p. 587; and George Kriehn, "The City Beautiful," *Municipal Affairs* III (December 1899), p. 599.

FIG. 5
*Arch of the Rising Sun from the
Court of the Universe,*
Panama-Pacific
International Exposition, San
Francisco,
1915. McKim, Mead and White,
architects.
Rendering by Jules Guerin
(1866–1946).
Watercolor on paper;
101.6 x 96.5 cm. (40 x 38 in.).
COLLECTION: San Francisco Public
Library, California.
PHOTO: Schopplein Studio.

FIG. 6
Viking ship with Manufactures
and Liberal Arts Building in
background, World's Columbian
Exposition, Chicago, 1893.
Charles Dudley Arnold (b. 1844),
photographer.
COLLECTION: Avery Library,
Columbia University, New York
City.

FIG. 7
Theodore Roosevelt, 1902.
John Singer Sargent (1856–1925).
Oil on canvas; 147.4 x 101.0 cm.
(58⅛ x 39¾ in.).
COLLECTION: The White House,
Washington, D.C.

FIG. 8
Columbia and Cuba, a study for a
magazine cover, *circa* 1898.
Kenyon Cox (1856–1919).
Pencil on paper; 31.8 x 20.3 cm.
(12½ x 8 in.).
COLLECTION: The Library of Congress,
Washington, D.C.

strolling on the Benjamin Franklin Parkway in Philadelphia, or visiting any of the dream cities of the great expositions that dotted the American landscape in these years: Buffalo, Saint Louis, San Francisco (Fig. 5), and others. Walking among the lagoons of the World's Columbian Exposition in Chicago, one could find a Viking ship (Fig. 6) lying next to backdrops of Imperial Rome, Renaissance Florence, Bourbon Paris, and the Far East. Literally all the history of mankind lay at the fingertips of Americans.

The American Renaissance can also be viewed as an imperialistic expression of American culture, not only in the appropriation of forms and symbols from foreign cultures, but also in the creation of the American empire. The Spanish-American War (Fig. 8), the Big Stick of Teddy Roosevelt (Fig. 7), the White Fleet (Fig. 9), the Panama Canal, the Latin American adventures of Woodrow Wilson, are all part of the breast-thumping spirit that could move the architect Stanford White, when reproached for importing so many art treasures to decorate homes, to claim: "In the past, dominant nations had always plundered works of art from their predecessors; . . . America was taking a leading place among nations and had, therefore, the right to obtain art wherever she could."[12]

12 Quoted in Lawrence G. White, *Sketches and Designs by Stanford White* (New York, 1920), pp. 24–25. The recognition of this aspect can be found in a number of places. One is a page from a European magazine of the period that is pasted in a McKim, Mead and White Office Album (vol. VII) devoted to the Charles H. Barney House (now in the Avery Library, Columbia University, New York City). Shown is a photo of a French Renaissance fireplace with the caption: "La cheminée d'Avignon dans la Salle d'Assemblée" and below this in large letters: "Dépouilles de la Vieille Europe Dans la Neuve Amérique." On the opposite page is a photograph of the same mantel in the Barney House. Also written in ink is the note, "W.R. Hearst—California," probably indicating that Hearst bought it from the Barney estate when the house was broken up. Edith Wharton was especially sensitive to this issue, and in *The Custom of the Country* (New York, 1913), she uses the forced sale of Boucher's famous Saint-Desert tapestries as a symbol of the transfer of power from the decaying old European aristocracy to the new American plutocrats.

businessmen's organizations. Patronage was especially the prerogative of the very rich. The Vanderbilt family, railroad and real estate entrepreneurs, were the quintessential patrons in the years 1876 to 1917, constructing a sequence of at least seventeen large houses, several of which cost in excess of $1,000,000, and at least one, Biltmore at Asheville, North Carolina, that cost $5,000,000. Society and wealth found an outlet in the vision of an American Renaissance, and among its patrons were the Astors, the Whitneys, the Morgans, the Goelets, the Rockefellers, the Fricks, the McCormicks, and others.

The artist played a leading role. He could provide a setting of leisured elegance bearing the patina of class and taste for people who were frequently one generation removed from overalls and shovel. Fittingly, the artist designed the currency of capitalism—Augustus Saint-Gaudens did the ten- and twenty-dollar gold pieces (Fig. 12), James E. Fraser did the Buffalo nickel, Victor D. Brenner did the Lincoln penny, Adolph Weinman did the Liberty dime, and Kenyon Cox did one-hundred–dollar bills (Fig. 13). The artist did not play an avant-garde role, rebelling against society and the inequalities of wealth. Rather, he became part of the elite, and Stanford White, John Singer Sargent, and Edith Wharton stare out from the photographs of costume balls, the opening of *Tosca*, and twelve-course dinners.

Integral to the elitism was a spirit of *noblesse oblige* that found a release in the grand public gestures of the American Renaissance. The period saw the foundation of many of America's major cultural institutions: libraries, museums, orchestras, operas, and universities. These were founded by the wealthy through direct gifts and philanthropic organizations. The large European Old Master holdings of many art museums were tied directly to

FIG. 12
Twenty-dollar gold piece,
Liberty side, 1907.
Augustus Saint-Gaudens (1848–1907).
Diameter 3.2 cm. (1¼ in.).
COLLECTION: American Numismatic
Society, New York City.

FIG. 13
Design for a one-hundred–dollar bill, 1912.
Kenyon Cox (1856–1919).
Pencil on paper; 30.1 x 45.7 cm.
(11⅞ x 18 in.).
COLLECTION: The Cleveland Museum of
Art, Ohio, Gift of J. D. Cox.

FIG. 14
*Chicago, View Looking West, of the
Proposed Civic Center Plaza and
Buildings, Showing It as the Center of
the System of Arteries of Circulation
and of the Surrounding Country.* From
The Plan of Chicago, 1909.
Daniel H. Burnham (1846–1912) and
Edward H. Bennett (1874–1954), planners.
Rendering by Jules Guerin (1866–1946).
Watercolor on paper; 74.6 x 104.8 cm.
(29 ³⁄₈ x 41 ¹⁄₄ in.).
COLLECTION: Burnham Library of
Architecture, The Art Institute of
Chicago, Illinois.

both a vision of America equaling the Old World in artistic property and to the pillaging activities of Bernard Berenson, Stanford White, and others. Reform and the City Beautiful movement interlocked; the same individuals promoted educating the immigrant and beautifying elevated railroad stations. Messages of patriotism and citizenship were implicit in all of the public art and architecture. Frequently funded by the wealthy, the gestures can be interpreted cynically as a subterfuge by the elite to patronize the masses or idealistically as an acknowledgment of wealth's responsibilities. [13]

In civic art—the City Beautiful movement—can be found a culmination of the aspirations of the American Renaissance impulse. The roots of the City Beautiful movement can be traced back to mid-century and the various park and sanitary commissions, but it was in the 1890s that the dual influences of the period's expositions and various reform movements crystallized a new sense of civic grandeur. The appeal in its widest bounds was "to bring order out of the chaos." [14] Across the country, municipal art leagues, civic improvement associations, and city art commissions were formed that combined the talents of businessmen, architects, artists, and the new professions of city planner and administrator. The movement followed the United States flag overseas to the new colony of the Philippines, where Daniel H. Burnham and Edward H. Bennett produced plans for Manila and the new capital at Baguio. Burnham and Bennett's plan for Chicago, 1906–1909, is certainly the best known and one of the most comprehensive of the City Beautiful plans (Fig. 14). The impressionistic renderings by Jules Guerin and Fernand Janin turn grubby commercial Chicago into Parisian boulevards and Venetian lagoons. Consummating the City Beautiful movement was Congress's establishment of the Commission of Fine Arts in 1910 to guide the development of Washington, D.C., and to carry forward the work of Senator James McMillan's Park Commission of 1901–1902 (Fig. 49).

The large civic beautification and decorative schemes were portrayed as quintessentially "American and democratic." [15] Will Low, a leading muralist, claimed that "every American artist . . . should be born with a missionary spirit," and with all seriousness wrote that the White City of Chicago represented "a realization that art of the people, for the people had come to us." [16] In the large public building with a comprehensive decorative scheme, the American identity was found; or as Edwin Blashfield, another muralist, wrote: "The names of public buildings are the century-marks of the ages. . . . wherever the footprints of the spirit of civilization have rested most firmly some milestone of human progress has risen to be called the Parthenon or Notre Dame, Giotto's Tower or Louvre, and to teach from within and without, by proportion and scale, by picture and statue, the history of the people who build it; to celebrate patriotism, inculcate morals, and to stand as the visible concrete symbol of high endeavor." [17]

In buildings such as The Boston Public Library (1887–1895; Fig. 15), can be grasped most firmly the aspirations of the American Renaissance. Financed with public funds but supported by the cultural and economic elite of Boston, the building, in their eyes and the eyes of its creator, Charles McKim, ranked on a par with any of the great monuments of the past. Built in the form of a large Renaissance palazzo, the calm form and light pink

13 In 1878 an article in *Atlantic Monthly* (quoted in Neil Harris, *The Land of Contrasts 1880–1901* [New York, 1970], p. 19) complained that workers had begun to regard "works of art and instruments of high culture, with all the possessions and surroundings of people of wealth and refinement, as causes and symbols of the laborer's poverty and degradation, and therefore as things to be hated."

14 Daniel H. Burnham and Edward H. Bennett, *The Plan of Chicago*, ed. Charles H. Moore (Chicago, 1909), pp. 1, 2.
15 Blashfield, "A Word for Municipal Art," p. 583.
16 Will H. Low, *A Painter's Progress* (New York, 1910), pp. 193, 251. A similar gloss on Lincoln's Gettysburg Address was used by Louis Sullivan in "The Tall Office Building Artistically Considered" (1896) in *Kindergarten Chats and Other Writings* (1947), p. 213.

17 Edwin H. Blashfield, *Mural Painting in America* (New York, 1913), p. 18.
18 The special significance of the public library can be found articulated in A.D.F. Hamlin, "The Ten Most Beautiful Buildings in the United States," *The Brochure Series of Architectural Illustrations* I (January 1900), p. 8; and Helen L. Horowitz, *Culture and the City: Cultural Philanthropy in Chicago from the 1880s to 1917* (Lexington, 1976), p. 113.

FIG. 15
The Boston Public Library, 1887–1895.
McKim, Mead and White, architects.
COLLECTION/PHOTO: The Library of
Congress, Washington, D.C.

FIG. 16
Entrance, The Boston Public Library,
1887–1895. McKim, Mead and White,
architects. Statues of *Science* and
Art by Bela Pratt (1867–1917); relief
panels over doors by Augustus
Saint-Gaudens (1848–1907); central
panel and seal designed by Kenyon
Cox (1856–1919) and executed by
Augustus Saint-Gaudens; rondels by
Domingo Mora.
COLLECTION/PHOTO: The Library of
Congress, Washington, D.C.

23

FIG. 17
Delivery room, The Boston Public
Library, 1887–1895. McKim, Mead and
White, architects. Murals: *The Quest of
the Holy Grail*, 1895–1901, by Edwin
Austin Abbey (1852–1911).
COLLECTION/PHOTO: The Library of
Congress, Washington, D.C.

Milford granite exterior contrast with the dark colors and excited pictur-
esqueness of its neighbors. Encrusted with fragments and memories of
European origins, the building stands aloof and withdrawn, a sanctum of
idealism against the clamor of Copley Square. To Ernest Fenollosa, the
library was "the veritable Assisi of American art."[19] At the entrance, twin
statues by Bela Pratt personifying Science and Art guard the main doors.
Above the central portal is the seal of the library, designed by Kenyon Cox
and carved by Augustus Saint-Gaudens. Also in the center, carved into the
belt course and the frieze are the phrases: "Free to All" and "Built by the
People and Dedicated to the Advancement of Learning" (Fig. 16). On the
inside, an elaborate spatial and decorative sequence contains statues and
memorials of heroes and patriots by Louis Saint-Gaudens and Frederick
MacMonnies and murals by artists such as Pierre Puvis de Chavannes (*Spirit
of Light*), Edwin Austin Abbey (*The Quest of the Holy Grail;* Fig. 17), and John
Singer Sargent (*The World's Religions*). Rich marbles, ceiling paintings in the
Venetian and Pompeiian styles, bronze doors by Daniel Chester French, the
noble spaces, the stairhall, the courtyard, and the great reading room across
the front give the message that this is not merely a building for housing
books, but a ritualistic center of civilization.

19 Ernest F. Fenollosa, *Mural Painting in the
Boston Public Library* (Boston, 1896), p. 25.

2

Cultural Conditions

Numerous terms and labels have been used to define the years between 1876 and 1917. They have ranged from colors: "Gilded," "Brown," and Mauve"; to themes: "Energy," "Confident," and "Excess." [1] For both the participants and for later commentators, the attempt has been to provide some sense of order and unity to a period of tremendous diversity and rapid change.

Rapid physical and social change has always been a characteristic of the United States, but in the later nineteenth century the tempo seemed to increase. In 1870 the country was essentially rural. Of its population of 39,905,000, only 24.8% could be classed as urban. America had little position in world affairs, and while the industrial revolution had produced some changes in work and transportation, still the majority of citizens did not live materially differently from their grandfathers. In 1910, forty years later, the population stood at 92,407,000 with the percentage of those living in urban areas at 45.5%. Cities had absorbed nearly a fivefold increase in population, from nine million in 1870 to forty-two million in 1910. Upward and outward moved the city. New or vastly enlarged communities came into being: the ghetto for the immigrant, the suburb for the middle and upper classes, and the resort or spa for those who could afford to escape. The United States became a major world power with overseas colonies; never again could it stand apart from international conflict. Life-styles were manifoldly affected by the industrial revolution and the accompanying technology—the flickering gas or kerosene lamp had given way to electricity and the light bulb, indoor plumbing came into use, telephones linked together great portions of the country, and in the hands of all classes of men and women were machines of previously unheard of ability and power: the washing machine, the typewriter, and the automobile. Socially, these changes were a product of the appearance of the large organization: the corporation, the large factory, the assembly line, and the faceless bureaucracy of the government. Men were now statistics—the individual disappeared to be replaced by the jargon of numbers, groups, and classes. To make an impact, you belonged to an organization, for work, for pleasure, for profession, or for interests. A sense of continuity, of knowing your employer, knowing who made your suit or grew your food, disappeared for many Americans. [2]

With the announcement in 1890 of the closing of the frontier, followed in 1893 by Frederick Jackson Turner's classic enunciation of the frontier's impact on American development (significantly, first delivered at the Congress of Historians at the World's Columbian Exposition), Americans could feel an era had ended. Certainly, the apparent rise of stratified classes—upper, middle, and lower—and the growing gap between the very wealthy and the poor belied the tenderly held myth of the worth of common man and equality. Faith in a government of impartial, intelligent, rational men was challenged by the rampant self-interest—if not outright corruption—shown by many politicians. On the surface, religion still seemed to be a unifying force, and tremendous building campaigns were undertaken, and church

1   Mark Twain (Samuel L. Clemens) and Charles D. Warner, *The Gilded Age: A Tale of Today* (New York, 1873); Lewis Mumford, *The Brown Decades: A Study of the Arts in America, 1865–1895* (New York, 1931); Thomas Beer, *The Mauve Decade: American Life at the End of the Nineteenth Century* (New York, 1926); Howard Mumford Jones, *The Age of Energy: Varieties of American Experience, 1865–1915* (New York, 1971); Van Wyck Brooks, *The Confident Years 1885–1915* (New York, 1952); and Ray W. Ginger, *Age of Excess: The United States from 1877 to 1914* (New York, 1965).

2   A number of these observations come from Daniel J. Boorstin, *The Americans: The Democratic Experience* (New York, 1973); H. Wayne Morgan, *Unity and Culture: The United States, 1877–1900* (Baltimore, 1971); and Robert H. Wiebe, *The Search for Order, 1877–1920* (New York, 1967).

attendance and the traditional pieties were still required for respectability. But underneath, cracks appeared. Darwinism and openly acknowledged atheism won converts, and secretly many people acknowledged a questioning attitude. Some Americans exuded a sense of confidence, a belief in the idea of progress, but beneath the surface, many felt "dislocation and bewilderment" and that unity or control appeared to be distended.[3]

Searching for unity or order, some Americans found an explanation in science, others found it in nature, both romantic, tamed nature and the raw Call of the Wild, and still others in history, which informed the present.[4] Henry Adams, one of the more thoughtful men of the era, could find no meaning for the age; his thesis "The movement from unity into multiplicity, between 1200 and 1900" expresses the lack of controlling order. In Adams's search for unity, an epiphany of sorts occurred during the summer of 1893 on the shores of Lake Michigan at the World's Columbian Exposition, where, he felt, the artists, architects, and landscape gardeners had seemingly "leaped directly from Corinth and Syracuse and Venice, over the heads of London and New York, to impose classical standards on plastic Chicago" (Fig. 10). Astonished, impressed, and hopeful, he felt "Chicago was the first expression of American thought as unity; one must start there." Musing beneath the dome of the Administration Building and looking out across the Court of Honor, Adams contemplated the fact that someday people would "talk about Hunt and Richardson, La Farge and St. Gaudens, Burnham and McKim, and Stanford White when their politicians and millionaires were otherwise forgotten."[5] Still, doubts occurred to Adams, and later, after visiting other expositions, he concluded that the order was illusory. But his initial sentiments give an insight into the attractive order the American Renaissance could provide for many people.

Physical and social dislocation may explain some of the appeal of the American Renaissance, but ultimately the movement and the question of identification can only be understood in relation to the cultural currents of the period. Three strong strains, interrelated and yet separate, are important: the rampant nationalism, a belief in idealism and the genteel tradition, and finally, the increasing attraction of foreign cultures, or cosmopolitanism.

Nationalism has a long history, but it was in the nineteenth century that national identity and the modern consciousness of an allegiance to a national state emerged as powerful factors in art as well as in politics. Americans had always been prone to a boastfulness about their capabilities and divine endowment. However, the main substance of antebellum nationalism revolved around the uniqueness of the political system and the new, uncontaminated quality of the American experience.[6] Beginning in the 1870s, American nationalism came to be defined in historical terms, with a corresponding increase in mystical and religious allusions. With the approach of the Centennial, the American past could almost be said to have been discovered. Organizations emerged that presented in different ways the American past: The American Historical Association (1882), The American Protective Association (1887), the Association for the Preservation of Virginia Antiquities (1888), the Daughters of the American Revolution (1890), and the Colonial Dames (1890). Some were hereditary, others were academic and

3   Wiebe, *Search for Order*, pp. 12, 44.
4   Roderick Nash, ed., *The Call of the Wild (1900–1916)* (New York, 1970).
5   Henry Adams, *The Education of Henry Adams* (1918; reprint ed., New York, 1931), pp. 498, 340, 343, 341.
6   Jones, *Age of Energy*, pp. 31–33.

scholarly, and some were devoted to preserving American qualities and the superiority of the race. The clamor of nationalism as the twentieth century approached became deafening. Any anniversary, centennial, or sesquicentennial became the occasion for erecting memorials, flying flags, writing hackneyed poetry, and giving sermons. Art played a vital role in promoting nationalism. Cass Gilbert, the architect of two state capitols and numerous public buildings, wrote that the State should satisfy man's "natural craving" for art, and thereby secure "patriotism and good citizenship."[7]

At first glance, the genteel tradition may seem opposed to nationalism, but in actuality both arose from similar ambitions to ensure the moral superiority of America. Concerned with elevating aesthetic standards, the genteel tradition contained many of the operative elements of "high culture" of the period; it sought an art filled with moral content that would keep the forces of barbarism at bay.[8] Underlying the genteel tradition was a fear of national inferiority, a belief that culture and art were indexes of civilization. The French critic Hippolyte Taine's concept that art rather than individual gifts expressed the genius of nations found a sympathetic ear in the United States. A reviewer of James Jackson Jarves's *Art Hints* proclaimed: "In other words, the history of art is the history of nations."[9] Charles Eliot Norton, professor of art history at Harvard, observed that the "highest achievements in the arts" were not so much the products of "solitary individual artists" as the expressions of a nation's "faith," "loftiness of spirit," and the "embodiment of its ideals."[10] Art was the chief expression of every age, Charles Hutchinson, the President of The Art Institute of Chicago, claimed. It expressed "that which was the deepest and the most sincere in the life of its people."[11] By understanding art, a more truthful view of a people's achievement could be gained, or as John La Farge argued, "The record of art passes beyond the record of the historians."[12] Vernacular, homespun culture was, in general, to be avoided in favor of an art that had visible traditions and ties to the past. Dissemination of the genteel viewpoint, didactic in nature, came through artists, poets, novelists, critics, and in the pulpit, the classroom, and the museum.

The standards that the genteel commentators attempted to impose were drawn from the Old World; Ruskin, Hegel, Pater, Viollet-le-Duc, and others spoke of a religion of high culture and art. Matthew Arnold had particular relevance. His works such as *Culture and Anarchy* (1869) and his concept of a "saving remnant" that would interpret "the best that has been thought and said in the world" found many followers in the United States.[13] During one of his visits, Arnold challenged the United States: "Do not tell me only of the magnitude of your industry and commerce; of the beneficence of your institutions, your freedom, your equality; of the great and growing number of your churches and schools, libraries and newspapers; tell me also if your civilization—which is the grand name you give to all this development—tell me if your civilization is *interesting*."[14] Both the individual and society could be improved by art. This was the lesson of Europe, or as one commentator claimed: "From babyhood to decrepit age all [Europeans] revel in art, and this daily contact with the beautiful quietly moulds the character and creates an unerring taste, not only in things artistic, but in the properties of life."[15]

7   Cass Gilbert, "The Greatest Element of Monumental Architecture," *The American Architect* CXXXVI (August 5, 1929), pp. 143–144.
8   The original concept of a genteel tradition was used negatively by George Santayana in "The Genteel Tradition in American Philosophy," *Winds of Doctrine* (London, 1913), pp. 186–215. Later scholars have viewed it more positively; see Jones, *Age of Energy*, chap. 6; and John Tomsich, *The Genteel Endeavor* (Stanford, 1971).

9   John Neal, *North American Review* 71 (October 1855), p. 440.
10   Quoted in Kermit Vanderbilt, *Charles Eliot Norton: Apostle of Culture in a Democracy* (Cambridge, Mass., 1959), p. 205.
11   Quoted from an address at the Art Institute in 1888 in Helen L. Horowitz, *Culture and the City: Cultural Philanthropy in Chicago from the 1880s to 1917* (Lexington, 1976), p. 74.
12   John La Farge, *One Hundred Masterpieces of Painting* (Garden City, 1913), p. viii.

13   Matthew Arnold, "Numbers: Of the Majority and the Remnant" (1884), reprinted in *The Complete Prose Works of Matthew Arnold*, vol. 10, ed. R.H. Super (Ann Arbor, 1974), p. 163; and Matthew Arnold, *Culture and Anarchy* (reprint ed., Cambridge, Mass., 1960), p. 6.
14   Matthew Arnold, *Civilization in the United States* (Boston, 1888), p. 170.
15   George E. Bissell, "Art and Education," *Municipal Affairs* VI (June 1902), p. 185.

The elevation of the spiritual life of the nation through art came not simply by more art, but art of a specific type that incorporated elements of the ideal; or as Charles Hutchinson of The Art Institute of Chicago said: "It is not the sole mission of art to amuse or to furnish moral instruction. The true mission of *ART*, as Hagel [*sic*] says, is to discover and present the ideal." [16] Throughout nineteenth-century American art, the *ideal* existed as a rather diffuse concept that received a great deal of commentary in the American Renaissance period. Basically, it was elevated thought and virtue presented in images that were beautiful, noble, and universal in application. Consequently, ideal art drew upon the past and not upon observation of nature. For instance, Charles Hutchinson could claim that "the secret of the greatness of the *Art* of the Italian Renaissance is to be found in the fact that it was the ideal realization of Italian reality" and that great art in all ages went behind reality "to present the ideal." [17] Most critics and artists would agree with William James Stillman, writing in *Old Italian Masters* (1892). He argued that the greatness of individual works was due to the concept of beauty, "not to be confounded with the actual and probably never existing in nature." [18] Only by a study of the past and tradition could the ideal be learned, or as Stillman noted: "The ideal was slowly worked out by the universal process of evolution, generation after generation working out the same problem of the ideal, the pupil carrying the work of his master a little further." [19]

Learning from the past, from the great themes and techniques of predecessors, the duty of the American artist was to create a new composition. John La Farge sought "Authority: the influence of the best" and added, "That, I suppose is what we mean by civilization." The past would not be a hindrance. On the contrary, "That call is not one to imitation; it is rather the revelation of one's real intellectual desires, the initiation into one's real home and family." [20]

Idealistic subjects received a variety of expressions depending upon the medium. Architecturally, it meant buildings with a clear relation to the great works of the past through domes, triumphal arches, the orders, colonnades, and temple fronts. In painting and sculpture, the human figure, nude or draped, was either an abstract allegory personifying Truth, Agriculture, or the State, or a real person symbolizing higher virtues. While specific incidents could be portrayed, the scene, removed from specific incidents, was felt to be more elevated, as exemplified by the Sherman Monument, Grand Army Plaza, New York City, by Augustus Saint-Gaudens. A realistic though slightly simplified equestrian Sherman is led towards eternity by the figure of Victory. Trappings of allegory are the drapery, shields, wreaths, and wings. Abbott Thayer explained his use of wings on many female figures: "Doubtless my lifelong passion for birds has helped to incline me to work wings into my pictures; but primarily I have put on wings probably more to symbolize an exalted atmosphere (above the realm of genre painting) where one need not explain the action of his figures" [21] (Fig. 37).

Abstract idealism did not of course encompass all the art of the American Renaissance: not all buildings were elevated and monumental, and in sculpture and painting, genre and historical subjects continued. But even so, the influence of the idea can be sensed in art's removal from the world of

16 Quoted from a 1916 address in Horowitz, *Culture and the City*, p. 88.

17 Quoted from a 1916 address in Horowitz, *Culture and the City*, p. 88. Another said, "We have seen that these artists of the Early Renaissance . . . seized the ideal in that actual, employed the truth they won from nature in the higher forms of the imagination" (James M. Hoppin, *The Early Renaissance and Other Essays on Art Subjects* [Boston, 1892], pp. 50–51).

18 William James Stillman, *Old Italian Masters* (New York, 1892), p. vi.

19 William James Stillman, "The Revival of Art," *The Old Rome and the New and Other Studies* (Boston, 1898), p. 211.

20 John La Farge, "The American Academy at Rome," The Field of Art, *Scribner's Magazine* 28 (August 1900), p. 253.

21 Quoted from a letter of 1912, Thayer to the director of the Hillyer Art Gallery, *Bulletin of Smith College Hillyer Art Gallery*, March 10, 1937.

FIG. 18
Edward Robinson, 1903.
John Singer Sargent (1856–1925).
Oil on canvas; 143.5 x 92.1 cm.
(56½ x 36¼ in.).
COLLECTION: The Metropolitan Museum
of Art, New York City.

FIG. 19
How the Gossip Grew, 1890.
Francis Millet (1846–1912).
Photograph of a work in the Millet
Scrapbook, page 19.
COLLECTION: Art and Architecture Division,
The New York Public Library, Astor, Lenox
and Tilden Foundations, New York City.

FIGS. 20 AND 21   *Facing page*
Entry hall, H.W. Poor house, New
York City, 1899–1901. McKim, Mead and
White, architects.
COLLECTION/PHOTO: Museum of the
City of New York.

mundane realities. John Singer Sargent's portrait of Edward Robinson (Fig. 18), a classical archaeologist and director of The Metropolitan Museum of Art, New York City, has an air of superiority, while the little genre scene of Francis Millet, *How the Gossip Grew* (Fig. 19), has an air of neatness and primness impossible to achieve in life. Avoided and ignored was actual reality—the urban scene—that later would be celebrated by a new generation of painters, the Ashcan School.

Seeking to acquire all "the best that had been thought and said in the world" generally meant, for genteel Americans, European examples of art, architecture, literature, and music. The artistic and sophisticated segments of American society had always been attracted by the Old World; however, in the period after 1870, a very changed cosmopolitan spirit was in evidence.[22] Cosmopolitanism differed from the genteel tradition in its lack of didactic and highly moralistic content; cosmopolitanism sought the exotic and beautiful no matter where it lay. Hence the eclectic, sensuous, and vivacious quality of many interiors of the period, where Roman sarcophagi, Venetian ceilings, Louis XIII mantels, large China vases, Goeblin tapestries, and polar bear rugs could all be used in an entrance hall (Figs. 20 and 21). The shift in attitude can be noted in a variety of ways. Earlier, Europeans were generally distrusted by Americans as immoral; however, by late in the century, Europeans were actively courted for their status, and European nobility (frequently down on their luck) became objects of competition for

22   Jones, *Age of Energy*, chap. 7.

FIG. 22
Samoan Girl in a Canoe, circa 1890–1891.
John La Farge (1835–1910).
Watercolor on paper; 36.8 x 53.3 cm.
(14½ x 21 in.).
COLLECTION: Corcoran Gallery of Art,
Washington, D.C.

FIG. 23 *Facing page*
Entrance hall, Henry Villard house,
New York City, 1882–1886. McKim, Mead
and White, architects.
COLLECTION/PHOTO: Museum of the
City of New York.

daughters of American millionaires.[23] Wealthy Americans sought foreign titles and purchased large historic estates abroad. In American literature there was, towards the end of the century, an increasing flood of travel sketches, novels set in foreign lands, and historical accounts of non-American subjects. The earlier Yankee distrust of Emerson and Twain disappeared to be replaced by the word pictures of William Dean Howells, F. Marion Crawford, F. Hopkinson Smith, Edith Wharton, Henry James, and Richard Harding Davis.

Cosmopolitanism cannot be exclusively defined as an American infatuation with Europe. The Orient, the South Seas, and the Near East also came under scrutiny, and ultimately these more foreign regions felt Americans' lust for acquisition. The attraction lay in the exotic, perhaps erotic, and ultimately mysterious quality of these cultures that betrayed little connection to the West. The harem fantasies of H. Siddons Mowbray from the 1880s, *History of Religion* by John Singer Sargent, and the hieroglyphic puzzles of Elihu Vedder were indebted to this aspect of cosmopolitanism. From the mid-1870s onwards can be found Japanese elements in painting, architecture, and decoration. The works of Whistler and McKim, Mead and White show traces of the study of Japanese prints. Some of the first substantive accounts of Oriental art are by Americans: James Jackson Jarves, Ernest F. Fenollosa, and Edward S. Morse.[24] John La Farge, in company with Henry Adams, traveled extensively in the South Seas and the Far East, producing a memorable series of watercolors (Fig. 22) and accounts. Confronted with an unfamiliar culture and art, La Farge's responses were those of the genteel

23 Dixon Wecter, *The Saga of American Society* (New York, 1937), chap. 10; Edith Wharton notes the new attraction of Europe in *A Backward Glance* (New York, 1934), p. 62.
24 Edward S. Morse, *Japanese Homes and Their Surroundings* (New York, 1886); Ernest F. Fenollosa, *Epochs of Chinese and Japanese Art* (New York, 1911); and James Jackson Jarves, *A Glimpse of the Art of Japan* (New York, 1876).

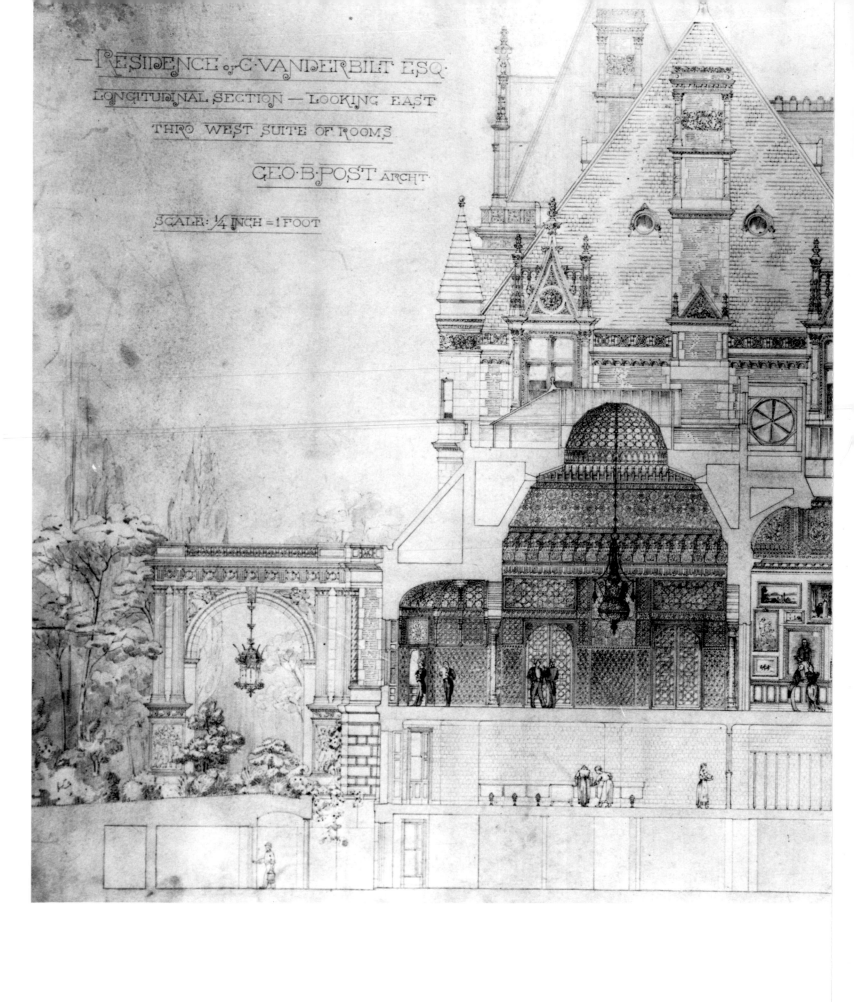

—RESIDENCE of C. VANDERBILT E.SQ.

LONGITUDINAL SECTION — LOOKING EAST

THRO WEST SUITE OF ROOMS

GEO·B·POST ARCHT·

SCALE· ¼ INCH = 1 FOOT

3

Presence of the Past

The physical and social changes, the new nationalism, the genteel tradition, and cosmopolitanism were cultural conditions that prepared the way for the American Renaissance, but it was a new sense of history that most directly formed the mental set of the American Renaissance. One element of American mythology has always been the American Adam stepping ashore at Jamestown or Plymouth without a past. Alternatively, there were those Americans who, from the very beginning, attempted to record and preserve selected aspects of the past. In the 1870s a change took place, and Americans discovered that history did not mean the far distant Holy Land, Greece, Rome, local geneology, and a few selected Revolutionary heroes, but that a more immediate past existed in both European and American history.

Discovery of the concept of the Renaissance as a historical-cultural event occurred in the mid and later nineteenth century. The word "Renaissance," referring to the Italian revival of classic antiquity in art, architecture, and letters in the fourteenth through the sixteenth centuries, first came into English usage in the 1840s.[1] For many English commentators and artists attracted by the Middle Ages, and especially the Gothic past, the classical Renaissance was an anathema, a modern revival of paganism. John Ruskin and his disciples of the 1850s and 1860s such as James Jackson Jarves, Charles Eliot Norton, and Russell Sturgis led the way. While Ruskin could admit a small amount of genius in the Pre-Raphaelite Renaissance, in his view the high point of culture and civilization occurred in late medieval Venice and Pisa.

Beginning in the 1870s, books and articles appeared that viewed the Renaissance period in a positive light and set in motion the American infatuation with it. Several books were of particular importance: two by Englishmen, Walter Pater's *Studies in the History of the Renaissance* (1873) and John Addington Symonds's *The Renaissance in Italy, The Fine Arts* (1877; the third volume of a five-part work), and two by the Swiss historian Jakob Burckhardt, *The Cicerone: A Guide to the Works of Art in Italy* (1873; originally published in German in 1855) and *The Civilization of the Renaissance in Italy* (1878; originally published in German in 1860).[2] Unifying the different approaches was the theme that a high point of Western civilization, especially in the arts, occurred in Italy during the Renaissance. American reaction in general was positive; a reviewer of Symonds claimed that the "mark" of the Renaissance could be found not only in Italy "but upon the productions of the whole Western World" and that the artistic force of Greece, which Symonds saw as the generating element of the Renaissance, "is travelling onward with ever-increasing vigor along a path which is constantly tending upwards, but whose end is lost in the dim distance of the future."[3] A reviewer of Burckhardt for the *New York Herald* claimed: "We are children of the Renaissance. And not only are we children of the Renaissance, but as Burckhardt truly says the influence of that mother age is still at work among us."[4]

---

1   Jones, "The Renaissance and American Origins," p. 147; see also *The Compact Edition of the Oxford English Dictionary*, s.v. "Renaissance."
2   Pater's book appeared under a New York imprint in 1877; Symonds's vol. 3 appeared under a New York imprint in 1879. Burckhardt's *Civilization* appeared with a New York imprint in 1879; his *Cicerone* did not appear in the United States until 1908 but had several London editions.

3   *The Art Interchange* 2 (May 14, 1879), p. 81.
4   *New York Herald*, October 18, 1880.

Other publications appeared in the late 1870s, the 1880s, and the 1890s that further served to bring the Renaissance into perspective. In popular magazines such as *Scribner's*, there were articles on pictures of the French Renaissance, Savonarola, Leonardo da Vinci, and others.[5] Former medievalists and followers of Ruskin frequently reoriented their assessment of the Renaissance. Charles C. Perkins, a Bostonian and prolific writer on the arts, published in 1878 *Raphael and Michelangelo: A Critical and Biographical Essay*, and then in 1883, *Historical Handbook of Italian Sculpture*. William James Stillman, the editor of the very Ruskinian art journal *The Crayon* (1855–1861) and a personal friend of the master, became less enamored in his later years and wrote on the importance of the Renaissance. For *The Century Magazine* Stillman prepared notes to accompany a series of engravings by Timothy Cole that were later published under the title *Old Italian Masters* (1892). At Yale University, James M. Hoppin, an avowed "true disciple" of Ruskin, felt the need to correct him and claimed: "The Early Renaissance [of Florence, 1420–1500] may be compared to morning after night—the night of barbarism, ignorance and intellectual bondage."[6]

Simultaneous with the discovery of the Renaissance by historians and critics, American artists who had been studying at various European academies returned with new knowledge. Italy had earlier been a popular spot for work by American artists, but mainly for the poetry of ruins and atmosphere, not for any concentrated, intense study of the Renaissance period. The generation of American artists that returned home in the 1870s and 1880s learned about the Renaissance through art schools in Dusseldorf, Munich, The Hague, and Paris. Differences existed between the academies, between instructors, and certainly students absorbed and carried away different emphases. In general, however, most of the academies saw the fountainhead of modern art as the Florence and Rome of the Renaissance. Hence the various prizes and the national academies in Rome.

Paris and the École des Beaux-Arts were the most popular places to study, and there American students were exposed to the architecture of the Italian Renaissance through the lavish *envoi* drawings of *Prix de Rome* winners or the accurate steel plate renderings of elevations and details of the Palazzo Cancelleria in Paul Marie Letarouilly's *Edifices de Rome moderne* (1840–1857) or the Pitti Palace in Auguste Grandjean de Montigny's *Architecture Toscaine* (1815). Augustus Saint-Gaudens studied in the atelier of François Jouffroy, who led the movement away from cold neoclassicism to the naturalism of the Italian Renaissance. Painters such as Walter Gay, Henry O. Walker, and Edwin H. Blashfield studied in the atelier of Léon Bonnat, who in his salon pictures openly quoted from Velazquez and Michelangelo. Jean León Gérôme, known for convincing historical illustration, attracted the largest contingent: Kenyon Cox, Thomas Eakins, Abbott Thayer, George de Forest Brush, Robert Blum, and others.

Not every American artist and architect studied on the continent, and in England a sizable group paused—at least briefly—and discovered the Renaissance. The Pre-Raphaelite movement and its successor, the Aesthetic movement, were important in awakening Americans to the art of decoration and also in directing them towards their own Colonial past and ultimately to

5   Linda Villari, "The Plain Story of Savonarola's Life," *Scribner's Monthly* 20 (August 1880), pp. 503–522; Wendell Lamorous, "Pictures of the French Renaissance," *Scribner's Monthly* 11 (January 1879), pp. 337–362.
6   James M. Hoppin, *The Early Renaissance and other Essays on Art Subjects* (Boston, 1892), pp. iii, 8.

FIG. 25
Minute Man, 1871–1875,
Concord, Massachusetts.
Daniel Chester French (1850–1931).
Bronze; statue height 213.3 cm.
(84 in.).
COLLECTION/PHOTO: The Library of
Congress, Washington, D.C.

the Italian Renaissance. Painters such as Frederic Leighton, Alma-Tadema, Edward John Poynter, and Albert Moore exploited Greek and Roman motifs in their work. The vast decorative program and historical paintings for the Houses of Parliament, even though stylistically different, undoubtedly helped inspire American visitors. Some chose to stay, and among the American colony were Francis Millet, Edwin Austin Abbey, John Singer Sargent, James McNeill Whistler, and George H. Boughton.

Concurrent with the discovery of the Renaissance, Americans found another past: their own of the seventeenth and eighteenth centuries. To most Americans, even the highly educated, American history had meant ancestor worship, a few heroes (George Washington mainly), and the explorers. Other aspects of the past were a blank. Beginning in the 1870s, however, Americans discovered their past. This discovery can be traced to several causes: the burgeoning nationalism, the genteel concern that a lack of history meant decadence, and finally the year 1876. At the Centennial celebration in Philadelphia, Americans saw not only curiosities such as Washington's false teeth, but eighteenth-century portraits, a survey of American painting, an "Old New England Kitchen" (a log cabin), antique spinning wheels, and Queen Anne chairs. Other aspects of the inquiry into the American past took the form of articles in *Harper's* and *Scribner's* on life, battles, and towns in the eighteenth century; serious scholarship such as Moses Coit Tyler's books on early American literature; S.W.G. Benjamin's on early portraitists; and *The Magazine of American History* (1877–1893).[7]

Artists and architects also participated in this rite of self-discovery: they created in wood, paint, stone, and bronze images by which Americans could identify themselves. One of the first and certainly the best known of the patriotic symbols was Daniel Chester French's *Minute Man*, unveiled in 1875 (Fig. 25). The work was based at least in part upon the antique statue *Apollo*

7   Aspects of this discovery of the American past are treated in Richard Guy Wilson, "Charles F. McKim and the Renaissance in America," (Ph.D. diss., University of Michigan, 1972), chap. 4; and Vincent Scully, Jr., *The Shingle Style* (New Haven, 1955), chap. 2.

Belvedere, and French invested his work with emblems of peace and war; the plow and the gun.[8] Simultaneously, Charles F. McKim commissioned the first photographic record of Colonial architecture and produced the first example of the Colonial Revival in the remodeling of the Robinson house in Newport, Rhode Island. The value of studying the Colonial past was noted by many architects, such as Robert S. Peabody, who in 1877 rather rhetorically asked: "With our Centennial year have we not discovered that we have a past worthy of study?"[9] Painters responded to the increased historical sensibility with iconic visions. Monumentality exists with accuracy of detail in paintings such as George Boughton's *Puritans Going to Church* (1867; Fig. 26) and Thomas Eakins's *William Rush Carving the Allegorical Figure of the Schuylkill River* (1877). Another vital expression came through the illustrators for the popular periodicals, such as Edwin Austin Abbey and Howard Pyle, who would soon emerge as leading history painters.

The monumentalization and memorialization of the American Colonial and Revolutionary past increased in force in the succeeding decades; and in the 1880s the Civil War, too, entered the realm of history. Time had softened many of the brutal memories and had begun to claim many of the survivors

FIG. 26
Puritans Going to Church, 1867.
George H. Boughton (1833–1905).
Oil on canvas; 35.9 x 63.8 cm.
(14⅛ x 25⅛ in.).
COLLECTION: The Toledo Museum of Art, Ohio, Gift of Florence Scott Libbey.

8   New York, The Metropolitan Museum of Art, *Daniel Chester French: An American Sculptor,* by Michael Richman, 1976, pp. 43–44.
9   Quoted in Richard Guy Wilson, "American Architecture and the Search for a National Style in the 1870s," *Nineteenth Century 3* (Autumn 1977), p. 74–80.

of the carnage. The conflict was viewed in a new light, as the acting out of archetypal themes of brother versus brother, of ritualistic initiations under fire, of badges of courage and manhood. For the United States, it secured admission into a pantheon of nations possessing a stock of noble themes. Augustus Saint-Gaudens's Admiral Farragut Memorial in Madison Square Park, New York City (1877–1881; Fig. 27), set the stage with a simplified naturalism learned from fifteenth-century Florentine sculpture. Caught in a moment of action on the bridge of his ship with the wind tugging at his coat, Farragut transcends the place and action with his expression and carriage to become a symbol of stoic heroism and commitment. The pedestal designed by Stanford White and the carvings by Saint-Gaudens explicitly refer to the Renaissance in the calligraphy, the emblems, and the twin semireclining figures personifying Courage and Loyalty.

As the War Between the States passed into history, grand army plazas, soldiers' and sailors' monuments, memorials to regiments, tombs, and statues of leaders and heroes became omnipresent. Both leaders and foot soldiers were recognized, and in Saint-Gaudens's monument to Colonel Robert Shaw in Boston, the black soldier's contribution was memorialized.

FIG. 27
Admiral David Glasgow Farragut Memorial, Madison Square Park, New York City, 1877–1881. Augustus Saint-Gaudens (1848–1907). Design of base by Stanford White (1853–1906). Bronze and granite. PHOTO: Bob Zucker.

FIG. 28
Robert E. Lee Monument, Richmond,
Virginia, 1890.
Jean A. Mercié (1845–1916).
Bronze.
PHOTO: Metropolitan Richmond
Chamber of Commerce.

44

The South began to remember its version of the conflict. In 1890 an equestrian statue of Robert E. Lee (Fig. 28) by the French sculptor Jean A. Mercié (a fellow student and a friend of Saint-Gaudens's from the atelier Jouffroy) was unveiled in Richmond, Virginia, on a square that became the head of Monument Avenue, a grand boulevard punctuated with statues to other members of the Lost Cause.[10]

Seeking symbols for American civilization, artists and architects naturally fastened on the Renaissance and the classic past; a historical symbiosis existed. The origins of American Georgian and Early Republican architecture lay not just in England but in Rome and the Renaissance. Senator James McMillan noted that the Capitol and the Treasury Department's headquarters were "in the classical style of architecture" and should serve as a precedent for the twentieth century. "All great art borrows from the Past," McMillan claimed, and he explained: "In architecture, the work of the individual is confined mainly to adapting to the conditions of his particular problem forms that have already been perfected."[11] Joy Wheeler Dow, an architect and writer, advanced a similar argument in his appropriately titled book, *American Renaissance* (1904): "We want to belong somewhere and to something, not to be entirely cut off by ourselves as stray atoms." To Dow, Renaissance architecture meant all styles, including local variations such as American Georgian, Greek Revival, and Federal, that could be traced back to the Old World. All countries had drawn on the same source. Dow said of Richard Morris Hunt's Biltmore: "We call Biltmore French Renaissance now; it will be American Renaissance later on."[12]

Many artists attempted to use the iconography of the classic past in their American works, since ideal art required a universal language. Will Low, the muralist, indicated the frustrations when he said: "I am almost as tired of the 'early settlers' as I am of 'Justice', 'Science', and 'Art': but there is a rich field in the myths and history which we have inherited in common with all the modern world."[13] To Kenyon Cox, American history was too short and "unfitted" and "modern costume [too] formless and ugly" to be a part of ideal art.[14] A similar resentment was expressed by Augustus Saint-Gaudens, working on the Farragut in Rome: "It gives me a curious mixture (to see all these glories of the 'Renaissance') of a wish to do something good and of the hopelessness of it—what artists they were—'They weren't anything else.' I've been pegging away at my Farragut, but it's a hard 'tug' with our infernal modern dress—I only have the cap, sword, belt and buttons—and the resource of trying to strike away from the stuff we have in America."[15]

Edwin Blashfield reconciled American subject matter with the ideal by proclaiming that the conflict was bogus, that all art "is at one and the same time realistic and idealistic." Symbolic figures, drawn realistically, "like nature," could be idealistic if "informed with a sense of beauty." They received their identity by emblems, and if the *pickelhaube,* or the spiked helmet, meant Germany and the Phrygian liberty cap represented France, then one could "Americanize a figure with the Union Shield." Blashfield went on to claim: "The Attributes and the Graces have not settled by the Seine or the Rhine; the Muse is just as willing to take up the Lyre at Concord or Cambridge as at Florence or by the Fountain of Valcluse."[16]

10 Saint-Gaudens served on the Lee monument jury and certainly gave the commission to Mercié; see Homer Saint-Gaudens, ed., *The Reminiscences of Augustus Saint-Gaudens*, vol. 2 (New York, 1913), p. 47; and "Equestrian Monuments" XLIV, *American Architect and Building News* 34 (November 1891), pp. 104–105. Research on this problem was carried out by Carden McGehee, Jr.

11 Senator James McMillan, "The American Academy in Rome," *The North American Review* 174 (May 1902), p. 627.
12 Joy Wheeler Dow, *American Renaissance: A Review of Domestic Architecture* (New York, 1904), pp. 19, 167.
13 Quoted in William Walton, "Mural Painting in this Country Since 1898," The Field of Art, *Scribner's Magazine* 40 (November 1906), p. 637.
14 Kenyon Cox, *The Classic Point of View* (New York, 1911), p. 70.

15 Saint-Gaudens to Stanford White, March 1878, Saint-Gaudens Collection, Dartmouth College, Hanover, N. H. Reprinted with changed punctuation and emphasis in *Reminiscences of Augustus Saint-Gaudens*, vol. 1, p. 256.
16 Edwin Blashfield, "A Word for Municipal Art," *Municipal Affairs* III (December 1899), p. 588.

FIG. 29
*Washington Laying Down His Command
at the Feet of Columbia*, 1902,
a mural in the Baltimore Courthouse.
Edwin H. Blashfield (1848–1936).

Washington Laying Down His Command at the Feet of Columbia (1902; Fig. 29), a mural in the Baltimore Courthouse by Blashfield, is such an Americanization. Instead of painting a narrative picture of the event, Blashfield attempted to immortalize the meaning by placing Columbia as a central figure and surrounding her with personifications of the Virtues dressed in medieval and classic costumes carrying emblems of War, Peace, Abundance, and Glory. Washington dressed in a historical costume of buff and blue is equally removed from the present, and as Kenyon Cox claimed: "The larger implications of the story to be told are much more clearly expressed than they could be by a realistic representation of the scene that occurred at Annapolis in 1783." [17]

Flawed and filled with clichés, the American Renaissance search for symbolism came close to achieving an identifiable form with the American Virgin motif. The woman as a repository for higher virtues had a long history in nineteenth-century American culture, and earlier she had taken the form of Columbia, Liberty, and/or America. [18] But in the later nineteenth and early twentieth centuries, the female form in art was revitalized and the image presented was one of a beautiful, glowing-with-health young woman. She was elegant and noble, a woman from whose mind and lips there would never issue a crude thought or word. Unaware of her own sexuality and never overtly sold in carnal terms, she undeniably possessed a sexual presence. The American Virgin can be found at all levels of American culture, from the Swift Packing Company's "Premium Calendar" to the languishing, drifting girls of Thomas Dewing's paintings (Fig. 30). In literature, the American girl was a major presence. Henry James created a great controversy with *Daisy Miller* (1879), in which a misunderstanding by the American Virgin abroad leads to her death. Numerous critics and authors felt it necessary to defend the honor of the American girl. [19] Many of James's

17 Cox, *Classic Point of View*, p. 76.
18 Joshua C. Taylor, "America as Symbol," *America as Art* (Washington, D.C., 1976).
19 One example is William Dean Howells, *The Rise of Silas Lapham* (1885; reprint ed., New York, 1951), p. 19, where a character mentions the need "to honor the name of American Woman, and to redeem it from the national reproach of Daisy Millerism."

FIG. 30
The Days, 1887.
Thomas Dewing (1851–1938).
Oil on canvas; 109.6 x 180.8 cm.
(43 ³/₁₆ x 72 in.).
COLLECTION: Wadsworth Atheneum,
Hartford, Connecticut.

FIG. 31 *Right*
Bacchante, 1894.
Frederick MacMonnies (1863–1937).
Marble; height 219.7 cm. (86½ in.).
COLLECTION: The Brooklyn Museum,
New York, Ella C. Woodward Fund.

FIG. 32 *Facing page*
Columbian Fountain, World's Columbian
Exposition, Chicago, 1893. Frederick
MacMonnies (1863–1937). Charles
Dudley Arnold (b. 1844), photographer.
COLLECTION: Avery Library, Columbia
University, New York City.

FIG. 33
A Daughter of the South, a drawing
for *Collier's Weekly* (July 31, 1909).
Charles Dana Gibson (1867–1944).
Ink on paper; 76.2 x 63.5 cm.
(30 x 25 in.).
COLLECTION: The Library of Congress,
Washington, D.C.

later stories concern the naive American Virgin confronting Old World evil.[20] Explorations of the nature of the American Beauty can be seen in the novels of Edith Wharton, in which the innocent Lily Bart of *The House of Mirth* (1905) is contrasted with the scheming materialist Undine Sprague of *The Custom of the Country* (1913). For Henry Adams, infatuated with the Virgin of the twelfth century, the female symbol could never exercise such power in the nineteenth. He noted ironically, "An American Virgin would never dare command; an American Venus would never dare exist."[21]

Yet command she did. Foreign critics noted the uniqueness of the woman theme in American art as different renditions were made by Frederick MacMonnies (Fig. 31), Abbott Thayer (Fig. 37), and George de Forest Brush.[22] For the World's Columbian Exposition, MacMonnies created the sixty-foot–long Columbian Fountain that contained in the prow a Feminine Fame, aft, an old man as Father Time, and amidships on a high throne, a seminude Columbia (Fig. 32). Power was supplied by eight scantily clad females representing the Arts and Sciences and assisted by outriders on seahorses, mermaids, putti, and dolphins. Will Low, in commenting on this representation of "our as yet experimental civilization," caught the central theme: "It is the young girl who fills such a large part of our experiment who is really to the fore. It is Smith and Wellesley who row with the young girl enthroned."[23]

The quintessence of the American Virgin can be found in the magazine illustrations of Charles Dana Gibson (Fig. 33), Alonzo Kimball, and Howard Chandler Christy. Aloof, statuesque, and yet sensuous, they were "the perfecting of the highest type of womanhood," as Christy wrote in his paean, *The American Girl* (1906).[24] However, the sad reality of the American Virgin became painfully evident in the case of Evelyn Nesbit, a celebrated beauty, a model for the Gibson Girl. Posing in Japanese kimonos, Grecian gowns, and on bearskin rugs, she was a subject for the cameras of Gertrude Käsebier and Rudolf Eickemeyer (Fig. 34). And, of course, she was ultimately the nemesis of Stanford White.[25]

20 Henry James, *The Portrait of a Lady* (New York, 1881); and Henry James, *The Golden Bowl* (New York, 1904).
21 Henry Adams, *The Education of Henry Adams* (1918; reprint ed., New York, 1931), p. 385.
22 New York, The Metropolitan Museum of Art, *American Impressionist and Realist Paintings and Drawings from the Collection of Mr. and Mrs. Raymond J. Horowitz*, by Dianne H. Pilgrim, 1973, p. 77.
23 Will H. Low, "The Art of the White City," *Scribner's Magazine* 14 (October 1893), p. 511.

24 Howard Chandler Christy, *The American Girl* (New York, 1906), pp. 11–12.
25 The death of Stanford White has received a variety of treatments, from the 1958 movie, *The Girl in the Red Velvet Swing;* to factual accounts, Gerald Langford, *The Murder of Stanford White* (Indianapolis, 1962); and Michael Mooney, *Evelyn Nesbit and Stanford White: Their Love and Death in the Gilded Age* (New York, 1976); to novels, E.L. Doctorow, *Ragtime* (New York, 1975); and several others.

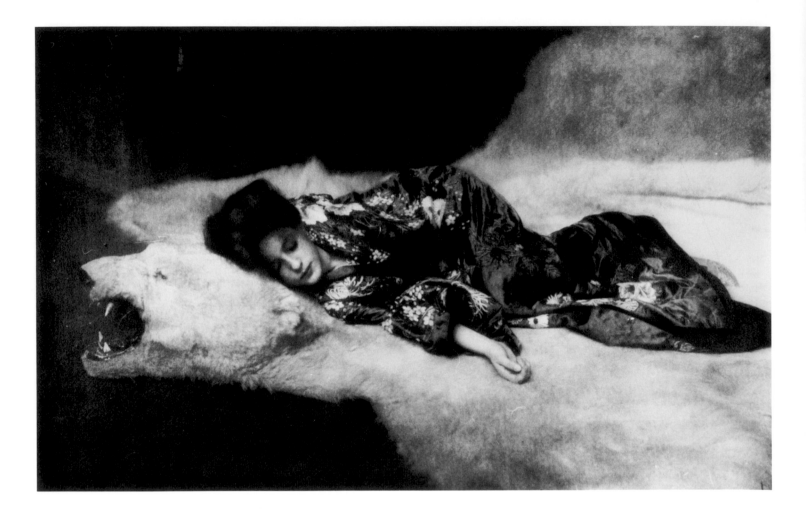

FIG. 34 *Above*
In My Studio (Evelyn Nesbit), 1901.
Rudolf Eickemeyer, Jr. (1831–1895).
Photograph.
COLLECTION: Hudson River Museum,
Yonkers, New York.

FIG. 35 *Facing page*
Accepted design for the new Rhode
Island State Capitol, Providence,
circa 1892. McKim, Mead and White,
architects. Rendering by Hughson
Hawley (1850–1936).
Watercolor on paper; 81.3 x 109.2 cm.
(32 x 43 in.).
COLLECTION: State of Rhode Island
and Providence Plantations.

FIG. 37
Caritas, 1894–1895.
Abbott Thayer (1849–1921).
Oil on canvas; 215.9 x 139.7 cm.
(85 x 55 in.).
COLLECTION: Museum of Fine Arts,
Boston, Massachusetts, The Warren
Collection and contributions through
the Paint and Clay Club.

4

Scientific Eclecticism

E clecticism, the selection and usage of styles, motifs, and details drawn from a variety of sources, defines an element of the aesthetic of the American Renaissance. Certainly not new in American art, the uniqueness of American Renaissance eclecticism came from a "scientific spirit" that guided both the selection and the ultimate usage.

For participants in the American Renaissance, the nadir of American art and architecture had occurred in the period of the 1840s to the 1880s. A "nightmare" was one description of the bulbous Second Empire of Mullet, the thin Gothic of Renwick, the anecdotal sculpture of Rogers, and the imitations of nature by the Hudson River School. Francis Millet claimed that a confusion of "novelty" with "genius" had come from the celebration of "intuition" rather than the "sound lessons of antique art." Arguing that the American Academy in Rome could provide an alternative, Millet wrote: "Our artists are only half educated. . . . they have not had the traditions of art as a birthright. . . . what we want in our artists is cultivation. That we must have . . . as a substitute for tradition."[1]

Exactly the same sentiments were expressed by Edith Wharton and Ogden Codman, Jr., in *The Decoration of Houses* (1897). They believed that the abasement of American furniture came from "unscientific methods" of "piling up heterogeneous ornament, [and] a multiplication of incongruous effects. . . . The worst defects of the furniture now made in America are due to an Athenian thirst for novelty," Wharton and Codman wrote, "not always regulated by an Athenian sense of fitness." The solution proposed in *The Decoration of Houses* was a "study of the best models," and not "dubious eclecticism."[2]

The work despised by members of the American Renaissance generation were examples of synthetic eclecticism, or painting, building, and furniture that combined a variety of different motifs drawn from various sources betraying mixed parentage.[3] The new guideline was a scholarly knowledge of history, and while seldom if ever (except in the case of some furniture) was exact copying promoted, the attitude toward the past was almost scientific.

In the later nineteenth century, science, in addition to its traditional role of describing and explaining the physical world, began to be applied to other activities. Fused and confused were natural history and national history, biological selection and racial superiority. Social concepts received scientific credentials under new terms: "political science," "sociology," and "scientific management." In all areas of learning, and especially in those defined as liberal arts—literature, history, religion, and art—a spirit of scientific rigor, inquiry, and definition became evident.[4]

To some degree, the scientific spirit was indebted to the rise of experts and professionals: the attempt by a younger generation to distinguish themselves from an older generation's amateurishness by claiming a more profound understanding of the "science of modern city-making" or the history of art.[5] While the scientific spirit may appear antithetical to genteel notions of

1   Francis Millet, "The American Academy in Rome," *Review of Reviews* 31 (June 1905), pp. 713–714.
2   Edith Wharton and Ogden Codman, Jr., *The Decoration of Houses* (New York, 1897), pp. xx, 27, 2.
3   Some of my thinking on eclecticism has been influenced by the only historian to approach it at all critically, Carroll L.V. Meeks. While I differ on several points, I am indebted to his "Picturesque Eclecticism," *Art Bulletin* 32 (1950), pp. 226–235; and "Wright's Eastern Seaboard Contemporaries: Creative Eclecticism in the United States Around 1900," in *Acts of the Twentieth International Congress of the History of Art* (Princeton, 1963), pp. 64–77.
4   For some of these ideas see John Higham, *Strangers in the Land: Patterns of American Nativism 1860–1925* (New Brunswick, 1955), pp. 134–135; Merle Curti, *The Growth of American Thought*, 2nd ed. (New York, 1951), p. 593; and Edgar Kaufman, Jr., "Nineteenth Century Design," *Perspecta* 6 (1960), pp. 56–67.
5   Charles Mulford Robinson, *Modern Civic Art or the City Made Beautiful*, 4th ed. (New York, 1918), p. 4. On the rise of the expert see Mel Scott, *American City Planning Since 1890* (Berkeley, 1971), p. 42; and Robert H. Wiebe, *The Search for Order, 1877–1920* (New York, 1967), chaps. 5–7.

the ideal in art, many commentators recognized in scientific research a similar devotion to higher intellectual truths.[6] The expositions of the period, with the numerous pavilions devoted to the higher realms of progress, were examples of the harmony of scholarship, science, and the arts.

Museums of natural history and art history developed almost contemporaneously and were supported by the same philanthropists. By the 1890s similar methods of display had developed in both art and natural history museums. Museums aspired to be encyclopedic and systematic; their collections were to be appreciated for intellectual and educational values and not as entertainment. The unity sought can be seen in the Brooklyn Institute of Arts and Sciences (Fig. 2), which in 1893 commissioned from McKim, Mead and White a building of 1,500,000 square feet, the largest building in the world to house under one roof all types of collections of art and science.

For art museums founded in the 1870s, such as the Museum of Fine Arts, Boston, and The Metropolitan Museum of Art in New York, a reorientation took place in the 1890s. Modeled on the lines of the South Kensington Institute in London, with the intention of not only educating but reforming industrial production, collections were made up of copies of paintings, casts of sculptures, and assorted *objets d'art* of doubtful parentage.[7] Serious scholarship threw out the spurious, and instead of a primary goal of fostering good craftsmanship for home and industry, the collection and formal appreciation of "masterpieces" and Old Masters became the main objective.[8]

Art history came into being in the nineteenth century, a product not only of an increased historical sense but of a scientific methodology. Academic connoisseurship and serious literature replaced dilettantish appreciation. The classifying, cataloguing, filing, and recording of styles, motifs, and details became almost obsessive. An accurate method of representation was necessary for study purposes, and while measured drawings and copies were one method, photography—which came into widespread use after 1870—gave Americans a chance to study the original models with a degree of accuracy previously unknown.

The effect of science upon the actual production of paintings, sculpture, architecture, furniture, and other objects would be to replace the earlier synthetic eclecticism of strange novelties and combinations with a new eclecticism of scholarly and scientific pretensions. Wharton and Codman sprinkle the term "scientific" through *The Decoration of Houses,* and at one point, in attempting to prove the superiority of Renaissance modes of interior decoration over medieval, call upon "all students of sociology" to acknowledge that "the instinct for symmetry . . . is the most strongly developed in those races which have reached the highest artistic civilization." Proper room design came from "mathematical calculation" and "scientific adjustment of voids and masses."[9] Even Kenyon Cox, who decried the modern "scientific spirit" that appeared to deny tradition and produce the horrors of Post-Impressionism, Cubism, and Futurism, found he had to admit that painting and sculpture, being "imitative arts," were "therefore more dependent than any others upon exact knowledge, more tinged with the quality of science."[10] Cox was arguing for a classic art of tradition, perfection, and self-control. The "primary business of painting is to create a

FIG. 38 *Facing page*
Western end, Church of the Ascension, New York City. Remodeled, 1884–1887. Architectural details designed by Stanford White (1853–1906); mural by John La Farge (1835–1910); sculpture by Louis Saint-Gaudens (1853–1913); mosaics by D. Maitland Armstrong (1836–1918).
PHOTO: Scott Hyde.

6   Helen L. Horowitz, *Culture and the City: Cultural Philanthropy in Chicago from the 1880s to 1917* (Lexington, 1976), pp. 25–26, 89–106.
7   Neil Harris, "The Gilded Age Revisited: Boston and the Museum Movement," *American Quarterly* 14 (Winter 1962), pp. 545–566.
8   Harris, "The Gilded Age Revisited," pp. 545–566; and Horowitz, *Culture and the City,* pp. 22–24. Admittedly, John Ruskin had created a predisposition for some of this.

9   Wharton and Codman, *Decoration of Houses,* pp. 31, 44, 34.
10   Kenyon Cox, "The Illusion of Progress," in his *Artist and Public* (New York, 1914), p. 89, see also p. 78; and Kenyon Cox, *The Classic Point of View* (New York, 1911), pp. 14–16, 22.

beautiful surface," Cox wrote, but its "secondary business is to remind the spectator of things he has seen and admired in nature, and to create the illusion of truth."[11] Sculpture depended upon the laws of proportion and the science of the human body, but painting, being more "complicated," depended upon science even more. "The science it [painting] professes is no less than that of the visible aspect of the whole of nature—a science so vast that it never has been and perhaps never can be mastered in its totality."[12]

Present in scientific eclecticism was an intensity of study and accuracy of detail. The high and very consistent quality of architectural ornament has often been commented upon, and although to some degree it may have been a result of mass production of terracotta and fibrous plaster and other mechanical processes, an equal uniformity in hand-cut stone argues that it was an element of the architect's concern and aesthetic.[13] For the J. P. Morgan Library, Charles McKim ordered a "squeeze," or a wax impression, of the joints of the Erechtheum in Athens as a study model.[14] Daniel Chester

FIG. 39
Transfiguration, circa 1518.
Raphael (1483–1520).
Panel; 405.0 x 278.0 cm.
(159½ x 109½ in.).
COLLECTION: The Vatican Museum, Italy.
PHOTO: Alinari/Editorial Photocolor
Archives.

11 Cox, *Classic Point of View*, p. 23, see also pp. 3–4.
12 Cox, "Illusion of Progress," pp. 91–92.
13 Charles H. Reilly, "The Modern Renaissance in American Architecture," *Royal Institute of British Architects Journal* 17 (June 25, 1910), p. 633; Peter Smithson, "The Fine and Folk: An Essay on McKim, Mead and White and the American Tradition," *Architectural Review* 35 (August 1965), pp. 394–397; and William Jordy, *American Buildings and Their Architects: Progressive and Academic Ideals at the Turn of the Twentieth Century*, vol. 3 (New York, 1972), p. 348.
14 Charles McKim to Gorham Stevens, December 14, 1903, McKim, Mead and White Collection, The New-York Historical Society, New York City.

French had similar concerns when he created his statue of John Harvard (1883–1884): lacking a portrait of the subject, he asked scholars for information on period details of clothing, hair styles, and facial types. For the monumental Lincoln in Washington, D.C. (Fig. 50), French used Mathew Brady photographs, casts of the death mask and hands, and studied Lincoln's shoes.[15] To Edwin Austin Abbey, the "science" of painting was the fastidious replication of details of armor, costumes, furniture, and old fabrics, and he asserted: "I feel it my duty as well as my pleasure to be guilty of as few historical inaccuracies as this antiquarian age permits."[16] In 1908 Gari Melchers received a commission to paint a full-length portrait of the Revolutionary War hero General Nathanael Greene to hang as a pendant with one of Gilbert Stuart's portraits of Washington, which was in the governor's reception room at the new Rhode Island Statehouse. He revealed the attraction of historical study in a letter: "I am trying to do it—in the same spirit of the pictures of that period, so that it may be in harmony with the portrait of Washington."[17] The result was a new portrait of Greene, done in a style that crosses Stuart with Charles Willson Peale.

The method of scientific eclecticism produced artists, artisans, and architects who had a facility for evoking different styles and periods. H. Siddons Mowbray moved from the Gérôme realism of *Crystal Gazers* (Fig. 40) to the decorative style of Pinturicchio for the library of the University Club, New York, and to the model of Raphael for the entrance hall to the Morgan Library. Cass Gilbert designed in the commercial vernacular, the Georgian, the Imperial Roman, and the Gothic. John La Farge's large mural, *Ascension* (1886–1888), in the Church of the Ascension in New York, has an obvious source in Raphael's *Transfiguration* in the Vatican (Fig. 39), but it draws upon a variety of other works: the figures of the apostles are derived from Palma Vecchio's *Assumption of the Virgin* (Venice, Accademia), the background is indebted to Japanese landscape, and the painting style comes from Titian and Delacroix. Set into a Gothic Revival church (Upjohn, 1841) with architectural surrounds of pilasters and decoration by Stanford White recalling Bramante, high relief flying angels by Louis Saint-Gaudens recalling Donatello, and mosaic kneeling angels by D. Maitland Armstrong recalling Giotto, the entire composition, in scale and confidence of sources, speaks of the scientific eclecticism that made all the past the property of the American Renaissance (Fig. 38).[18]

Charles McKim spoke for many when he wrote to Edith Wharton: "The designer should not be too slavish, whether in the composition of a building or a room, in his adherence to the letter of tradition. By conscientious study of the best examples of classic periods, including those of antiquity, it is possible to conceive a perfect result suggestive of a particular period, . . . but inspired by the study of them all."[19]

McKim's Boston Public Library illustrates this dictum. It draws upon a variety of sources—Labrouste's Bibliothèque Sainte-Genevieve in Paris, Leon Alberti's San Francisco in Rimini, and the Colosseum in Rome—but in the mind of Samuel A.B. Abbott, the President of the Library Trustees and the principal patron: "It will hold its own beside any of the great works of the great architects of the Renaissance."[20]

FIG. 40
Crystal Gazers, circa 1895.
H. Siddons Mowbray (1858–1928).
Oil on canvas; 35.6 x 15.6 cm.
(14 x 6⅛ in.).
COLLECTION: Kresge Art Center Gallery, Michigan State University, East Lansing, Gift of Gladys Olds Anderson.

15 New York, The Metropolitan Museum of Art, *Daniel Chester French: An American Sculptor*, by Michael Richman, 1976, pp. 56–58, 171–181.
16 E.V. Lucas, *The Life and Work of Edwin Austin Abbey* (London and New York, 1921), pp. 381–382.
17 Gari Melchers to Charles F. McKim, March 5, 1908, McKim, Mead and White Collection, The New-York Historical Society, New York City.

18 Some of the notations on sources come from Helene Barbara Weinberg, *The Decorative Work of John La Farge* (New York, 1977), pp. 174–193; and Robert Rosenblum, "New York Revisited: Church of the Ascension," *Art Digest* XXVIII (March 15, 1954), p. 29.
19 Charles F. McKim, "Memoranda to Mrs. Wharton," *circa* February 2, 1897, McKim Collection, The Library of Congress, Washington, D.C.
20 S.A.B. Abbott to Charles F. McKim, November 28, 1889, McKim Collection, The Library of Congress, Washington, D.C.

Periods and Organizations

The core of the American Renaissance can be seen as an elite group of East Coast, frequently New York–based, artists, architects, craftsmen, critics, and patrons. By example and polemics they carried the message of the American Renaissance to all parts of the country. Essential to this was a large network of organizations and institutions that propagated the idea of a Renaissance. But the idea of the American Renaissance did not emerge full-blown; rather, it grew out of the raised art consciousness of the 1870s. Several different periods are observable: a prelude period from the mid-1870s to the mid-1880s, a period of intense interest and activity in all the arts from the later 1880s to World War I, and a later period of declining spirit from 1918 to the mid-1930s.

Characterizing the prelude period were the development of patterns of collaboration, increased scale and luxury, direct quotation from the work of Old Masters, and the beginning of an organizational framework. Stylistic consensus did not exist, though the appearance of numerous historical works on the Italian Renaissance gave a direction. Private commissions were the norm.

The choice of 1876 as the beginning of the American Renaissance is arbitrary, but many of the participants later would mark the Centennial as the inauguration of a new interest in art.[1] By 1880 the term "American Renaissance" appeared with reference to recent art activities.[2] Central to this was the formation of several organizations: the Society of American Artists (1877), founded as a rebuke to the practices of the National Academy of Design (1826), the Art Students League of New York (1875), The Tile Club (1877), the New York Etching Club (1878), and the Society of Decorative Art (1877). Each drew upon the same membership and had similar interests in artistic collaboration, and the Italian Renaissance was frequently pointed to as a worthwhile source of study. These societies were followed in the early 1880s by the Society of Painters in Pastel (1883–1884) and the Architectural League of New York (1881). During the 1870s and 1880s, numerous museums and schools of art were founded. Also reflecting the heightened art consciousness were publications: books on interior decoration and art history, columns in popular magazines, and specialized periodicals such as *The American Architect and Building News* (1876), *The Art Interchange* (1878), *The Art Review* (1879), and *The Art Amateur* (1878).

The stylistic diffuseness of the prelude period can be seen in a variety of mediums. In mural painting, the contrast between John La Farge's work for H. H. Richardson at Trinity Church in Boston (1876–1877; Fig. 41) and William Morris Hunt's for Richardson and Leopold Eidlitz on the New York State Capitol (1878) indicate divergent sources: La Farge reflects an English Pre-Raphaelite sensibility while Hunt draws on French allegorical painting.[3] The differences between the lingering neo-classicism of Daniel Chester French and the enlivened Renaissance naturalism of Augustus Saint-Gaudens are other examples of disparate sources. In architecture, stylistic diffuseness is apparent in resort and suburban houses. The shaggy, shingle-covered early

FIG. 41 *Facing page*
Trinity Church, Boston, Massachusetts, 1872–1877. Henry Hobson Richardson (1838–1886), architect. Murals by John La Farge (1835–1910). PHOTO: Richard W. Cheek.

1   George William Sheldon, "Prefactory Note," *Artistic Country Seats: Types of Recent American Villas and Cottage Architecture with Instances of Country Club Houses* (New York, 1886–1887); W.C. Brownell, "The Younger Painters of America: First Paper," *Scribner's Monthly* 20 (May 1880), p. 1; Louis J. Millet, "Interior Decoration: Its Development in America," *The Inland Architect* 1 (February 1883), p. 3; and "Art and Life in New York City," *Lippincott's Magazine* 29 (June 1882), pp. 597–605.

2   The first usage of the term "American Renaissance" was in *The Californian* 1 (June 1880), pp. 1–2.
3   La Farge was assisted by Augustus Saint-Gaudens, Francis Lathrop, George Maynard, and Francis Millet.

FIG. 42
Palazzo Cancelleria, Rome,
circa 1485–1495.
PHOTO: Alinari/Editorial Photocolor
Archives.

Colonial Revival of the 1870s and early 1880s gave way to the more sophisticated and urbane Georgian of the H.A.C. Taylor house (1883–1886) in Newport, Rhode Island, by McKim, Mead and White. City houses also reflected a shifting identity, from the French and Italianate of the three Vanderbilt houses of the late 1870s to a direct reliance on High Renaissance palazzos, as can be seen in the relation between the Cancelleria in Rome and the Villard houses, 1882–1886 (Figs. 42 and 43). In all of these monumental city palaces, the designers (McKim, Mead and White for the Villard, Richard Morris Hunt for the W.K. Vanderbilt, George B. Post for the Cornelius Vanderbilt II, and Herter Brothers and Charles B. Atwood for the W.H. Vanderbilt [Figs. 23, 24, and 44–46]) commissioned murals, windows, sculptural details, and furniture from various artists.

The Boston Public Library, 1887–1895, inaugurated the high or mature period of the American Renaissance and the shift to a wider range of vision. Private commissions continued and increased in magnificence (as with the Newport "cottages"), but a new, all-embracing public spirit was also evident as the entire landscape became a scene for action through the replanning of cities and the erection of monumental edifices to the glory of American civilization. The construction of The Boston Public Library marked the beginning of an examination of the public possibilities of art and architecture that became fully recognized at the World's Columbian Exposition of 1893.

FIG. 43 *Above*
Henry Villard houses, New York City,
1882–1886. McKim, Mead and White,
architects.
PHOTO: Vincent S. Villard.

FIG. 44 *Left*
Dining room, Henry Villard house,
New York City, 1882–1886. Fireplace
sculpture by Augustus Saint-Gaudens
(1848–1907).

FIG. 45 *Left*
Cornelius Vanderbilt II house, New York
City, 1878–1882. George B. Post
(1837–1913), architect.
COLLECTION/PHOTO: The Library of
Congress, Washington, D.C.

FIG. 46 *Above*
Fifth Avenue, north from Fifty-first
Street, New York City, showing
W.H. Vanderbilt house, 1879–1881,
Herter Brothers (after 1865–*circa*
1900) and Charles B. Atwood
(1848–1895), architects, and
W.K. Vanderbilt house, 1877–1881,
Richard Morris Hunt (1827–1895),
architect.
COLLECTION/PHOTO: The Library of
Congress, Washington, D.C.

Seen initially as a "fight between the West and East," the White City ultimately became a symbol of national unity.[4] Eastern and Western artists and architects worked in harmony, and although later some would decry the image presented, at the time few spoke out.[5] Stylistically, the high period is governed by scientific eclecticism; the older, synthetic, romantic approach that had still existed in the prelude period disappeared as artists, architects, and furniture designers studied sources and precedents more closely. In general, classicism in image and compositional rules governed more firmly.

Chicago opened the way for numerous expositions in the next twenty-two years: the Tennessee Centennial at Nashville (1897), the Trans-Mississippi and International Exposition at Omaha (1898), the Pan American Exposition at Buffalo (1901), the Louisiana Purchase Exposition at Saint Louis (1904), the Alaska-Yukon-Pacific Exposition at Seattle (1910), the Panama-Pacific International Exposition at San Francisco (1915), the Panama California International Exposition at San Diego (1915), and several more. None ever rivaled Chicago in popularity, and only minor expositions were held on the East Coast.[6] But their impact was tremendous. As a cumulative body they brought the word of the American Renaissance to people of all classes from all parts of the country. Each exposition had unique features: Nashville, large copies of the Parthenon and a pyramid; Buffalo, a Tower of Light; and Saint Louis, a model city. Certain elements became standards: large, central bodies of water, buildings grouped in cohesive arrangements, statuary, mural and wall painting, and some form of the classical style. Appropriately, the greatest freedom from the classical idiom can be seen in the California expositions with their confectionary appliqué of newly created styles.

Accompanying the exposition mania was the formation of organizations and institutions that advanced the American Renaissance. The organizations can be categorized as art medium–oriented: the National Sculpture Society (1893), the National Society of Mural Painters (1895), and the Society of Beaux-Arts Architects (1894); oriented towards advancement of all the arts: The American Federation of Arts (1909), the American Fine Arts Society (1889), and the Fine Arts Federation of New York (1897); those devoted to schooling and study: the American Academy in Rome (1897; originally formed as the American School of Architecture in Rome, 1894), The American School of Classical Studies, Rome (1895); and those devoted to civic art: the Municipal Art Society of New York (1893) and the Municipal Art Leagues of Cincinnati (1894) and Chicago (1899). Accompanying this increased formalization was the foundation of learned societies and academies in which artists participated and designed the medals and seals. Museums and art schools experienced a similar growth; *The American Art Annual* for 1910–1911 listed 944 art museums, art societies, and art schools against 403 in 1907.[7] Museums, as noted, changed their orientation in this period away from reproductions and towards collecting Old Masters. Across the country, Toledo to New Orleans, San Francisco to Brooklyn, many of the major regional museums were founded and grew into new classical quarters. Appropriately, the image of the museum changed: the Gothic Revival red brick and terracotta of the 1870s structures (Fig. 47) was replaced by Roman swagger, as in Boston and New York (Fig. 48).

4   *Chicago Tribune*, September 25, 1889, quoted in Mel Scott, *American City Planning Since 1890* (Berkeley, 1971), p. 32.
5   The best-known criticism appears in Louis Sullivan, *Autobiography of an Idea* (Washington, D.C., 1924). However, this was penned nearly thirty years later and Sullivan blames on the fair his own failings, which were personal. At the time, the most questioning critic was Montgomery Schuyler in "Last Words about the World's Fair" (1895), reprinted in his *American Architecture and Other Writings*, vol. 2, ed. W.H. Jordy and Ralph Coe (Cambridge, Mass., 1961), pp. 556–574.
6   Only a few East Coast expositions have been located: The Jamestown Tricentennial, 1907, and the New York State Fair, Syracuse, 1910.
7   William Walton, "Art Institutions in the United States," The Field of Art, *Scribner's Magazine* 50 (August 1911), p. 253.

The late period of the American Renaissance began in 1917 with the United States's entry into the Great War. After the war, art and culture were no longer exclusively the property of the past—Greek, Roman, or Renaissance. Cracks had appeared earlier; the Armory Show of 1913 is but one of many instances. American Renaissance commentators who previously had stated positive objectives became retrograde, reacting against Cubism, Expressionism, and the Bauhaus. The American Renaissance still existed as the official ideal, as various monuments to the war, the West Virginia State Capitol (1922–1932), Mount Rushmore (1927–1941), and the National Gallery of Art (1937–1941) illustrate. In some cases there was even an attempt to modernize the American Renaissance image, as in the stripped classicism of Paul Cret, the Art Deco of Paul Manship, and the regional portrayals of many of the WPA post office murals. However, for many, an art that drew so conspicuously on the past and refused to recognize the facts of modern technological society (except for a Muse posing as Electricity) had no place, and rebellion and avant-garde attitudes became part of the institution of culture. By the late 1930s, with the influx of European modernists and a corresponding change in American expectations of European art, the American Renaissance no longer existed.

FIG. 47   *Left*
The Metropolitan Museum of Art, New York City, 1874–1880. Calvert Vaux (1824–1895) and Jacob Wrey Mold, architects.
PHOTO: The Metropolitan Museum of Art.

FIG. 48   *Below*
The Metropolitan Museum of Art, New York City. Fifth Avenue facade, 1895–1902, by Richard Morris Hunt (1827–1895) and Richard Howland Hunt (1862–1931), architects.
Wings, 1904–1926, by McKim, Mead and White, architects.
PHOTO: The Metropolitan Museum of Art.

While the American Renaissance died out in the 1930s, certain of its elements have continued even today. Institutionally, organizations such as the Municipal Art Society of New York, the American Academy in Rome, and the many art schools, Brooklyn to San Francisco, still exist, though with refocused aesthetics. In Washington, D.C., the U. S. Commission of Fine Arts remains concerned with the design of the minute to the grand, lampposts to building complexes, as it pursues the goals of Daniel Burnham, Charles McKim, Augustus Saint-Gaudens, Frederick Law Olmsted, Jr., and Senator James McMillan. Serious systematic study of the Italian Renaissance and its progeny is a durable mainstay of college and university history and art history departments. Many major museum and library collections of art, books, and other objects can be traced back to the American Renaissance. And finally, there are the actual physical artifacts, the large parks, grand boulevards, plazas and squares, public buildings, city and country houses, that constitute a tangible heritage.

Since the 1930s the aesthetics and the vision of the American Renaissance have been the subject of derision by many of the artistic and cultural establishment of the United States. The artifacts of the American Renaissance were disposable. The works of Will Low, Daniel Chester French, and their compatriots were either thrown out or hidden in basements and attics; Edwin Blashfield murals were painted over or allowed to decay; and buildings such as McKim, Mead and White's Pennsylvania Station in New York were destroyed with wanton abandon. Infatuated with European modernism and attempting to create a unique American art of abstraction and total originality, the artistic elite were opposed to the goals and methods of the American Renaissance. The history of American art and architecture received an interpretation that either ignored or deplored the American Renaissance.

However, in the past several years, there has been growing interest in realism and the human figure in painting and sculpture. Meanwhile, architects have been found exploring eclecticism, formal composition of the Beaux-Arts variety, and ornament. The preservation movement has gained strength, and there has been a movement towards the recognition of the value of Beaux-Arts monuments.

The American metropolis has changed dramatically since the turn-of-the-century, and certainly the City Beautiful vision could not then, and can not now, solve many of the American urban ills. Yet the fact remains that the most enjoyable and comprehensible elements of cities are frequently those portions created during the American Renaissance period. The sense of visual delight through ornament and decoration and the sense of scale and proportion in both the classical orders and sculptural figures are being discovered as important. While large stairwells, mural paintings, forecourts, and plazas can be viewed as economically indefensible by the functional pragmatist, as spatial entities they are enlivening. Passing through the grand vaulted spaces of railroad stations recalling Roman thermae or pausing to view a Civil War memorial, one can glimpse the ennobling vision of the American Renaissance. A vision of a great civilization was created; a high culture was expressed.

PART II STATEMENTS OF CULTURE

6 Architecture, Landscape, and City Planning

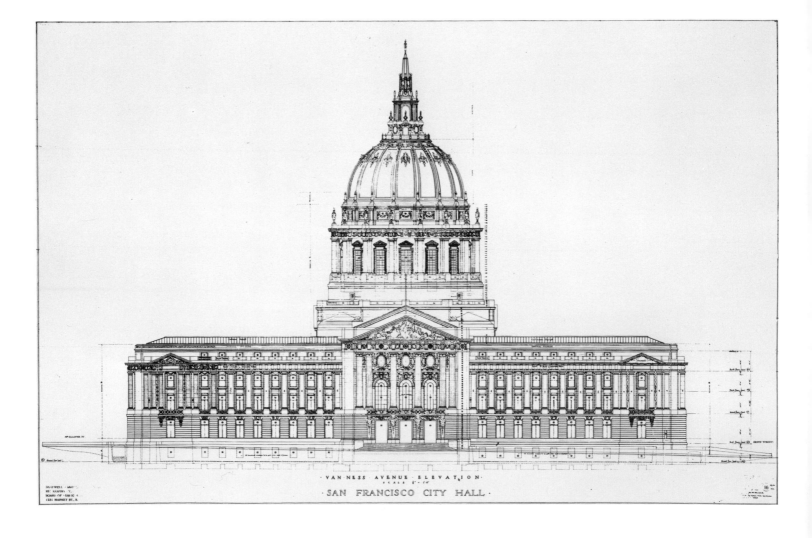

· VAN NESS · AVENUE · ELEVATION ·
SCALE 1"=1'0"

· SAN FRANCISCO CITY HALL ·

Architecture dominated the American Renaissance. The vision of a great civilization became reality with monumental public buildings such as Arthur Brown, Jr.'s San Francisco City Hall (Fig. 51), large commercial structures decorated with murals and sculpture, such as George Post's Bank of Pittsburgh (Fig. 52), and country and resort houses rivaling those of Europe, such as Richard Morris Hunt's Breakers for Cornelius Vanderbilt II (Fig. 72). Great portions of the landscape, from small resting places along the Hudson River (Fig. 53) to entire civic centers, became part of the architectural vision. Cities from coast to coast—New York, Washington, D.C. (Fig. 49), Chicago (Fig. 14), Denver, and San Francisco—were transformed into backdrops for the projected rituals of nationalism and civilization. Architecture played the key role. Against the clatter and grim poverty of the street there could stand the eternal and pure vision of the American Renaissance building (Fig. 54).

Architecture as the controlling art form influenced the closely allied disciplines of landscape architecture and city planning, as well as the other arts. Artists frequently saw their role as subservient to that of the architect. Architecture, simply by size, scale, and confidence of appearance, tended to overpower all else. The architect led, he created the unity—the three dimensional entity—into which would be put the work of the stained glass artist, the mural painter, the decorative sculptor, and the interior decorator.

The dominance and power of the architectural approach resulted from several factors. The architect encompassed the worlds of the artist and of the businessman. Men such as Charles McKim, Daniel Burnham, and Cass Gilbert were at home in the corporate boardroom, the university trustees' meeting, the club room, the mayor's office, the drafting room, the building site, and the artist's studio. In an age seeking a high culture, architecture provided the most permanent expression of the American arrival as a great civilization. The vituperation heaped upon the buildings of the American Renaissance by a later generation seeking the modern image is testimony to the power of these buildings.

A symbiotic relationship existed between architecture, landscape architecture, and city planning. Although scale and materials differed for each medium, the creation of spaces for human activity concerned all three disciplines. Mutual attitudes of scientific eclecticism, or the assemblage of pieces from the past—usually the classic past—to create harmonious wholes, provided a common basis. A strong sense of social and moral responsibility activated these three modes of expression, even though the aesthetic viewpoint dominated. The term "City Beautiful" indicates an orientation of city planning in the period. Stanford White summed up the outlook of many designers when he told a client: "The architects who have made their mark in the world are artists and designers of buildings, and not engineers and businessmen—the latter I suppose you know to your cost."[1] Finally, the products, whether a building, a city plan, or a garden, required not simply the activity of a designer making beautiful drawings but a patron

1 Stanford White to C.T. Barney, September 18, 1901, McKim, Mead and White Collection, The New-York Historical Society, New York City.

Richard Guy Wilson

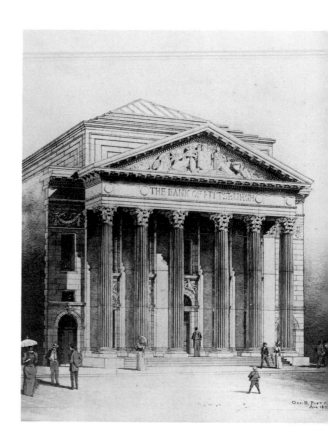

FIG. 51 *Facing page:*
Van Ness Avenue elevation, San Francisco City Hall, 1912–1915. Blakewell and Brown, architects.
COLLECTION: Sylvia Brown Jensen, California.
PHOTO: The Arthur Brown, Jr., Collection.

FIG. 52 *Above:*
Front elevation of the Bank of Pittsburgh, 1894. George B. Post (1837–1913), architect. Ink and watercolor on paper; 91.4 x 61.0 cm. (36 x 24 in.).
COLLECTION: The New-York Historical Society, New York City.

to finance the project and executants. The dominance of the architectural approach can best be understood through an examination of the relative status of the three disciplines; the actual method of creation through training, design, and drawings; and finally the buildings themselves.

Architecture

Among the three disciplines, architecture was the most highly developed, both professionally and educationally. The founding of the American Institute of Architects in 1857 stands in contrast to the organization of the American Society of Landscape Architects and the American City Planning Institute in 1899 and 1917 respectively. Over the years a few rival organizations developed, but by the 1890s most architects were firmly united behind the AIA.[2] In education there was little specific development in the areas of landscape architecture and city planning until after 1900. Architecture, though, had a firmly established system of training, and architects viewed themselves as capable of handling the entire landscape.

Until the 1850s formal architectural training in the United States was nonexistent. Most architects learned through self-education, apprenticeship with a self-taught architect, or from a foreign immigrant. In 1855 Richard Morris Hunt returned from study at the École des Beaux-Arts, one of the few architectural schools in existence. Three years later, in 1858, Hunt organized in New York a private atelier. Several of Hunt's students—William Robert Ware, Henry Van Brunt, and George B. Post—later became leaders of the American Renaissance. Van Brunt remembered the prospect nostalgically: "Thus we together entered upon an era so rich, so full of surprise and delight that it seems, as we look back upon it, as if once more in the world the joy of the Renaissance, the white light of knowledge, had broken in upon the superstitions of romance."[3] In 1865 the first American school of architecture was founded at the Massachusetts Institute of Technology in Boston with William Robert Ware as the director. Before the first classes were held, Ware visited Paris to study the methods of the École des Beaux-Arts and, a few years later, hired as a critic and instructor of design Eugene Letang, a recent graduate of the École. Subsequent American schools of architecture generally followed the École pattern of training (Cornell, 1871; Syracuse, 1873; Michigan, 1876; Pennsylvania, 1890; Armour Institute, 1895; and Harvard, 1895).[4] They also followed the tradition of hiring French critics: Maurice J. Prevot and Jean Hebrard at Cornell, Paul Cret at Pennsylvania, and E.S.A. Duquesne and Jacques Haffner at Harvard. In 1881 William Robert Ware moved to New York and set up the Columbia School of Architecture.

Concurrently, many Americans followed the example of Hunt, who had attended the École from 1846 to 1853, and Richardson, who had attended between 1859 and 1863. Charles F. McKim and Robert Peabody were there from 1867 to 1870, Whitney Warren from 1888 to 1893, and Arthur Brown, Jr., from 1897 to 1900. The height of the American attendance came in the period between 1890 and 1914.[5] The American Academy in Rome was established at the same time, which helped to continue the focus of American architectural education on European precedents.

2   The history of American professionals and specifically that of architects is too complex to treat in detail here. In the 1880s one rival organization, the Western Association of Architects, had grown up—but the breach healed. In the later 1890s and early 1900s a strong drive was made to increase the prestige of the AIA. The acquisition of the Octagon in Washington, D.C., under the presidency of Charles McKim in 1902, is one indication of this attempt.

3   Henry Van Brunt, "Richard Morris Hunt" (1895), reprinted in *Architecture and Society, Selected Essays of Henry Van Brunt*, ed. W.A. Coles (Cambridge, Mass., 1969), p. 332. On Hunt's atelier see also W.A. Coles, "Richard Morris Hunt and His Library as Revealed in the Studio Sketchbooks of Henry Van Brunt," *The Art Quarterly* XXX (Fall–Winter 1967), pp. 224–238; and Alan Burnham, "The New York Architecture of Richard Morris Hunt," *Journal of the Society of Architectural Historians* 11 (May 1952),

pp. 9–15. Other students included Charles Dexter Gambrill, Frank Furness, and Edmund Quincy.
4   The University of Illinois School of Architecture, founded in 1868 and for many years guided by Nathan C. Ricker, was the only early school not strongly influenced by the Beaux-Arts method. See James Philip Noffsinger, *The Influence of the École des Beaux-Arts on the Architects of the United States* (Washington, D.C., 1955).
5   Noffsinger, *Influence of the École des Beaux-Arts*, pp. 106–110.

FIG. 53   *Left:*
Study for Inspiration Point, Riverside Drive,
New York, circa 1905. Arnold W. Brunner
(1857–1925), architect; Frederick Law
Olmsted, Jr. (1870–1957), landscape
architect.
Watercolor and ink on board; 87.7 x 56.8 cm.
(34½ x 22⅓ in.).
COLLECTION: Cooper-Hewitt Museum, the
Smithsonian Institution's National
Museum of Design, New York City.
PHOTO: Scott Hyde.

FIG. 54   *Below:*
The Bowery, New York. The Bowery Savings
Bank, New York City, 1893–1895. McKim,
Mead and White, architects.
COLLECTION / PHOTO: The Library of
Congress, Washington, D.C.

FIG. 55
Plan of building group for an urban square,
circa 1900, a student project by
William Adams Delano (1874–1960).
Ink and wash on paper; 73.7 x 92.7 cm.
(29 x 36½ in.).
COLLECTION: Avery Library, Columbia
University, New York City.

Not all architects received formal training. Stanford White, for example, received preliminary instruction as a painter from John La Farge, apprenticed with H.H. Richardson, traveled in Europe for a year, and then in September of 1879 joined McKim and Mead in partnership. Cass Gilbert's education consisted of a short period with a Saint Paul architect, one year at MIT, a trip abroad, two years with McKim, Mead and White, and then in 1885 he formed a partnership with James Knox Taylor in Saint Paul. The apprentice method lost favor as formal education developed, but time spent in a large, well-known office after schooling was always considered an integral element. McKim, Mead and White ran the best-known training

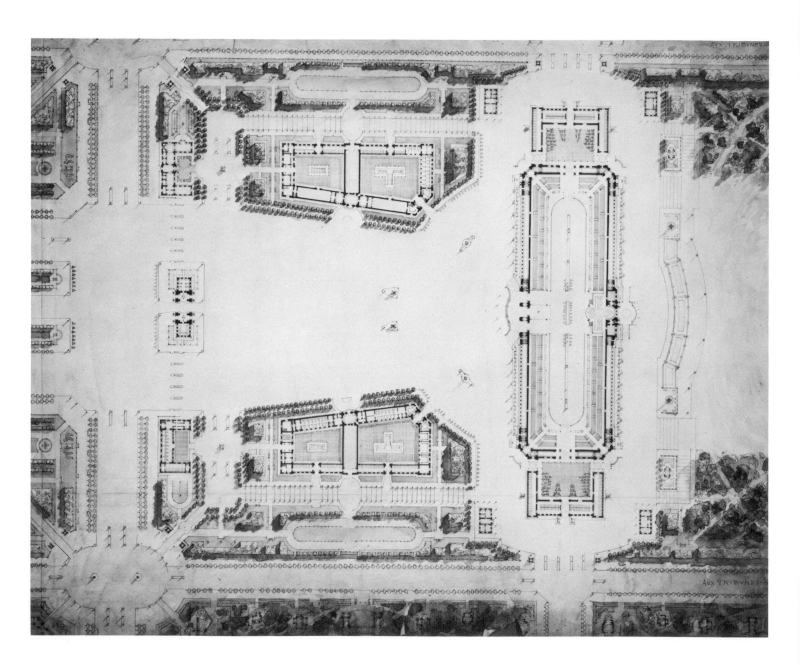

6   The involvement of Olmsted can be seen in letters of McKim to him, reprinted in Charles Moore, *The Life and Times of Charles Follen McKim* (Boston, 1929), pp. 264–265. Francesco Passanti, "The Design of Columbia in the 1890s: McKim and His Client," *Journal of the Society of Architectural Historians* XXXVI (May 1977), pp. 69–84, reconstructs the sequence of the design's development and indicates that Olmsted played a very small role.

office, and in addition to Gilbert, office alumni included John M. Carrère, Thomas Hastings, Francis L.V. Hoppin, Terrance A. Koen, George F. Babb, William E. Whidden, A. Page Brown, A.D.F. Hamlin, Royal Cortissoz, Louis Kamper, Hobart Weeks, Henry Bacon, Edward P. York, Philip Sawyer, and Egerton Swartwout, among many. These men carried the message of the American Renaissance to all parts of the country: San Francisco, Detroit, Portland, Saint Augustine, and elsewhere.

Integral to the dominance of architecture was the attitude that the architect not only designed buildings but decided on the site and the molding of outer space. School projects such as that done by William Adams Delano while at the École for an exhibition center (Fig. 55) gave the architect the sole responsibility for creating important centers of public gathering. In the real world of commissions and buildings, a landscape architect might be consulted and probably would be charged with recommending planting and minor ornamentation, but the architect remained in charge. The creation of university and college campuses in the American Renaissance offers an example of the dominance of the architect's approach. McKim, Mead and White designed the campuses of Columbia University at Morningside Heights in Manhattan and New York University in the Bronx, made major additions to Harvard University and The University of Virginia, and added buildings or architectural elements of gates, fences, and terraces to numerous others. In most cases, the involvement of landscape architects was minimal. The best-known scheme was at Columbia. Frederick Law Olmsted, Sr., served on the advisory board and actually tried to create a compromise plan. But Olmsted was only an adviser; the final plan was almost exclusively Charles McKim's and projected a processional path through urban spaces bounded by buildings, a path that culminated in the pantheonic Low Library (Fig. 56).[6]

FIG. 56
The Library of Columbia College (Low Library), New York City, 1894. McKim, Mead and White, architects.
COLLECTION: The New-York Historical Society, New York City.

The Court of Honor for the World's Columbian Exposition at Chicago (Figs. 10 and 84) further reveals the dominance of the architectural vision. Olmsted is generally credited with the plan; however, he projected an "informal water effect."[7] The final decision for the formal Court of Honor came from the need to group the major exhibition buildings, the determination by the architects (Daniel Burnham and John Wellborn Root) of the actual shape and disposition of the buildings, and finally the unanimous and apparently spontaneous agreement by the invited architects (Richard Morris Hunt, Charles F. McKim, George B. Post, Robert S. Peabody, and Henry Van Brunt) for a total unity of style, color, and cornice height. Henry Sargent Codman, Olmsted's assistant, suggested the arrangement of terraces, bridges, canals, and landings.[8] The original "informal water effect" emerged only in the outer reaches of the Exposition. Olmsted certainly never envisioned the imperial pomp of the Court of Honor, and he deplored it.[9]

Daniel Burnham's career represents clearly the architectural dominance.[10] Beginning as an architect in Chicago in 1873 with John Wellborn Root (who died in January 1891), Burnham's first major involvement in landscape and city planning came with the Columbian Exposition, where he served first as consultant architect and then as director of works and construction and chairman of the consulting board of architects, artists, engineers, and landscape architects. After the Exposition, D.H. Burnham and Company became the largest architectural firm in the United States, concentrating almost exclusively upon commercial and public buildings. At the same time, Burnham developed a career as a city planner, serving as chairman of the McMillan Commission for Washington, D.C. (1901–1902; Fig. 49) and then producing plans for Cleveland (1902–1903), San Francisco (1904–1906), Manila and Baguio in the Philippines (1905), and ultimately Chicago (1906–1909; Fig. 14), along with a host of minor plans and recommendations. In 1910 he became the first chairman of the U.S. Commission of Fine Arts in Washington, D.C. In all of these endeavors Burnham was assisted by many talented people, but he was no mere figurehead. A portion of his effectiveness came from his ability as a pragmatic organizer and his ability to think large, or as has been attributed to him: "Make no little plans; they have no magic to stir men's blood. . . . Make big plans; aim high in hope and work. . . . Let your watchword be order and your beacon beauty."[11] Burnham made decisions not only on architectural style or the placement of buildings, but also on the design of open spaces, the development of park systems, road patterns, replanning of slums, and on the political issues central to the successful implementation of any plan. Frequently, Burnham has been criticized as merely an organizer lacking any firm aesthetic convictions, simply a parrot of the ideas of his Eastern cohorts, especially Charles McKim. Yet all evidence indicates he firmly believed in the moral purpose of the "Classical Renaissance," as he termed the style, and he became one of the strongest spokesmen for the American Academy in Rome.[12]

Many other architects conceived of their job as encompassing the entire man-made landscape. Arnold Brunner attended architecture school at MIT, graduated in 1879, worked for George B. Post, and then set up an office that became well-known for City Beautiful plans and notable structures. In

7   Quoted in Cynthia Field, "The City Planning of Daniel Hudson Burnham" (Ph.D. diss., Columbia University, 1974), p. 69.
8   This responsibility for the design has been controversial. However, from the public statements of Burnham at the time, Olmsted apparently played a small role in the Court of Honor. See Daniel H. Burnham, "The Organization of the World's Columbian Exposition," *The Inland Architect* 22 (August 1893), pp. 5–8. This was originally read before the World's Congresses of

Architects at Chicago on August 1, 1893, and subsequently widely republished. The public tributes later paid to Olmsted by Burnham ("In the highest sense he is the planner of the Exposition") and others reflect the usual hyperbole of the period (Charles Moore, *Daniel H. Burnham, Architect, Planner of Cities* [Boston, 1921], vol. 1, p. 74). A further consideration can be found in Titus M. Karlowicz, "D.H. Burnham's Role in the Selection of Architects for the World's Columbian Exposition," *Journal of the Society of Ar-*

FIG. 57
*View of Courtroom, U.S. Federal Building,
Cleveland (Ohio), circa* 1909. Arnold W.
Brunner (1857–1925), architect.
Pencil on heavy board; 66.5 x 77.1 cm.
(26¼ x 30⅜ in.).
COLLECTION: Cooper-Hewitt Museum, the
Smithsonian Institution's National
Museum of Design, New York City.

Cleveland he served with Burnham on the Plan Commission and also designed the Federal Building (Fig. 57). He also worked on plans for Toledo, Albany, Pittsburgh, Baltimore, Rochester, and Denver. For New York City he did a variety of schemes including parks such as Inspiration Point on Riverside Drive (in conjunction with Frederick Law Olmsted, Jr. [Fig. 53]). The partners John M. Carrère and Thomas Hastings, architects of The New York Public Library, were involved in a variety of planning schemes, both individually and in tandem, including the Cleveland Plan, plans for Atlantic City, Hartford, and Grand Rapids, and the Pan American Exposition in Buffalo.

The dominance of architecture over landscape architecture and city planning tended to be confirmed by criticism and publications. Periodicals such as *The American Architect and Building News* (founded in 1876), *The Architectural Record* (founded in 1891) and *The Brickbuilder* (founded in 1897) frequently featured articles on landscape and urban design. On the other hand, *Landscape Architecture*, the first such specialized periodical, was not founded until 1910, and there was no American journal specifically devoted to city planning until 1925.[13]

Writers and critics such as Russell Sturgis, Mariana Griswold Van Rensselaer, Harry Desmond, Herbert Croly, and Montgomery Schuyler, normally identified with architecture, felt no compunction in addressing

chitectural Historians XXIX (October 1970), pp. 247–254.
9   Laura Wood Roper, *FLO: A Biography of Frederick Law Olmsted* (Baltimore, 1973), pp. 437, 446.
10   See Moore, *Burnham,* vols. 1 and 2; and Thomas H. Hines, *Burnham of Chicago, Architect and Planner* (New York, 1974).
11   Moore, *Burnham,* vol. 2, p. 147. Apparently this is a rephrasing by Willis Polk, an associate; see Field, "City Planning of Daniel Hudson Burnham," p. 413.

12   Moore, *Burnham,* vol. 2, p. 56.
13   *City Planning* first appeared in 1925. *The Journal of the American Institute of Planners* began in 1935. There had been previous periodicals dealing with the city—*Municipal Affairs* (1897–1903) and *The American City* (1909–1975)—but none devoted specifically to city planning. For landscape design, two earlier periodicals should be noted, *Garden and Forest* (1888–1897) and *The Horticulturist* (1846–1875).

landscape design, city planning, and ultimately the other arts as well. Some, such as Van Rensselaer, Croly, and Desmond, became unwavering supporters of the American Renaissance, though Croly did question the lavish display of wealth by the rich in their dwellings.[14] Russell Sturgis, an unreconciled Ruskinite, could never accept the formalism of McKim, Mead and White and others.[15] Schuyler also reflected the medieval critical viewpoint into the 1890s, but by 1902 he became a staunch admirer of the City Beautiful movement and defended the McMillan Commission's plans for Washington, D.C., in *The Architectural Record* and on the editorial page of the *New York Times*.[16] He even proposed a scheme for New York City of two diagonal avenues between Fourteenth and Fifty-ninth streets that would, he claimed, offer "sites for stately buildings where they could really be seen."[17]

Development of Landscape Architecture

The subservience of landscape architecture to architecture resulted from its relative youth as a profession and the lack of a clear definition of purpose. The term "landscape architect" first appeared in 1863 in a report by Frederick Law Olmsted, Sr., and Calvert Vaux concerning New York's Central Park.[18] More commonly used terms were "landscape gardener" or "nurseryman," reflecting the diverse origins of the discipline. Most landscape architects originated from one of three backgrounds: they were converted architects, they had apprenticed with a park or garden designer, or finally, they were glorified horticulturists, knowledgeable about plant materials and cultivation but lacking a design orientation. Not until 1899 was the American Society of Landscape Architects founded, and a year later the first professional curriculum in landscape architecture was organized at Harvard under Frederick Law Olmsted, Jr. Well into the twentieth century many landscape architecture programs, especially at Midwestern universities, went under the name "Landscape Gardening" and were attached to schools of agriculture rather than to schools of design.[19]

A historical background for landscape design in the United States was almost nonexistent. Leaving aside the minor episodes of planned gardens in the Colonial and Early Republic periods, conscious landscape design really began in the 1840s with the writings and work of Andrew Jackson Downing and his contemporaries.[20] In image, Downing's designs followed the picturesque, romantic approach popularized by Humphrey Repton and John Claudius Loudon in England. Parks, cemeteries, suburbs, and the grounds surrounding houses were laid out in a soft, easy flowing, curving, and often spatially undefined manner. The work of Frederick Law Olmsted, Sr., and Calvert Vaux continued this trend, though with more spatial structure and a higher moral purpose, attempting to effect social change through physical form. Olmsted's work reflected the utilitarian-transcendentalist currents of the mid-nineteenth century, and he saw his work as quintessentially American and democratic. Consequently, he fought against the monumental arched gateways—aristocratic, pompous, and foreign—that Richard Morris Hunt proposed for Central Park in the period from 1863 to 1865.[21] In works stretching from Prospect Park in Brooklyn to Belle Isle in Detroit, Olmsted reached a wide public, but the underlying meanings and intentions were

14 Harry Desmond and Herbert Croly, *Stately Homes in America* (New York, 1903) presents the positive picture; however, Croly's "Rich Men and Their Houses," *The Architectural Record* 12 (May 1902), pp. 27–32, is more critical.
15 Russell Sturgis, "McKim, Mead and White" in "Great American Architects," *The Architectural Record* (May 1895), pp. 1–111.
16 Charles McKim to Montgomery Schuyler, February 28, 1902, McKim Collection, The Library of Congress, Washington, D.C., contains a thank you "for your admirable presentation of the Washington scheme."

17 Montgomery Schuyler, "The Art of City Making," *The Architectural Record* 12 (May 1902), p. 25.
18 Norman T. Newton, *Design on the Land: The Development of Landscape Architecture* (Cambridge, Mass., 1971), p. 273; see also Roper, *FLO*, p. 292.
19 The Morrill Land Grant College Act, 1862, established many colleges in the Midwest with two primary divisions, Agriculture and Mechanics; hence the "A & M" school.
20 On the early history of American landscape design see Newton, *Design on the Land*, chap. 18;

Carlton B. Lees, "The Golden Age of Horticulture," *Historic Preservation* 24 (October–December 1972), pp. 32–37; David B. Chase, "The Beginnings of the Landscape Tradition in America," *Historic Preservation* 25 (January–March 1973), pp. 34–41; and George B. Tatum, "The Emergence of an American School of Landscape Design," *Historic Preservation* 25 (April–June 1973), pp. 34–41.
21 Albert Fein, *Frederick Law Olmsted and the American Environmental Tradition* (New York, 1972), pp. 11–13, figs. 7, 8. The originals for these drawings are in the American Institute of Architects Foundation Collection.

imperfectly understood at best; his mentality was that of a mid-century reformer persisting into the 1890s. Late in Olmsted's career a shift in orientation of landscape design became evident; formal compositions of symmetrical axes, cross axes, and imagery specifically derived from classical sources appeared in the gardens at Biltmore (Fig. 58).

On the level of spatial structure, the increased formality of landscape architecture resulted from changes in American architecture. Up until the 1880s the irregular spatial organizations of most American buildings reflected picturesque planning. A setting of soft, amorphous outer space was appropriate for the building. The irregular, picturesque outline and plan of buildings and grounds directly reflected the dominance of painting, especially landscape painting, in the period from 1830 to 1880. In contrast, the increasing dominance of architecture from the mid-1880s onwards can be seen in the new axiality and formal distribution of spaces according to notions of an ideal classic order in both buildings and grounds. Formally ordered architecture, whether McKim, Mead and White's Rhode Island Statehouse (Fig. 35) or Charles Adams Platt's Harold F. McCormick house (Fig. 59), in Lake Forest, Illinois, projected outwards a system of straight lines, axes, and cross axes that were reflected in landscape design.

On the level of intention, the increased formality indicated a shift in purpose. Landscape architecture still had the dimension of social betterment and improvement, but now celebrated were images of power, organization, and control. Reflecting the change was Frederick Law Olmsted, Jr., who carried on his father's firm after 1895 in company with a half-brother, John

FIG. 58
Gardens at Biltmore, George Washington Vanderbilt house, Asheville, North Carolina, 1888–1895. Frederick Law Olmsted, Sr. (1822–1903), landscape architect; Richard Morris Hunt (1827–1895), architect.
COLLECTION: Biltmore House and Gardens.

Charles Olmsted. In 1900 the younger Olmsted addressed the AIA conference in Washington, D.C., and pleaded for an understanding of L'Enfant's original plan and observed: "Great public edifices must be strongly formal, whether they are perfectly symmetrical or not, and this formal quality ought to be recognized in the plan of their surroundings if the total effect is to be consistent."[22] He was appointed to the McMillan Commission in 1901, and with Burnham, McKim, and Charles Moore (the secretary of the Commission), he traveled in Europe to study firsthand the sources that influenced the original scheme and that again might provide inspiration. They visited the Bois de Boulogne, the Tuileries, Fontainebleau, Versailles, Vaux-le-Vicomte, the Luxembourg Gardens, Villa d'Este, Hadrian's Villa, the Piazza di San Pietro, the Piazza San Marco, Hatfield House, and Hampton Court Palace, among other sites. The trip revealed, according to Charles Moore,

FIG. 59
Block Plan of House, Gardens and Service Buildings, Estate for Harold F. McCormick, Lake Forest, Illinois 1908–1911. Charles Adams Platt (1861–1933), architect.
Ink on linen; 130.1 x 89.5 cm. (51¼ x 35¼ in.).
COLLECTION: Avery Library, Columbia University, New York City.

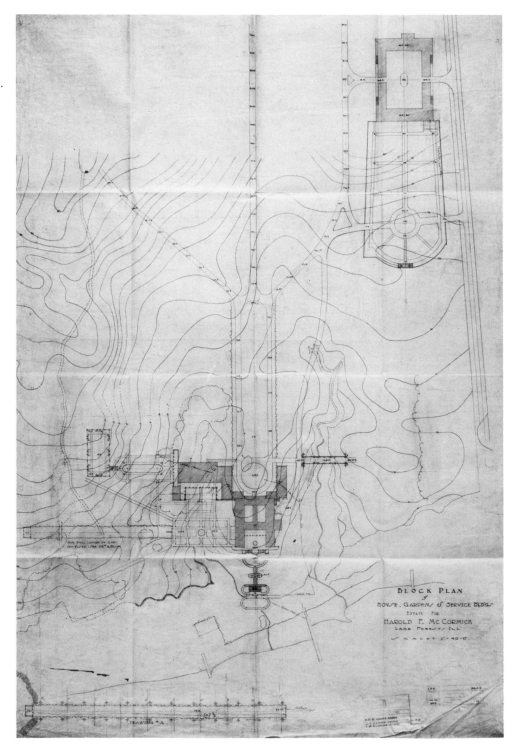

"that the problems in Washington must be worked out along Roman rather than Parisian lines."[23] The McMillan Commission's scheme, with the reassertion of the shaft of space of the Mall, the projection of major memorials to Lincoln and to other national heroes as terminations of the reclaimed axes, the Union Square in front of the Capitol, the Memorial Bridge, and the twin alleys of four-abreast American elms all derived from the European tour. The younger Olmsted fully supported these classical gestures and took charge of the landscaping features such as the sunken—Italian derived—gardens around the Washington Monument. The McMillan Commission Plan for Washington, D.C. (Fig. 49), celebrates a mighty nation linked to the classical past.

The informal, picturesque method of landscape design did not completely disappear in the 1890s and 1900s, but the dominant image was the clear language of geometric order derived from the classical past. Among those who worked in the new formalism were the European émigrés—Jacques Greber and Diego Suárez—and native Americans—the Olmsteds, Beatrix Jones Farrand, Nathan Barrett, Guy Lowell, and George Burnap. Popularization of formal landscape design came through several publications, first the writings of Charles Adams Platt and then Edith Wharton, who in 1904 published *Italian Villas and Their Gardens*, with illustrations by Maxfield Parrish (Fig. 151).

Charles Adams Platt's career illustrates the transcendence of landscape design into architecture. Trained neither as an architect nor as a landscape architect, but as a painter at the École des Beaux-Arts, he became interested in landscape design through both painting and a younger brother who had been briefly in the Olmsted office. In 1892 Charles and William Platt visited Italy to draw, measure, and photograph gardens and villas dating from the fifteenth through the eighteenth centuries. William died shortly after they returned home; Charles published their findings in two articles for *Harper's Magazine* in 1893 and as a book the following year.[24] The building and the grounds were considered as a totality, or as Platt wrote: "The word 'villa' is used in the Italian sense, implying all the formal parts of the grounds arranged in direct relation to the house, the house itself being as much a part of it as the garden or the grove." His conclusion claimed a similarity of landscape types between the United States and Italy and called for a "revival of the same method."[25] In the next few years Platt developed a substantial landscape practice and by 1900 graduated to designing houses as well as gardens.

The "Villa at Lake Forest" (the Harold F. McCormick house and grounds at Lake Forest, Illinois, built from 1908 to 1911 with additions made in 1917 [Figs. 59–61]) was one of Platt's finest and most notorious projects,

FIG. 60 *Below:*
Harold F. McCormick house and gardens, Lake Forest, Illinois, 1908–1911.

FIG. 61 *Below, bottom:*
1917 entrance gates of the Harold F. McCormick house, Lake Forest, Illinois, 1908–1911.
Drawing by Schell Lewis.
Pencil on tracing paper; 43.5 x 74.9 cm. (17⅛ x 29½ in.).
COLLECTION: Avery Library, Columbia University, New York City.

22 Frederick Law Olmsted, Jr., "Landscape in Connection with Public Buildings in Washington," *Papers Relating to the Improvement of the City of Washington, District of Columbia*, ed. Glen Brown (Washington, 1901), p. 25.
23 Moore, *McKim*, p. 192; see also John Reps, *Monumental Washington* (Princeton, 1967), chap. 4.
24 Charles Adams Platt, "Italian Gardens," *Harper's New Monthly Magazine* 87 (July and August 1893), pp. 165–180, 393–406.
25 Charles Adams Platt, *Italian Gardens* (New York, 1894), pp. 6, 154.

since the commission had originally belonged to Frank Lloyd Wright.[26] Described as an example of "The Renaissance Villa of Italy Developed into a Complete Residential Type for Use in America," the house terminated a long drive and masked a view of Lake Michigan beyond.[27] The formal division of the grounds into gardens, lawns, woods, and terraces was an outward projection of the house's internal organization. The system of fountains, steps, and terraces on the lakeside that continued the entrance axis, although not a copy, recalled many of the Italian examples Platt knew—the Villa d'Este, the Villa Lante, and the Villa Caprarola. From country houses and gardens Platt would later graduate to full-scale commercial and public commissions. Landscape design was left far behind.

The Birth of City Planning

City planning as a discipline and a profession emerged around the year 1900. In Austria, Germany, Spain, France, England, and the United States a new concern with the physical form of cities became evident. The causes of this simultaneous explosion of interest were the astronomical growth of cities in the later nineteenth century, the rotting of cities' older cores and industrial sectors, and the desire by different segments of the population—rulers, politicians, businessmen, philanthropists, and artists—to give an artistic dimension to cities and improve the living environment.[28] In the United States the City Beautiful movement provided the immediate background for the development of city planning, although much of the concern was directed towards civic or municipal art, and not towards complete city plans like Chicago's (Fig. 14). The great arches erected for memorials or celebrations, permanent or temporary, such as the Soldiers' and Sailors' Monument in Grand Army Plaza in Brooklyn (1889–1892; Fig. 4) and the Dewey Arch in Madison Square in New York City (1899; Fig. 62) indicate the essentially artistic nature of the enterprises.

Historically, city or town planning in the United States had existed in a rather nebulous area. Architects, landscape gardeners, politicians, soldiers, speculators, surveyors, and gentlemen all had participated in the process for the previous three hundred years. Except for the almost universal usage of the gridiron plan, little continuity had existed in American city planning.[29] Planning was seen as primarily an activity to subdivide land, arrange streets, and locate municipal buildings. Only a few real triumphs could be pointed to, such as L'Enfant's plan for Washington, D.C., 1791, and the work of the senior Olmsted. Some of Olmsted's designs constituted a precedent for the City Beautiful movement: tree-lined boulevards such as Eastern Parkway in Brooklyn, the boulevards in Buffalo, and the park as a continuous system throughout the city, as with the Fenways, Franklin, and Jamaica Pond Park in Boston.[30] Contemporaries of Olmsted—Horace Cleveland, Jacob Weidenman, and the more youthful Charles Eliot and George E. Kessler— had developed or used many of the same ideas and laid the basis for park systems and municipal betterment in other areas—Minneapolis, Minnesota; Hartford, Connecticut; and Kansas City, Missouri.

The immediate crystallization of the City Beautiful movement can be laid to the World's Columbian Exposition and the wide approbation it

FIG. 62 *Facing page:*
Dewey Triumphal Arch and Colonnade, Madison Square, New York City, 1899 (demolished). Charles R. Lamb, architect. Frederic W. Ruckstull (1853–1942), sculptor-in-charge. Quadria, *Victory at Sea*, by J.Q.A. Ward (1830–1910). South face: pier sculpture, left: *Triumphant Return* by Charles B. Niehaus (1855–1935); right: *War*, or *The Combat*, by Karl Bitter (1867–1915). Attic figures: left to right: *Commodore Perry* by Jonathan S. Hartley (1845–1912); *Admiral Farragut* by W.O. Partridge (1861–1930); *Commodore John Paul Jones* by E.C. Potter (1857–1923); *Commodore Decatur* by George T. Brewster (1862–1943). Keystone: *Great Eagle* by Frederic W. Ruckstull. Spandrels: *North and East Rivers* by Isidor Konti (1862–1938). South colonnade: left: *Navy* by George Bissel (1839–1920); right: *Army* by Frederic W. Ruckstull. North face: pier sculpture: *Peace* by Daniel Chester French (1850–1931) and *Departure for War* by Philip Martiny (1858–1927). Attic figures: *Commodore McDonough* by Thomas S. Clarke (1860–1920); *Commodore Porter* by J.J. Boyle; *Commodore Hull* by Henry K. Bush-Brown (1857–1935); *Lieutenant Cushing* by H. Augustus Lukeman (1871–1935). Spandrels: *Atlantic and Pacific Oceans* by Roland H. Perry (1870–1941). Keystone: *Great Eagle* by Frederic W. Ruckstull. Sides of arch: alto relievo panels: East: *Protection of Country* by William Couper (1853–1942); West: *Advancement of Civilization* by Johannes Gellert. Medallions above: *Commodore Bainbridge* by Ralph Goddard (1861–1936); *Commodore Preble* by F.C. Hamann; *Commodore Barry* and *Admiral Davis* by F.W. Kaldenberg; *Captain Lawrence* by Henry Baerer; *Admiral Dahlgren* by Casper Buberl; *Admiral Worden* and *Admiral Foote* by Frederick Moynihan.
COLLECTION/PHOTO: The Library of Congress, Washington, D.C.

26 Henry-Russell Hitchcock, *In the Nature of Materials: The Buildings of Frank Lloyd Wright, 1887–1941* (New York, 1941), pp. 47–48, 60, figs. 139–141.
27 "The Renaissance Villa of Italy Developed into a Complete Residential Type for Use in America," *The Architectural Record* 31 (March 1912), p. 201–223.
28 In 1873 Chicago had a population of 325,000, by 1910 it stood at 2,185,283. London in 1871 had a population of 3,254,260, and by 1910 it

stood at 4,522,000. Vienna in 1868 had a population of 607,514, and in 1910 it had 2,031,000 residents.
29 The best source on American planning history is John Reps, *The Making of Urban America* (Princeton, 1965).
30 For the immediate background of the City Beautiful movement, see Albert Fein, "The American City: The Ideal and the Real," in *The Rise of an American Architecture*, ed. Edgar Kaufmann, Jr. (New York, 1970), pp. 51–111.

received.[31] "Here," Daniel Burnham claimed, "a great truth, set forth by great artists, was taught to all our people. This truth is the supreme one of the need of design and plan for whole cities."[32] The White City struck a chord with Americans and suggested the possibility of replanning and beautifying entire cities. European prototypes were frequently pointed to as models: Imperial Rome, Renaissance Venice, and Second Empire Paris. Paris and the work of Baron Haussmann from 1852 to 1870 became especially important to Americans at the turn of the century and received much favorable comment.[33] Finally, as a literary prototype, Edward Bellamy's *Looking Backward, 2000–1887* (1888) offered the vision of "miles of broad streets, shaded by trees and lined with fine buildings, . . . large open squares filled with trees, among which statues glistened and fountains flashed . . . [and] Public buildings of a colossal size and an architectural grandeur unparalleled."[34] The appeal of this utopian vision and the subsequent spread of Nationalistic Clubs helped to fuel the notion of remaking American cities.

Comprehensive replanning on the scale of Washington, D.C., San Francisco, or Chicago represented only one side of the City Beautiful movement. On a far smaller scale were projects for library decoration (Fig. 153), park shelters, and sculpture. The Municipal Art Society of New York concerned itself with commissioning and finding locations for sculpture, placing mural paintings in civic buildings and schools, and providing street furniture and did not concern itself with a total plan for the city.[35] Chicago's White City, with its elaborate electroliers, colonnades, and monumental and genre sculpture and murals, was certainly a source, but there was also the earlier tradition of village and town improvement societies. Existing as far back as mid-century and largely concerned with tidying up front yards, planting, and paving roads, these societies had been frequently dominated by women and amateurs.[36] The local groups began to gain a national voice in 1897 with the founding of the American Park and Outdoor Art Association in Louisville, Kentucky, and in 1900 with the organization of the National League of Improvement Associations in Springfield, Ohio (to be renamed in 1901 the American League for Civic Improvement). In 1904 they merged as the American Civic Association and pushed for both municipal beautification and reform.

Reform, whether of the progressive or the conservative variety, was an integral element of most City Beautiful campaigns. Turn-of-the-century reform encompassed a variety of activities: Teddy Roosevelt's trust busting, Mayor of Cleveland Tom Johnson's fight with the traction interests, and Herbert Croly's *The Promise of American Life* (1909). The photographs of Jacob Riis showing the degrading conditions and filth that many men, women, and children lived in appeared in popular magazines and books and spurred many reformers to concentrate on cleanliness and beauty (Fig. 63).[37] Both private and government-sponsored committees studied the tenement house question, the causes of epidemics, and the problems of educating the poor and the immigrant. "Social conscience" varied with the individual and the organizations involved, but a cleaner and more moral environment certainly existed as a goal of most City Beautiful activities. Charles Mulford Robinson, the great popularizer of the City Beautiful, claimed: "Statues, monuments,

31   "The World's Fair in Chicago in 1893 marks the beginning of city planning in America. People left it with the inquiry: 'Why cannot cities be built like a world's fair; why should we not employ architects and artists in their designing; why should we not live in cities as beautiful as this fugitive play city, that will disappear at the end of the summer?'" (Frederick C. Howe, *The Modern City and Its Problems* [New York, 1915], p. 200). "To say that the world's fair created the subsequent aesthetic effort in municipal life were [sic] therefore false; to say that it immensely strengthened, quickened, and encour-

aged it would be true" (Charles Mulford Robinson, "Improvement in City Life," *Atlantic Monthly* 83 [June 1899], p. 771).
32   Daniel H. Burnham, "White City and Capital City," *The Century* 63 (February 1902), p. 619.
33   Howe, *Modern City*, p. 213; Jean Schopfer, "Art in the City," *The Architectural Record* 12 (November 1902), pp. 573–583; Jean Schopfer, "Open-Air Life in a Great City," *The Architectural Record* 13 (February 1903), pp. 157–168; "Letter from Boston," *The American Architect and Building News* 23 (April 21, 1888), pp. 188–189; Barr Ferree, "Architecture," *Engineering Magazine* 3

(August 1893), pp. 722–723; and Albert Shaw, "Paris: The Typical Modern City," *The Century* 42 (July 1892), pp. 448–466.
34   Edward Bellamy, *Looking Backward, 2000–1887* (New York, n.d.), p. 30.
35   Lillie H. French, "Municipal Art," *Harper's Weekly* 37 (April 18, 1893), p. 371. In mentioning some new windows installed in the Cincinnati City Hall, French concludes: "In these windows one finds probably the first example in America of strictly municipal art, as it was understood by the great commonwealth of Renaissance Italy." See also Harvey A. Kantor, "Modern Urban

skyline can wait; but bodies and minds must be fed. . . . aesthetic improvement comes last."[38]

The close connection between the City Beautiful and social reform was most graphically demonstrated in several publications. One was the *Charities and the Commons* (later *The Survey*), which had on its advisory board wealthy plutocrats such as Robert W. De Forest and William E. Guggenheim of New York and Robert Treat Paine of Boston, along with the reformers Jane Addams and Jacob Riis. Robert W. De Forest combined an interest in both social welfare and civic beauty. He was one of the wealthiest men in the United States, a noted corporate lawyer, the founder and for many years the

FIG. 63
Baxter Street Alley in Mulberry Bend.
Originally published in *The Battle with the Slum*, 1902.
Jacob Riis (1849–1914).
Photograph.
COLLECTION: Museum of the City of New York.

Planning in New York City: Origins and Evolution, 1890–1933" (Ph.D. diss., New York University, 1971), pp. 33–37; Harvey A. Kantor, "The City Beautiful in New York," *The New-York Historical Society Quarterly* 67 (April 1973), pp. 148–171; and Natalie Dana, *The Municipal Art Society, 1892–1967* (New York, 1967).

36 Mary Caroline Robbins, "The Art of Public Improvement," *Atlantic Monthly* 78 (December 1898), pp. 742–751; Sylvester Baxter, "The Beautifying of Village and Town," *The Century* 63 (April 1902), pp. 844–851; Andrew Jackson Downing, "On the Improvement of Country Vil-

lages" (1849), in his *Rural Essays*, ed. George W. Curtis (New York, 1858), pp. 229–243; and Jon A. Peterson, "The City Beautiful Movement: Forgotten Origins and Lost Meanings," *Journal of Urban History* 2 (August 1976), pp. 415–434. For the history of a local group see Margaret French Cresson, *The Laurel Hill Association, 1853–1953* (Pittsfield, Mass., 1953).

37 The best known works by Jacob A. Riis were *The Battle with the Slum* (New York, 1902) and *How the Other Half Lives* (New York, 1890), both of which appeared originally in the form of articles. The proximity of Riis's work to the City

Beautiful can be seen in the juxtaposition in *Atlantic Monthly* 83 (June 1899) of his "The Tenement House Blight," pp. 760–771, and Charles Mulford Robinson's "Improvement in City Life III: Aesthetic Progress," pp. 771–785.

38 Robinson, "Improvement in City Life I: Philanthropic Progress," *Atlantic Monthly* 83 (April 1899), p. 525.

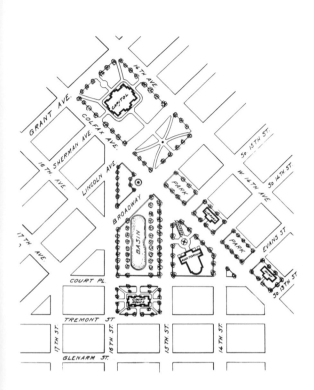

FIG. 64
Plan of the Center of Denver, Showing the Proposed Improvement, 1906. Charles Mulford Robinson (1869–1917), designer. COLLECTION: The Denver Art Museum, Colorado.

president of the New York Charity Organization, and variously a member of the Municipal Art Society, president of the Municipal Art Commission of the City of New York, president of the Russell Sage Foundation, president of the Welfare Council of New York, and for years a member and finally chairman of the Board of Trustees of The Metropolitan Museum of Art.[39] Vitally interested in architecture, De Forest recommended and stood by Stanford White's slightly heretical designs for the Madison Square Presbyterian Church (Fig. 83).[40] Over the years *Charities* ran many articles on the City Beautiful, conducted a "Civic Improvement Department" between 1907 and 1912, and in 1908 published an eighty-page "Civic Broadside" dealing with "The City Plan."[41] Another journal, *Municipal Affairs,* published by an old and prestigious organization, The Reform Club of New York, also lent weight to social causes and civic art. In addition to numerous articles, three separate issues of *Municipal Affairs* were devoted to the topics "Municipal Art," "The City Beautiful," and "Decoration of Cities."[42]

Most of the City Beautiful schemes were the products of architects and landscape architects, and generally the first professional city planners emerged from these backgrounds. The beginning of professional training appeared in 1909 when Harvard, through its Landscape Architecture Department, offered a course "The Principles of City Planning." Simultaneously, the first city planning conference convened in 1909 in Washington, D.C., to discuss the problems of congestion and types of city plans.[43] This and subsequent conferences were attended by many diverse individuals: politicians, financeers, reformers, engineers, and others; but the dominant figures at the early conferences were architects and landscape architects.

Of the nondesigners who rose to prominence with the City Beautiful movement, Charles Mulford Robinson was the major figure. Robinson emerged from obscurity in upstate New York, where he had graduated from the University of Rochester with a liberal arts degree and then worked for a local newspaper.[44] His three articles for *Atlantic Monthly* in 1899 entitled "Improvement in City Life" staked out the territory of civic art. He went on to popularize the movement in several books, among them *The Improvement of Towns and Cities; or, the Practical Basis of Civic Aesthetics* (1901) and *Modern Civic Art; or, The City Made Beautiful* (1903), in over a hundred articles, and in at least twenty-five improvement reports for different municipalities. Visual and spatial form were emphasized, with careful notation of European precedents for squares, bridges, canals, parks, street furnishings, and architecture. Although the approach lay along aesthetic lines, Robinson broadened the appeal by references to "the science of city building," to "engineering," and to "social benefits." He always addressed, at least briefly, "tenements," "problems of hygiene," and the "useful" and the "utilitarian" features that allowed him to conclude hyperbolically: "Personified, modern civic art appears as a sort of social reformer, for if the eye be that of the artist, there yet is surely in it the tear of the philanthropist."[45]

In 1910 Robinson attended the Harvard School of Landscape Architecture for a few months, and then in 1913 he accepted a chair as a professor of Civic Design in the Landscape Gardening Department at the University of Illinois. Inevitably, he became involved in actual city plans and worked on

39 *Dictionary of American Biography* (New York, 1944), Supplement 1, p. 230–233; and Mel Scott, *American City Planning Since 1900* (Berkeley and Los Angeles, 1971), p. 81.
40 Robert W. De Forest to Arthur James, April 21, 1903; to Stanford White, May 26, 1903, and January 20, 1904, McKim, Mead and White Collection, The New-York Historical Society, New York City.
41 Charles Mulford Robinson, ed. "The City Plan," *Charities and the Commons* 19 (February 1, 1908), pp. 1487–1562.

42 "Municipal Art Number," *Municipal Affairs* 2 (March 1898); "The City Beautiful," *Municipal Affairs* 3 (December 1899); and "Decoration of Cities," *Municipal Affairs* 5 (Fall 1901). On the Reform Club see Kantor, *Modern Urban Planning,* pp. 59–60.
43 Scott, *American City Planning,* pp. 101, 95.
44 "American Society of Landscape Architects: Minute on the Life and Services of Charles Mulford Robinson, Associate Member," *Landscape Architecture* 9 (July 1919), pp. 180–193.

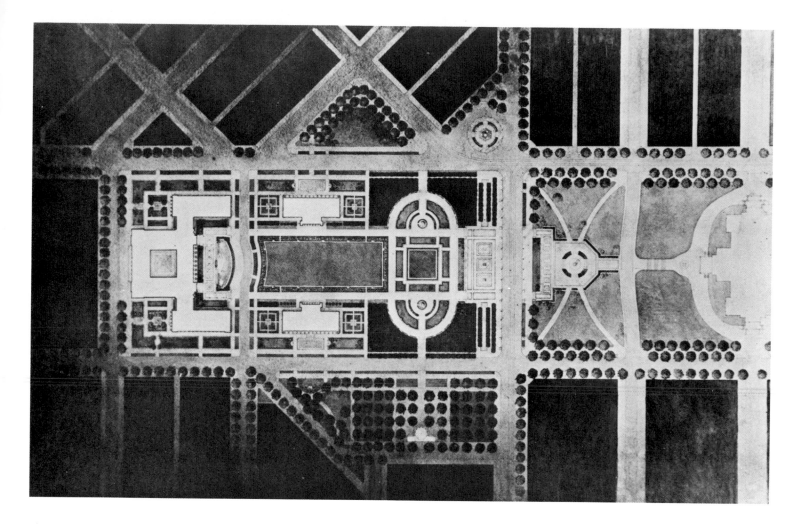

schemes for Buffalo; Detroit; Columbus, Ohio; Honolulu; Omaha; Los Angeles; and other cities. His importance, though, was as a publicist and not as a designer, as is revealed in a comparison of his plan for the civic center of Denver of 1906 with that of Arnold Brunner and Frederick Law Olmsted, Jr., of six years later (Figs. 64 and 65). For the problem of placing a set of important public buildings, Robinson attempted to reconcile two opposing street patterns and created a confusion of unrelated and ultimately dispersed buildings placed on oblique axes.[46] In contrast, Brunner and Olmsted forthrightly created a mall with emphatic termination points and a continuity of space. Robinson's death at the age of forty-nine on December 30, 1917, symbolically marks the end of the City Beautiful movement.

By 1917 American city planning had begun to move away from the City Beautiful ideals towards more strictly pragmatic issues of housing, delivery of services, zoning, and social statistics. Visual and spatial aesthetics continued to play a role for a while, and actually the major book on the City Beautiful, Werner Hegemann and Elbert Peets's *The American Vitruvius: An Architect's Handbook of Civic Art,* would not be published until 1922. Significantly, in 1917 the American City Planning Institute (now the American

FIG. 65
Denver, Colorado. Plan of Proposed Civic Center, 1912. Arnold W. Brunner (1857–1925) and Frederick Law Olmsted, Jr. (1870–1957), architect and landscape architect.
PHOTO: Reproduced from *Arnold W. Brunner and His Work,* 1926. Courtesy of the American Institute of Architects, Inc.

45 Charles Mulford Robinson, *Modern Civic Art; or, The City Made Beautiful* (New York, 1903), pp. 10, 12, 25, chap. 13, pp. 29, 25, 58.
46 C.M.R. [Charles Mulford Robinson], "Opening the Center of Denver," *The Architectural Record* 19 (May 1906), pp. 365–367; Charles Mulford Robinson, *Proposed Plans for the Improvement of the City of Denver* (Denver, 1906); and *A Short History of the Civic Center, Denver, Colorado* (Denver, 1912).

Institute of Planners) was founded. The complex problems facing the modern metropolis were not solvable by architects, landscape architects, and journalists alone. The subsequent development of city planning would move in a different direction.

Training, Drawing, and Design

The architectural vision of the American Renaissance existed in physical, three-dimensional reality and not simply as pretty drawings and dream cityscapes of temporary buildings. The accomplishment of the reality came through a complex process of design, a process initially defined by academic education, modified by the exigencies of an architectural office, and complicated by the practicality of construction. An understanding of this process and the role of architectural drawing is necessary to measure the architectural achievements of the American Renaissance.

The educational system that trained architects, whether in the École des Beaux-Arts in Paris or in an American university, was based on the conception of architecture as resulting from a coherent, rational process, and while artistic talent was an integral ingredient, there were elements of order that could be mastered.[47] The elements of architectural order were passed to the student in two ways: first, through formal courses in history, construction, descriptive geometry, and physics; second, through the atelier or studio, where design and personal preferences were taught by an instructor.

The elements of architecture that the schools taught naturally varied with time and individuals, but certain commonalities of the period from 1876 to 1917 can be noted. Architecture, properly speaking, was a monumental art and drew upon the traditions of the past. Knowledge of history was essential; hence, not only courses and books but also detailed studies of buildings and ornament became necessary (Fig. 66). Informing the present were brilliantly rendered interpretations of antiquity. The result of this close analysis of the past was that prototypical buildings and elements were recognized. Both entire buildings and fragments of buildings—domes, columns, windows, attics, and moldings—were part of the vocabulary of design. A third element of the order was that the style possessed a recognizable grammar that could be manipulated. The usage of different styles depended upon circumstances of location, material, program, and client. Most schools taught many styles; Gothic, Byzantine, Islamic, and Romanesque were among those recognized, but classicism of the Roman, French, or Italian variety dominated. Classicism possessed not only the requisite cultural connections but it had an academic heritage, it was codified in books by Vitruvius, Alberti, Serlio, Palladio, and in *The American Vignola* (1902–1906) by William Robert Ware. A fourth element of architectural order was the formal compositional rules such as proportion, axis, symmetry, the golden section, and mass. Mass was seen as corresponding to the interior and volume. It was dogma that the major spaces or volumes of a building should be easily recognizable from the elevation and contribute to making the building understandable. The notion that the plan generated the mass was not consistently held, and while the plan exercised much control, frequently form was conceived of in concert with, or before, the plan. Space was

47 There are a number of descriptions of the École system; the best are: Edwin H. Denby, "The École des Beaux-Arts and Its Influence in America," *Legion D'Honneur* 3 (April 1933), pp. 217–227; Ernest Flagg, "The École des Beaux-Arts," *The Architectural Record* 3 (January–March 1894), pp. 303–313; (April–June 1894), pp. 419–428; 4 (July–September 1894), pp. 38–43; and Richard Chaffee, "The Teaching of Architecture at the École des Beaux-Arts," in *The Architecture of the École des Beaux-Arts*, edited by Arthur Drexler (New York, 1977), pp. 61–109.

conceived of as particulated and correspondent to specific activities. But also space existed in sequence, as a hierarchy of areas containing movement.

The method of design taught in schools normally consisted of three separate activities. First, the student studied the problem and rapidly conceived of a solution, or the *parti,* upon which the design was based. The *parti* was presented in the form of a sketch, or an *equisse.* A knowledge of prototypical solutions and the past was essential if one was to arrive at a solution within a specified period of time. If the *parti* was judged to be acceptable, it was investigated and developed in another sequence of drawings made over periods ranging from several weeks to months. Finally, the completed design was presented in large elaborate drawings of elevation, plan, and

FIG. 66
Roman Composite Order, 1896, a student drawing by M. Katherine Lines.
Ink and watercolor on paper;
53.3 x 71.1 cm. (21 x 28 in.).
COLLECTION: Avery Library, Columbia University, New York City.

ROMAN · COMPOSITE · ORDER.

93

FIG. 67
Front elevation of an archives building,
1852, a student project by Richard Morris
Hunt (1827–1895).
Ink and watercolor on paper;
66.0 x 116.8 cm. (26 x 46 in.).
COLLECTION: American Institute of
Architects Foundation, Washington, D.C.

FIG. 68
Section of an archives building, 1852, a
student project by Richard Morris Hunt
(1827–1895).
Ink and watercolor on paper;
66.0 x 116.8 cm. (26 x 46 in.).
COLLECTION: American Institute of
Architects Foundation, Washington, D.C.

section. The École des Beaux-Arts student drawings of an archives building
(Figs. 67–69) by Richard Morris Hunt represent the culmination of this
process. His initial *equisse* of the *parti* has not survived, but it may be
presumed to have shown a large central hall with articulated wings similar to
Roman basilicas and Renaissance churches. Hunt's detailing combines Renaissance motifs and the recently completed Bibliothèque Sainte-Genevieve
in Paris (1838–1850) by Henri Labrouste.

The importance of architectural drawing to the process of education and
to the design sequence is obvious. Drawings were the means by which
concepts were explored and then transmitted to other architects, patrons,

and builders. Strictly considered, architectural drawings were a means to an end—the completed building—but frequently they became art objects in their own right.[48] The studies of a Roman composite order by M. Katherine Lines, a student at the Columbia School of Architecture, and the presentation renderings of *Arch of the Rising Sun from the Court of the Universe* at the Panama-Pacific International Exposition by Jules Guerin pass beyond representations of physical reality and become beautiful objects, an end unto themselves (Figs. 66 and 5).

Architecture-related drawings can be divided into five categories: 1) conception sketches; 2) study and development drawings; 3) presentation drawings; 4) working drawings; and 5) travel drawings. With the exception of travel drawings, most of the other drawings were integral to the design process. Travel drawings were the products of an architect's observations during a trip and ranged from thumbnail sketches of a piece of ornament to more pretentious drawings suitable for hanging.

FIG. 69
Plan of an archives building, 1852, a student project by Richard Morris Hunt (1827–1895).
Ink and watercolor on paper; 66.0 x 116.8 cm. (26 x 46 in.).
COLLECTION: American Institute of Architects Foundation, Washington, D.C.

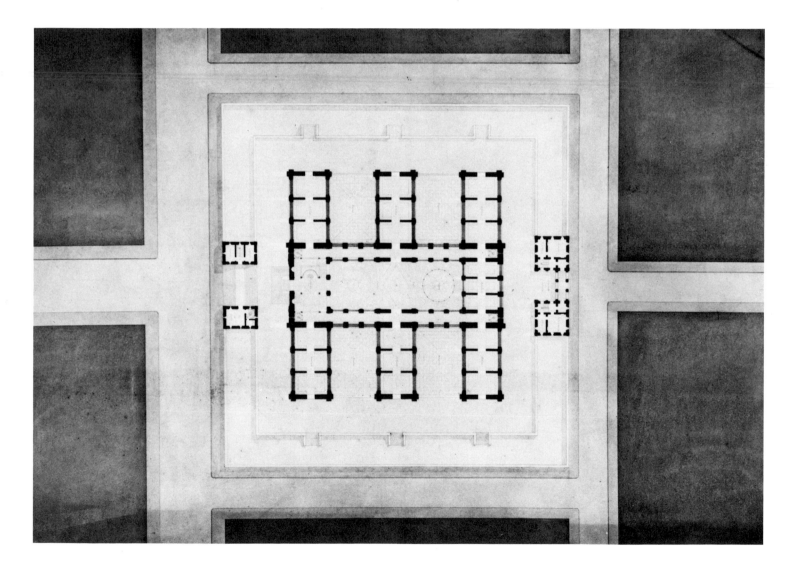

48 Historical treatment of architectural drawing, though generally as an art form, can be found in David Gebhard and Deborah Nevins, *200 Years of American Architectural Drawing* (New York, 1977); Eileen Michels, "Late Nineteenth-Century Published American Perspective Drawing," *Journal of the Society of Architectural Historians* 31 (December 1972), pp. 291–308; and Reginald Bloomfield, *Architectural Drawing and Draughtsmen* (London, 1912), p. 53.

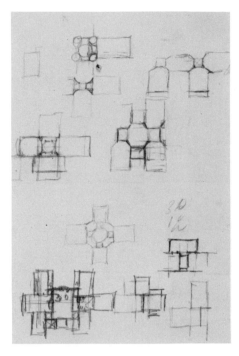

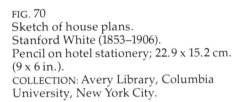

FIG. 70
Sketch of house plans.
Stanford White (1853–1906).
Pencil on hotel stationery; 22.9 x 15.2 cm.
(9 x 6 in.).
COLLECTION: Avery Library, Columbia
University, New York City.

American Renaissance architectural drawings, from conceptual sketches to grand presentation renderings, reveal certain characteristics beyond the emphasis on scale, quality, and bravura display. The influence of Impressionism and photography is evident in presentation drawings with full effects of atmosphere, haze, color, light, and shadow.[49] Earlier architectural drawing had used line to define form, and while in the late 1870s and the 1880s a textured style had developed that gave a sense of surface and light, the American Renaissance architectural drawing tended to emphasize bulk, volume, and mass. In spite of the tendency to present buildings in plan and elevation, the design was thought of as existing in three dimensions, of actual units occupying space. The predominence of sections indicates that, although interior perspectives were less frequent than exterior perspectives, space was conceived of as a dynamic entity, as a sequence of volumes arranged along an axis of procession.

The process by which American Renaissance architects designed buildings indicates the importance of education and drawing.[50] The initial concept of the designer was sketched out on scratch paper, an envelope back, or, as in the case of a Stanford White sketch, on hotel stationery (Fig. 70). White's intention to develop a large hall for a country house is fully revealed. Most concept sketches and the next class, study and development drawings, have not been preserved. They were simply sketches, and when their use ended, they were tossed out.

Depending on the designer and the size of the office involved, the concept sketches would be worked up into study drawings by either the original designer or an assistant. In small offices, such as Hoppin and Koen, the original designer would carry on, but in large offices such as McKim, Mead and White or Carrère and Hastings, assistants would generally take over and do the study and development drawings. Changes, shifts in emphasis, alternatives, would be explored; and if the building appeared to be unfeasible or unworkable, the entire project would revert back to the conceptual sketch level. Obviously, in a large office with many ongoing projects, who actually made decisions and the responsibility for different features became obscure. While nominally the original designer continued in charge, the process could become chaotic, as a remembrance of Stanford White by H. Van Buren Magonigle indicates: "He would tear into your alcove, perhaps push you off your stool with his body while he reached for pencil and tracing paper and in five minutes make a dozen sketches of some arrangement of detail or plan, slam his hand down on one of them—or perhaps two or three of them if they were close together—say 'Do that!' and tear off again. You had to guess what and which he meant."[51] On the other hand, Charles McKim's methods were equally unnerving, for as Magonigle recalled, McKim liked "to sit down at a draftsman's table, usually in his hat and immaculate shirt sleeves, and design out loud. . . . the room reverberated with architectual terms that sounded most recondite to a green boy of 20: Cyma Recta; Cyma Reversa; Fillet above; Fillet below, Dentils; Modillions, and so on." Then McKim would indicate to the draftsman where to draw lines and correct them: "He looked at them for a long time and then said 'Just take out that middle line and move it up a little. . . . No, put it back

49 H. Van Buren Magonigle, *Architectural Rendering in Wash* (New York, 1921) offers an excellent description of the technical processes involved.
50 As will become apparent below, much of this material is derived from my studies of the office of McKim, Mead and White, the preeminent firm of the period. For certain suggestions, I am indebted to James F. O'Gorman, "The

Making of a 'Richard Building,'" in *Selected Drawings: H.H. Richardson and His Office* (Cambridge, Mass., 1974), pp. 1–36.
51 H. Van Buren Magonigle, "A Half Century of Architecture, 3" *Pencil Points* 15 (March 1934), p. 117.
52 Magonigle, "A Half Century, 3" p. 116.

where it was—perhaps a little lower.'. . . it was quite a job to erase and remake the lines smeared in the process, and to repeat that sort of thing for hours on end was hard on the nerves of anyone."[52]

The next stage of the design process was working up the study drawings, generally done on tracing paper in plan and elevation, into a presentation rendering. Presentation drawings of projects displayed plans, elevations, sections, and sometimes perspectives and were on linen in ink or on heavy paper or board in ink, pencil, and sometimes wash.

Frequently, two different presentation schemes were prepared, such as Richard Morris Hunt's two alternative facades for the Breakers in Newport (Figs. 71 and 72). Although Hunt apparently favored the chateau style, the Vanderbilts admired the design based upon Northern Italian Renaissance sources, and the completed building followed this version, though with the

FIG. 71 *Left:*
Study for Breakers, Cornelius Vanderbilt II house, Newport, Rhode Island, 1892. Richard Morris Hunt (1827–1895), architect. Ink and watercolor on paper; 50.8 x 71.1 cm. (20 x 28 in.).
COLLECTION: American Institute of Architects Foundation, Washington, D.C.

FIG. 72 *Below:*
Study for Breakers, Cornelius Vanderbilt II house, Newport, Rhode Island, 1892. Richard Morris Hunt (1827–1895), architect. Ink and watercolor on paper; 50.8 x 71.1 cm. (20 x 28 in.).
COLLECTION: American Institute of Architects Foundation, Washington, D.C.

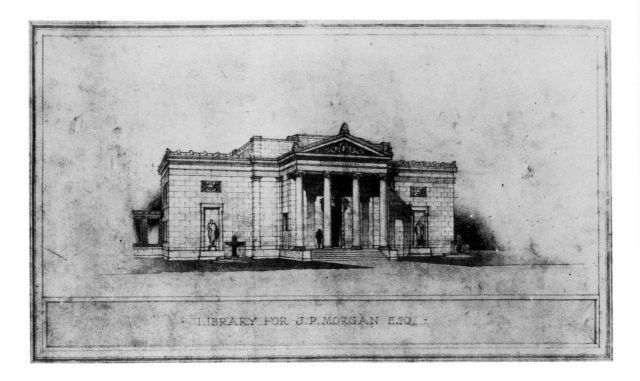

addition of a third story.[53] McKim, Mead and White presented two alternatives to J.P. Morgan for his library (Figs. 73 and 74), one essentially a Palladian villa, the other a more urban palazzo with recalls of Italian garden structures, which was the version that carried the day.[54] Of interest is Whitney Warren's project for the Morgan Library in a French Rococo style that was presented in elevation rather than perspective.

Presentation drawings acted as sales aids, as the magnificent perspective rendering of McKim, Mead and White's proposed Brooklyn Museum done by Francis L. V. Hoppin indicates (Fig. 2). The building committee must have been bowled over. Also presented at the same time was a series of elevations, sections, and plans whose tremendous size indicated that they had been made as impressive objects designed to convey a sense of scale and space.

The use of perspective drawings generally had two purposes. Architects discovered that some clients could not visualize designs presented in elevation, plan, and section, whereas a perspective indicated a three-dimensional body.[55] Second, perspectives provided a check on the abstraction of designing in flat, two-dimensional planes. A perspective drawing could reveal that elegant elevations lied and the design appeared poor in perspective. Plaster of paris models were also used as checks.[56] A further stage in this process was the actual erection of full-size sections to check depth, scale, and shadow. The architect of The Boston Public Library, The New York Public Library, and the Federal Building in Cleveland all had such models constructed (Fig. 75).

Drawing in perspective, especially for presentation, was a particular talent that became the province of specialists, either within an architectural

53 Antoinette Downing and Vincent J. Scully, Jr., *The Architectural Heritage of Newport, Rhode Island*, 2nd ed. (New York, 1967), p. 172.
54 Wayne Andrews, *Mr. Morgan and His Architect* (New York, 1957), p. 5., asserts the facade was derived from the Palazzo del Tei, Mantua; Leland Roth, "The Urban Architecture of McKim, Mead and White" (Ph.D. diss., Yale University, 1973), p. 641, claims as a source the upper level of the Nyphaeum of the Villa Papa Giulia, Rome.

55 Egerton Swartwout, "An Architectural Decade" (manuscript in the possession of Cain, Farrell, and Bell, New York, *circa* 1930), p. 34. I am indebted to John Gray Faron for permission to use the manuscript. Swartwout worked in the McKim, Mead and White office from 1892 to 1900 and recalled working on the designs for a house, "but the client, a very charming Boston woman, couldn't visualize it in elevation. . . . I hurriedly roughed out a perspective free hand, it wasn't nearly as good as the elevation, but the lady was delighted."

renderer. His ⸻
and reflection⸻
form and det⸻
while Guerin ⸻
City Beautiful ⸻
producing sev⸻
Lincoln Mem⸻

    The work ⸻
mitment to pa⸻
making of dr⸻
structed (Fig.⸻
drawings and ⸻
ings portrayed⸻
electrical and/⸻
varied on worl⸻
Working draw⸻
considered "s⸻
Italian immigr⸻
dered an appr⸻
how a building⸻
set down givir⸻
and all the oth⸻

    Beyond th⸻
construction. ⸻
for most archi⸻
the entire arcl⸻
architect lay n⸻
frequently the⸻
dinating the f⸻
interior decor⸻
actual design ⸻
Changes migl⸻
marble, the si⸻
Major alteratic⸻
as Charles Mc⸻
Columbian Ex⸻
After a series ⸻
vailed.[60]

The Building⸻

The interrelate⸻
both a unity ⸻
expression. Pe⸻
style differed ⸻
The result wa⸻
ties to Old W⸻

    A compa⸻
(1887–1895; Fi⸻

59 Samuel Swift,
tion of Architec⸻
Guerin," *The Brick⸻*
pp. 178–184. Mago⸻
frontispiece, write⸻
Guerin that he co⸻
more than anyone⸻
60 Henry Bacon, ⸻
Character Sketch,⸻
1910), p. 44.

FIG. 73 *Facing page:*
Alternative version for The Pierpont
Morgan Library, New York City, 1902.
McKim, Mead and White, architects.
Rendering attributed to Henry Bacon
(1840–1924).
Ink, pencil, and watercolor on paper;
35.6 x 61.0 cm. (14 x 24 in.).
COLLECTION: The New-York Historical
Society, New York City.

FIG. 74 *Left:*
The Pierpont Morgan Library, New York
City, 1902–1906, McKim, Mead and White,
architects.
COLLECTION: The Pierpont Morgan Library.

FIG. 75 *Below:*
Full-scale model of an architectural detail
of The New York Public Library, New York
City, 1897–1911. Carrère and Hastings,
architects.

office or from outside. Among architects that had a facility for perspective, Francis L. V. Hoppin stands out. Hoppin received his training at Brown University, MIT, and the École des Beaux-Arts before entering the McKim, Mead and White office in 1886, where he stayed until 1894. He became the office specialist in perspective, as drawings for the Century Club and The Brooklyn Museum indicate (Fig. 2). Egerton Swartwout, another office man, characterized Hoppin's drawings as "colored, blue sky and trees where there aren't any, and flying shadows, cloud shadows on the building you know, a real snappy piece of work."[57] Hoppin went on to a career with his own practice, designing the New York Police Department Headquarters and many country houses, including one for Edith Wharton in Lenox, Massachusetts, but his talents as a renderer were always on call, as the perspectives for the McMillan Plan indicate (Fig. 49).

    The final stage of preparing presentation drawings was to hire one of the free-lance specialists such as Hughson Hawley or Jules Guerin. Their work was exclusively pictorial representation, and they were in demand for competition entries, often producing drawings for several firms for the same competition. Neither actually did the building perspectives, which were supplied by the architect's office. Guerin and Hawley added the color, light, and atmosphere. Hawley, born in England and trained as a theater set painter, immigrated to the United States in 1879 and established himself as an architectural renderer. Near the end of his long career it was estimated that he had produced over eleven thousand architectural renderings.[58] His renderings were characterized by a solidity of form and a heaviness quite different from Jules Guerin's lighter approach (Figs. 35 and 5). Guerin was born in Saint Louis and studied painting in France before becoming a

56 "I purposely drew the perspective wrong. It was quite a complicated building, I forget just what it was, with angles that were not right angles, and set-backs and so on, and I knew it was beyond any one in the office except Ross maybe, to find my mistake. And when Mr. McKim saw it he was shocked—Here Mr. Kendall, this won't do at all. I had no idea it would shape up that way. . . . We might have a model made—and for a minute I thought my goose was cooked, but Mr. McKim, God bless him,

said No, I think we can do it a better way" (Swartwout, *An Architectural Decade*, p. 33).
57 Swartwout, *An Architectural Decade*, p. 28.
58 "Hughson Hawley, Scenic Artist and Architectural Painter," *Pencil Points* 9 (December 1928), pp. 761–774.

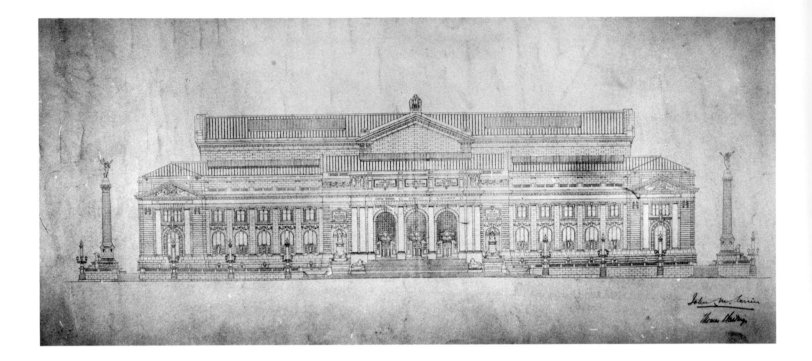

FIG. 77 *Above:*
Perspective of Fifth Avenue facade, The New York Public Library, New York City, 1897–1911. Carrère and Hastings, architects.
Ink on paper on board; 38.1 x 92.7 cm. (15 x 36½ in.).
COLLECTION: The New York Public Library.

FIG. 78 *Right:*
Floor plans for the first and second floors, The New York Public Library, New York City, 1897–1911. Carrère and Hastings, architects.

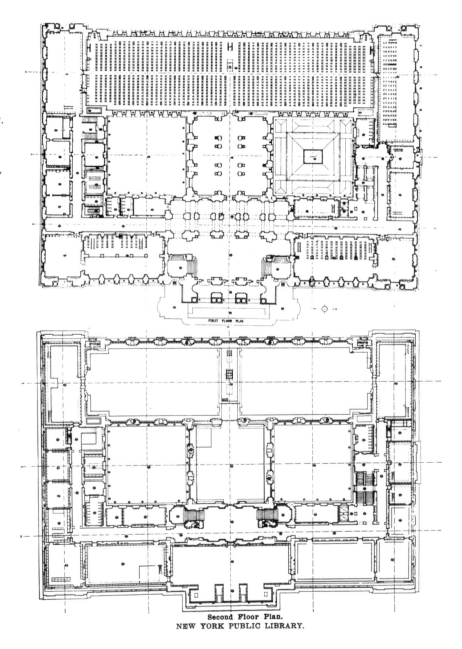

Second Floor Plan.
NEW YORK PUBLIC LIBRARY.

(1897–1911; Fig. 77) reveals alternative approaches to form, composition, and prototype. The Boston building is a solid block, the form derived from Italian Renaissance palazzos. All individual elements—the entrance, ornamentation, spatial movement, and function—are subservient to the unity of the total form. The interior organization is announced through different fenestration patterns, with the major space of the reading room revealed in the tall arches that march across the front. The New York Public Library, on the other hand, is not a solid block. An entrance pavilion, lower pierced walls with reiterated end pavilions and high pedimented roofs are composed in a hierarchy. The different functioning interior spaces of entrance, hall, card catalog room, reading room, and offices are revealed by the forms. The prototype of Claude Perault's east front of the Louvre for the Fifth Avenue facade of The New York Public Library accounts for some of the differences between it and Boston, but there is a further basic difference: the interior volumes and the spatial movement of the New York building determine the outer configuration. Carrère and Hastings began with a plan and enclosed the different spaces (Fig. 78); McKim, the designer of the Boston library, started with the solid block and inserted the spaces (Fig. 79). Appropriately, the New York building has a more coherent plan and works better as a library; the Boston library has a more memorable form.

FIG. 79
Floor plans for the first and second floors, The Boston Public Library, 1887–1895. McKim, Mead and White, architects.

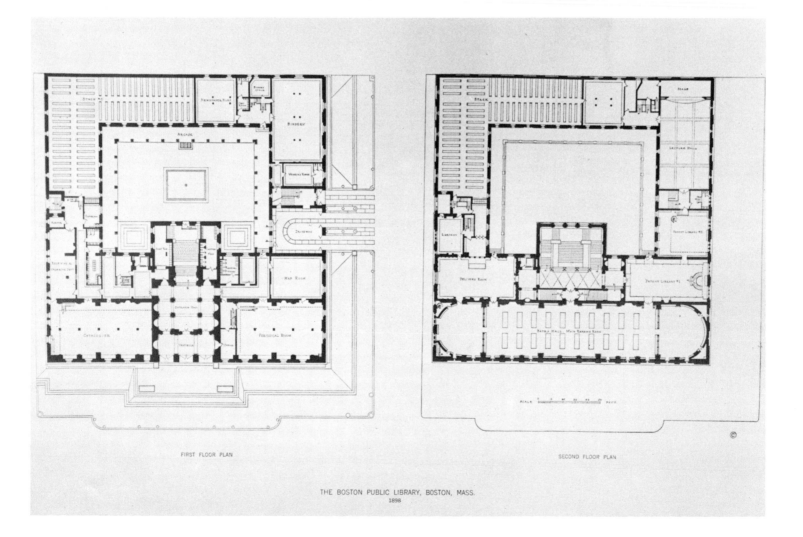

FIRST FLOOR PLAN

SECOND FLOOR PLAN

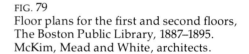

THE BOSTON PUBLIC LIBRARY, BOSTON, MASS.
1898

103

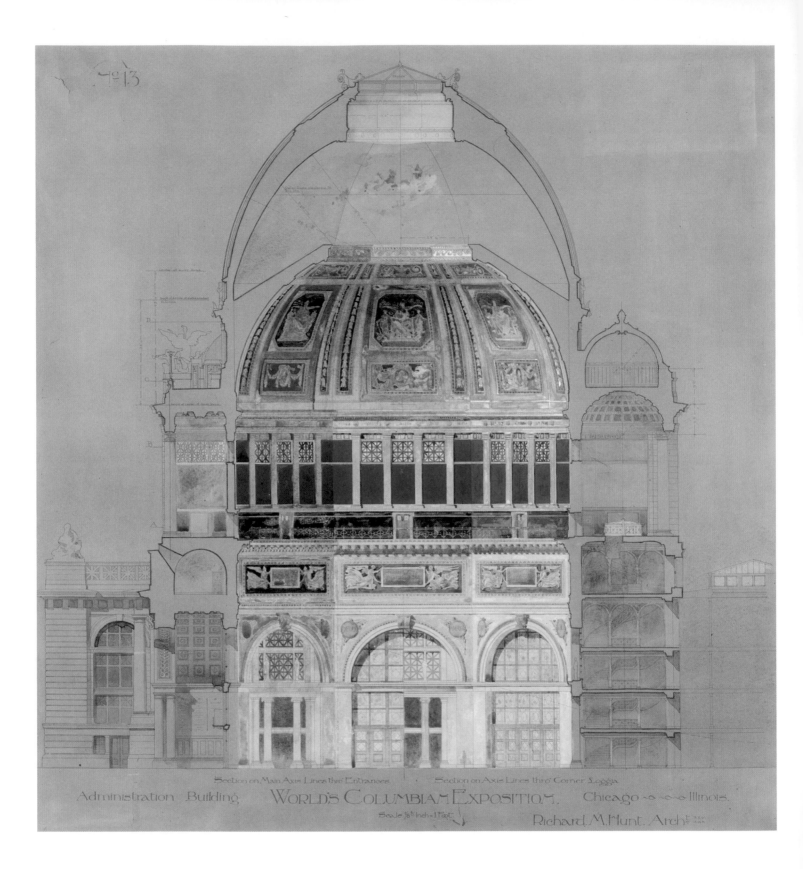

FIG. 80
Section of Administration Building,
World's Columbian Exposition, Chicago,
circa 1891. Richard Morris Hunt (1827–1895),
architect.
Ink and wash on paper; 91.4 x 61.0 cm.
(36 x 24 in.).
COLLECTION: American Institute of
Architects Foundation, Washington, D.C.

In contrast to the unity of the Boston and New York libraries stands The Library of Congress, which, strictly speaking, is only partially an American Renaissance building (Fig. 81). The product of a competition, the original design by Smithmeyer and Pelz dates from 1873.[61] Between the 1870s and the commencement of construction in 1889, many revisions and changes were introduced that did little to advance the end result. The building as completed in 1897 reflects American Renaissance only on the interior; the exterior is an anachronism from the 1870s.

John L. Smithmeyer and Paul J. Pelz were born in Austria and Germany respectively and received their training as apprentices with architects in Chicago and New York City before arriving in Washington, D.C., in the 1860s. Their design, euphemistically labeled "Italian Renaissance," represents the 1870s and the High Victorian attitude towards composition and form. Instead of the large subdivision of parts in The New York Public Library or the solid block of The Boston Public Library, The Library of Congress represents a picturesque attitude in which elaborate and extensive subdivision of parts dominates. This difference between the New York library's easily perceivable subdivisions and The Library of Congress's fractured multiplicity and lack of relationship of elements (for instance, the basement and the main and second floors) reflects the essential difference in attitude towards form in the two periods of the 1860s to the 1870s and the 1880s to the 1900s.

The American Renaissance quality of The Library of Congress derives solely from the interior (Fig. 155). Smithmeyer was fired in 1888 and Pelz in 1892. They were replaced by General Thomas Lincoln Casey, Chief of the

FIG. 81
Design for The Library of Congress, Washington, D.C., 1885. Smithmeyer and Pelz, architects. Rendering by Paul J. Pelz (1841–1918).
Ink and wash on paper; 55.9 x 74.9 cm. (22 x 29½ in.).
COLLECTION: The Library of Congress.

61 Helen-Anne Hilfer, "Monument to Civilization," John Y. Cole, "The Main Building of the Library of Congress," and Cole, "Smithmeyer & Pelz," in *The Quarterly Journal of the Library of Congress* 29 (October 1972), pp. 234–326.

Army Engineers, and Bernard L. Green, an engineer who jointly headed the construction effort and introduced numerous alterations, including the re-design of the dome. In 1892 Edward Pearce Casey, the twenty-eight–year–old son of General Casey, was appointed architect of the library and put in charge of the interior design and decoration. A graduate of Columbia University with a degree in engineering in 1886 and philosophy in 1888, he worked briefly in the McKim, Mead and White office, attended the École des Beaux-Arts for three years, and in 1892 set up an office in New York. Most of the interior circulation can be ascribed to Smithmeyer and Pelz, though revised by the Caseys and Green. The elaborate decorative treatment of sculpture and murals by many of the well-known American Renaissance artists—Cox, Vedder, Garnsey, Pratt, Warner, and others—was the province of Casey. The great spatial sequence of the exterior stairs, through the vestibule, into the great public hall and then—the climax—the great domed reading room surrounded with statues by Louis Saint-Gaudens, Daniel Chester French, Paul W. Bartlett, and others and overhead Edwin Blashfield's *The Progress of Civilization* is one of the great architectural journeys of the American Renaissance (cover and Figs. 155 and 76). Opening a book becomes an act of architectural homage.

The choice of style was another element of individual preference among American Renaissance architects. As noted earlier, many architects were adept at a number of styles, and although some form of classicism generally ruled, other choices were sometimes necessary. For the Vanderbilt family in the later 1880s and the early 1890s, Richard Morris Hunt used the Genoan Renaissance palazzo idiom for the Breakers in Newport (Fig. 72), a French neo-classical idiom for Marble House, also in Newport, and a chateauesque idiom for Biltmore in North Carolina (Fig. 58). McKim, Mead and White, best known for their advocacy of the Italian Renaissance style in city buildings, as with the Villard houses, the Century Club, and the Morgan Library, and the Georgian style, as with the H.A.C. Taylor house in Newport, tended to personalize style. Charles McKim's preference was towards heavy classicism, restrained and monumental, fitting his essentially reticent, carefully controlled, and somewhat pompous personality. The designs that he dominated were The Boston Public Library (Fig. 15), The Brooklyn Museum (Fig. 2), Pennsylvania Station in New York City (Fig. 82), and the Rhode Island Statehouse (Fig. 35). Stanford White, high-spirited, flamboyant man-about-town, tended towards a more lively and decorative effect, as with New York City's Century Club, the Madison Square Presbyterian Church (Fig. 83), and the State Savings Bank. The rich coloration of the Madison Square Church—a yellowish brick body, polished green granite columns, a yellow and green dome, a gold lantern, and terracotta ornament of blue, green, yellow, white, and buff—raised questions of appropriateness to Christian worship. Stanford White defended this personal selection with the claim that the style represented was "of the early Christians," and far more appropriate to ecclesiastical usage than the Gothic or other medieval styles.[62]

Stylistic associations and identification with specific prototypes was an important issue for the American Renaissance; however, many buildings did not contain specific stylistic sources and allusions. The Lincoln Memorial,

62 White, quoted in Charles Baldwin, *Stanford White* (New York, 1931), p. 236. A group of clippings and letters that White was responding to can be found in the McKim, Mead and White Collection, The New-York Historical Society, New York City. The question of the battle between conflicting ideologies over ecclesiastical appropriateness is too complicated to go into here, but Ralph Adams Cram should be seen as the opposite of Charles McKim or Stanford White, arguing for the medieval styles for America; see his *The Gothic Quest* (New York, 1907), pp. 139–164. Finally, it might be noted that Cram's approach to design and details is an example of scientific eclecticism.

PENNSYLVANIA STATION, NEW YORK CITY
Seventh Avenue and Thirty-Second Street

FIG. 82 *Above:*
Pennsylvania Station, New York City,
1902–1911. McKim, Mead and White,
architects.
From a drawing (1910) by Hughson Hawley
(1850–1936).
Lithograph mounted on cloth; sheet:
91.4 x 147.3 cm. (36 x 58 in.).
COLLECTION: The New-York Historical
Society, New York City.

FIG. 83 *Left:*
Madison Square Presbyterian Church,
New York City, 1903–1906. McKim, Mead
and White, architects. Drawing by
Frederick J. Adams (1879–1945).
Pencil on tracing paper; 116.8 x 81.3
(46 x 32 in.).
COLLECTION: The New-York Historical
Society, New York City.

107

the San Francisco City Hall (Fig. 51), the U.S. Customs House (Fig. 85), and the New York Police Department Headquarters are frequently identified with labels such as "Renaissance," "Beaux-Arts Eclectic," "eclectic Classicism," and other terms.[63] Certainly the drum and dome of Saint Peter's in Rome can be seen as an inspiration for the San Francisco City Hall's drum and dome, and the dome of Invalides in Paris might have been the original source for the dome of the New York Police Department Headquarters, but neither building is specifically Italian or French. Scientifically eclectic in regularity and accuracy of details over which much thought and labor went, the buildings were nonetheless completely original.

The Court of Honor at the World's Columbian Exposition indicates the scale at which the creative combination of different motifs and details was attempted. Specific sources can be picked out—the entrance arch of George Post's Manufactures and Liberal Arts Building, derived from the Arch of Septimius Severus in Rome, or the Spanish Renaissance towers on Peabody and Stearn's Machinery Building—but overall, none of the facades had pure stylistic origins (Fig. 10). The Administration Building (Figs. 80 and 84) by Richard Morris Hunt had an articulated base containing a giant order of Doric columns on top of which stood a high attic story of an open Ionic colonnade logia that recalled the tomb of Mausolus at Halicarnassus. The lofty drum and dome resembled in profile and proportions Brunelleschi's drum and dome for the Florence Cathedral, but Hunt enlivened them with some very French ornament. Against this monumental dignity, Karl Bitter posed his swirling sculptural groups that recalled the work of François Rude on the

FIG. 84
Administration Building, World's Columbian Exposition, Chicago, 1893. Richard Morris Hunt (1827–1895), architect; left rear: Machinery Building, Peabody and Stearns, architects; right: Electricity Building, Van Brunt and Howe, architects. Frances B. Johnston (1864–1952), photographer.
COLLECTION/PHOTO: The Library of Congress, Washington, D.C.

Arc de Triomphe in Paris. [64] Almost any item from the past could become American through the process of scientific eclecticism.

Specific stylistic references sometimes remained apparent, such as in George Post's Bank of Pittsburgh (Fig. 52), which recalls a Roman temple. In contrast, a building such as the U.S. Customs House by Cass Gilbert recalls only faintly the Old World in the decorative sculpture: the allegorical gowned figures of the continents or the forty-four heads of Mercury, the Roman god of commerce, that peer out from the capitals of the giant order of columns that girdle the Customs House (Fig. 85). The building, with its large physical presence and palpable processional route, is not European but American.

The architectural vision of the American Renaissance, expressed through elaborate drawings and the temporary cities of expositions, may give the impression of a dream world, but gardens, buildings, and cities were created. The impact was overwhelming, as can be judged by a concluding comment by a foreign observer.

In 1935 Le Corbusier, the French modern architect, visited the United States, prepared to admire the skyscrapers and other results of modernism. Instead, he found a different dominant vision and wrote: "In New York, then, I learn to appreciate the Italian Renaissance. It is so well done that you could believe it *to be genuine.* It even has a strange, new firmness which is not Italian, but American!" [65]

·VS· CVSTOM·HOVSE, NEW·YORK — BOWLING GREEN ELEVATION·
·CASS GILBERT, ARCHITECT — 111 FIFTH AVE, NEW YORK, N.Y. & ENDICOTT BLDG, ST PAUL, MINN·

FIG. 85
U.S. Customs House, New York City, 1899–1909. Cass Gilbert (1859–1934), architect.
Ink and watercolor on board; 71.1 x 89.0 (28 x 35 in.).
COLLECTION: The New-York Historical Society, New York City.

63   David Gebhard et al., *A Guide to Architecture in San Francisco and Northern California* (Santa Barbara and Salt Lake City, 1973), p. 81; Alan Burnham, *New York Landmarks* (Middletown, Conn., 1967), p. 49; Ralph Henry Gabriel, ed., *The Pageant of America*, vol. 13, "The American Spirit in Architecture," Talbot F. Hamlin (New Haven, 1926), p. 166.

64   James M. Dennis, *Karl Bitter, Architectural Sculptor, 1867–1915* (Madison, Wis., 1967), p. 46.
65   Le Corbusier [Charles-Édouard Jeanneret], *When Cathedrals Were White*, trans. F.E. Hyslop (New York, 1937, 1964), p. 60.

Decorative Art:
The Domestic Environment

Dianne H. Pilgrim

The American Renaissance was not so much a style as a mood, a spirit or state of mind, an age of transition intent on being different than the period before it. As the Italian Renaissance had looked back to a mythical era of the past, "a generalized classical age no more specifically of *one* date than is the scene of Raphael's *School of Athens*—and aspired to be not merely like that but in fact better: by synthesizing antique and modern knowledge there would come the most truthful philosophy, the best literature, the finest works of art,"[1] so did the generation of the late nineteenth century in America.

The decorative arts and the spaces they inhabit are indicative of the particular needs of a society. "The history of the home and its fittings is the history of man from the time when walls first sheltered his family."[2] During the Italian Renaissance, interiors were designed not only to illustrate the wealth and stature of their owners, but almost more importantly to stress their erudition. The aspirations and goals of many Americans during the period from 1876 to 1917 were not dissimilar to the hopes of Italians of the fifteenth and sixteenth centuries (Fig. 86). Not only was there a desire to display wealth and social prestige, but there was a sense of moral obligation to inform and educate the public as to what was good, beautiful, and in correct taste. In this atmosphere, the divisions between major and minor arts became less distinct. Until the nineteenth century, the so-called decorative arts were seen as an integral part of the social fabric.

The role of the decorative arts has changed throughout the ages. Until the Renaissance, what we today label as decorative arts were essentially the only arts. During the seventeenth and eighteenth centuries, the architect took a more prominent role in the plan of the interior decoration and the integration and location of objects within his structure. The craftsmen who executed the works were revered for their artistry and talent. The rising middle class and the increased use of mass production techniques during the nineteenth century gradually brought about a schism between the major and minor arts. The individual craftsman began to be replaced by large manufacturers, and one-of-a-kind objects began to be the exception. Furthermore, in this country the architect had always played a relatively minor role in determining the structure and contents of the interior spaces he designed. Until after the 1850s, most American architects did not have any formal training. Most private residences were designed and executed by builders, and it was left to the individual to select his own furnishings.

With the coming together of many diverse forces in the 1870s, however, there began a conscious effort of collaboration between architect, painter, sculptor, and artisan for a unified decorative effect, whether for the private, public, or religious structure. But as one might expect, this unity did not result in a single style. Through easier modes of transportation, expositions, and an increase in periodicals, instructional books, and photographs, the whole world became a source of design. To choose the best from all cultures, even our own, was seen as a way to create a great American civilization. But

FIG. 86 *Facing page:*
Drawing room with vista through atrium and picture gallery, William H. Vanderbilt house, New York City, 1879–1881.
Herter Brothers (after 1865–*circa* 1900), assisted by Charles B. Atwood (1848–1895), architects.
From Earl Shinn [Edward Strahan], *Mr. Vanderbilt's House and Collection,* Holland edition (New York, Boston, and Philadelphia, 1883–1884).

1   Michael Levey, *Early Renaissance* (New York, 1977), p. 15.
2   Helen Churchill Candee, *Decorative Styles and Periods in the Home* (New York, 1906), p. 6.

111

as one art historian has pointed out, this aspect of American art has been largely ignored as "hopelessly eclectic and unrepresentative of native attitudes. Works which were unabashedly dependent for iconographical and technical inspiration upon the art of the past are devalued by a modern taste which glorifies originality and fails to distinguish between creatively experimental eclecticism and slavish historicism. Projects which depended upon collaboration of a master and his assistants in straightforward emulation of Renaissance workshop practices are denigrated by a modern taste which emphasizes the hand of the individual artist. These works are rarely understood as examples of one of the most serious and optimistic movements in American art."[3]

This potpourri of disparate styles, particularly in interior design and the decorative arts, can be divided into two periods: one of relatively free historical adaptation during the 1870s and 1880s to one of a more scientific eclecticism of the 1890s going well into the twentieth century. An investigation of the background, interior decoration of the prelude period, the various decorative elements, and finally the more archaeological interiors will reveal the motivation, complexity, and intriguing quality of this long-ignored aspect of American art.

The spirit of the Renaissance, the idea of collaboration among artists, is seen most emphatically in the decoration of interior architectural environments. Beginning with Richardson's Trinity Church (1872–1877; Fig. 41), a new era in the history of American art began. For the first time, American and European artists made a conscious effort to create a unified decorative scheme. The word "decorative" has developed negative connotations during this century. *Webster's New Collegiate Dictionary* states that the word means "ornament, embellishment, adornment." However, it goes on to say: "making striking, often incongruous, additions to, to garnish."[4] However, during the late nineteenth century decorative art, which included mural painting, sculpture, stained glass, furniture, textiles, tiles, and collectables such as silver, glass, and ceramics, was considered worthy of attention by the best and most prominent artists and architects.

A coming together of many diverse forces contributed to this conscious unity and seriousness of all art forms. The Philadelphia Centennial Exposition of 1876 exposed the American public to a barrage of different styles and philosophies. So-called mid-century Rococo and Renaissance Revival furniture was seen along with objects inspired by the English Reform movement, which advocated a return to handcraftsmanship, honest construction, and a rectilinearity without excess of ornamentation. The works and writings of people such as William Morris, Bruce Talbert, E.W. Godwin, James Abbott McNeill Whistler, and Christopher Dresser eventually "fostered a period of concern about interior design, a period during which people talked about, wrote about, and spent vast sums in cultivating their taste."[5] The Aesthetic movement encompassed everything from painting to book covers, promoting "art furniture," "art pottery," "art glass." Thrown into this veritable medley were exhibitions of Oriental art. From the time of the London International Exposition of 1862, when Japanese displays were seen for the

3   Helene Barbara Weinberg, *The Decorative Work of John La Farge* (New York, 1977), pp. 14–15.
4   *Webster's New Collegiate Dictionary* (Springfield, Mass., 1958), s.v. "decorative."
5   Wilson H. Faude, "Associated Artists and the American Renaissance in the Decorative Arts," *Winterthur Portfolio* 10 (Charlottesville, Va., 1975), p. 102.

first time, exotica of all kinds became increasingly popular. The American Centennial celebration also focused attention on the American cultural heritage, and from the mid-1870s onwards, there was an increasing interest in studying, preserving, collecting, and reproducing designs from the American past (Fig. 87).

The seeming incongruity of styles and philosophies that manifested themselves during the period from the 1860s to 1880 have more in common than is apparent. Whether we talk about the English Reform movement or revival styles of the nineteenth century, there is a constant theme: a referral and emulation of some past cultural period. Even Charles Lock Eastlake, a chief exponent of the English Arts and Crafts movement, wrote in his book, *Hints on Household Taste* of 1868 (first published in America in 1872 and

FIG. 87
Compote, *Westward Ho!* (originally *Pioneer*) pattern, *circa* 1880.
James Gillinder and Sons (1861–present), Philadelphia, Pennsylvania.
Pressed and acid frosted glass;
29.2 x 22.3 x 14.0 cm. (11½ x 8¾ x 5½ in.).
COLLECTION: The Brooklyn Museum, New York.

rereleased seven times before 1890), that "the smallest example . . . of anything which illustrates good design and skilful [*sic*] workmanship, should be acquired whenever possible, and treasured with the greatest of care . . . [that they] may each become in turn a valuable lesson in decorative form and color."[6] Both Eastlake and the American Clarence Cook, whose book *The House Beautiful* (1877), which promulgated Eastlake's philosophy, illustrate examples of actual furnishings from Gothic to, in the case of Cook, American Colonial. The ways in which historical precedent has been utilized differ from one generation to the next. Charles Perkins in the 1877 preface to Eastlake's *Hints on Household Taste* summed up the feeling of many during the late nineteenth century: "We must then accept the conclusion, that the only legitimate use of past styles is such as was made by the artists of the Renaissance and aim as they did at putting the products of art and industry in harmony with the age in which we live."[7]

At the same time, American architects were beginning to seek professional training, either at the École des Beaux-Arts in Paris or at the first American school of architecture, founded in 1865, at the Massachusetts Institute of Technology. From these experiences and increased foreign travel, historical styles were more carefully studied and an appreciation and concern developed for architecture in its totality. From this point on, American architects began to take a more active role in the design of the interiors of their buildings.

During the 1860s and particularly in the 1870s and 1880s, there was a tremendous growth in the publication of art periodicals. These covered everything from fashion to how to mix a fixitive for pastels. *The Art Amateur: Devoted to the Cultivation of the Art of the Household* (1879–1903) published a wide range of informative articles: "French Empire and the Contributions of Percier and Fontaine," "Carpet Designing in America," "Tapestry Painting," "China Painting for Beginners," "Morality in Home Decoration," "The Sgraffiti of the Corsi Palace," and "Japanesque Decoration." The world was at the consumer's fingertips with illustrations of historical precedents and with practical "how-to-do-it" information. At the same time, a new type of instructional book such as Eastlake's or Cook's became increasingly popular. These replaced the pattern book of earlier centuries, which had been aimed at the cabinetmaker or designer. These new books were directed at the middle-class homeowner to help him improve his taste and style. Though these books differed in their stylistic points of view, they all were extremely serious, with strong moralistic overtones. It was sincerely felt that there was no longer an excuse for the bad taste which they saw in the art of the 1840s through the 1860s.[8]

The concept of unity and harmony of design fostered a new profession, that of the decorator. Although Leon Marcotte listed himself as a decorator for one year (1857), and starting in 1870 some furniture companies, such as Herter Brothers, Pottier and Stymus, and Alexander Roux, advertised themselves as manufacturers of furniture, upholstery, and decorations, the word "interior decorator" as we understand it today did not come into use until the late 1870s.[9] For the most part, interior decorators or decorating firms developed out of the large and expensive furniture manufacturers, which

6 Quoted in New York, The Metropolitan Museum of Art, *19th Century American Furniture and Other Decorative Arts*, 1970, p. xxvi. This was one of the first major exhibitions of nineteenth-century decorative arts, but it almost totally ignored the American Renaissance. This bias, expressed in the introduction, has been true throughout the twentieth century: "Because of our concern here with new concepts in furniture design evolving in the last two decades [of the nineteenth century] as a result of American architectural reform, we have omitted representation of these two revivals [Colonial and "Old World"]" p. xxvii.
7 Charles Lock Eastlake, *Hints on Household Taste* (Boston, 1877), p. xii.
8 The following are some of the more important early books: Harriet Prescott Spofford, *Art Decoration Applied to Furniture* (New York, 1878); Henry Hudson Holly, *Modern Dwellings in Town and Country Adapted to American Wants and Climate. With a Treatise of Furniture and Decoration* (New York, 1878); Jakob von Falke, *Art in the House* (Boston, 1879); Constance Cary Harrison, *Woman's Handiwork in Modern Homes* (New York, 1881); Maria Richards Oakey Dewing, *Beauty in the Household* (New York, 1882); Henry T. Williams and Mrs. C.S. Jones, *Beautiful Homes* (Boston, 1885); Arnold Brunner and Thomas Tryon, *Interior Decoration* (New York, 1887); Frederick Bartlett Goddard, *Furniture and the Art of Furnishing* (New York, 1887).
9 Trow's New York City Directories (published between 1786 and 1934) started using the term then.

FIG. 88
Armchair, 1872.
Thomas Brooks and Company (Brooks:
1811?–1887), Brooklyn, New York.
Walnut upholstered in blue silk damask;
97.1 x 82.5 x 78.7 cm. (38¼ x 32½ x 31 in.).
The chair is part of a group documented by
a bill of sale issued June 4, 1872, to Judge
Nathaniel Holmes Clement of Brooklyn.
COLLECTION: The Brooklyn Museum,
New York, Gift of Dr. Dorothea Curnow.

FIG. 89
Urn, (part of a six-piece tea and coffee service) *circa* 1875.
J.E. Caldwell and Company
(1839–present), Philadelphia,
Pennsylvania.
Silver; height: 52.9 cm. (20 13/16 in.).
COLLECTION: The Brooklyn Museum,
New York, H. Randolph Lever Fund.

had already started to expand their activities by the 1850s. Their business had at first been based on selling individual items to a client who chose from myriad styles without much sense of a unified design. The standard practice since the 1840s had been to sell furniture in sets or suites, whether in the Gothic, Rococo, Louis XVI, "Modern French" Renaissance, Neo-Grec, Eastlake, or numerous other styles. Mid-century stylistic terminology has never been clearly defined, for most of the styles were free adaptations of earlier periods, which in the nineteenth century overlapped one another, making clear distinctions extremely difficult. The Thomas Brooks armchair of 1872 (Fig. 88) went under the apocryphal title of Renaissance, but no fifteenth- or sixteenth-century chair ever resembled it in form, decoration, or comfort. Renaissance style furniture developed in France during the 1850s under the patronage of Emperor Napoleon III and Empress Eugénie. Henri Fourdinois, one of the leading cabinetmakers of the day, created the Renaissance style for Empress Eugénie, who felt a close identification with Marie Antoinette, and under her influence, a mix of many diverse forms developed. In contemporary literature this type of furniture was often referred to as "Marie Antoinette." This synthesizing of different historical styles was adapted to all forms of the decorative arts. The J.E. Caldwell and Company silver hot water urn of around 1875 (Fig. 89) successfully combines classical, Renaissance, and Egyptian motifs into a strong and original statement. Like Gothic, Egyptian was more of a survival from earlier in the century than a revival.

In one sense, the new direction in interior decoration continued a previous conviction about the appropriateness of certain styles for different room functions: for example, Gothic for libraries, Rococo for parlors. A.J. Downing, one of the first exponents of good taste, both in architecture and interiors, wrote as early as 1850 in his book *The Architecture of Country Houses* on this idea. But later, a room of the Louis XVI style, say, could contain articles of other cultures and times. Rooms became richer in detail, losing the sense of isolation so often present earlier.

Interior Decoration: Prelude Period

The first major collaborative efforts were in religious buildings. After Trinity Church, John La Farge and Augustus Saint-Gaudens completed the decoration of Saint Thomas Church in New York from 1877 to 1878. The scheme for the chancel of Saint Thomas "represents one of the earliest, if not the first adaptation of that [early Renaissance] style for church decoration in America." This new style "embodied the larger Renaissance attitude toward the role of the painter as a workman in the arts, a planner of unified decorative schemes, a participant in the work of decoration, and a collaborator with workmen in other media."[10]

The ornamentation of secular public buildings drew inspiration in the 1880s from the decoration of ecclesiastical and private structures. However, it was not until the next decade that architects responded to the elaborate murals seen at the World's Columbian Exposition in Chicago. Only then did they begin to plan decorative schemes for a wider range of public buildings, such as govermental and cultural structures.[11]

10 Weinberg, *The Decorative Work of John La Farge,* pp. 153–154.
11 Weinberg, *The Decorative Work of John La Farge,* p. 243.

The economic depression of 1873 curtailed most house building for about five years. But enormous wealth, the identification with the Renaissance, and the "new art idea" combined to create a new type of American domestic structure at the end of the 1870s—the urban palace. These large mansions offered new opportunities for the architect, artist, decorator, and patron to explore freely, without concern for cost, the new directions in art and design. In 1879 Louis Comfort Tiffany formed the firm of Associated Artists along with Samuel Colman, Lockwood de Forest, and Candace Thurber Wheeler. Tiffany, a painter, became convinced that there was more to being a professional decorator than just painting pictures. He found it more challenging to attempt to create a total environment than to create a single work of art. It is possible that he was familiar with Whistler's Peacock Room completed in 1877 and had probably seen the Primrose Room, which Whistler had decorated for his own house and had exhibited in Paris in 1878.[12] What influence, if any, these rooms had on other designers is difficult to assess.

Similar to a Renaissance workshop, each partner of Associated Artists was in charge of a specific department: Tiffany, glass; Colman, fabrics, wallpapers and ceiling papers, and general color arrangement; de Forest, carving and wood decoration; and Wheeler, textiles and embroideries. Mrs. Wheeler had been inspired at the Centennial by the work of England's Kensington School of Needlework. Her ambition to promote profitable industries for women led to the formation of the Society of Decorative Art in 1877. This organization held yearly exhibitions, and soon over thirty sister societies had formed across the country.

Tiffany has acquired a reputation as a pioneer and innovator, an artist far ahead of his age. But it is important to remember that Tiffany was a product of the same forces that formed his fellow artists. He desired to "surround himself with talented young people whom he would educate as he himself had been educated—by exposure to beautiful objects. His would be an atelier like that of Della Robbia or Rubens, where he would act as the master and where they would produce beautiful objects that could be seen and enjoyed in public as in private places."[13] To proclaim that Tiffany and Associated Artists "created a new style which, although not yet Art Nouveau, was based largely on the blending of exotic elements with Tiffany glass tiles, Islamic carvings, embroidered hangings and painted friezes"[14] is inaccurate. It dismisses the imaginative work of artists and firms such as La Farge, Will Low, Saint-Gaudens, Stanford White, Herter Brothers, Pottier and Stymus, D. Maitland Armstrong, and many others who worked at the same time.

It is worth pointing out how relatively small and in a certain sense incestuous the art world was during the American Renaissance. Everyone knew everyone else and at one time or another either studied or worked with one another. La Farge did commissions for McKim, Mead and White, was for two years (1880–1882) under contract to do stained glass for Herter Brothers, and had his own decorating firm from 1882 until shortly after 1885. After 1888 McKim, Mead and White tended to use Tiffany glass (by then the Tiffany Glass Company). Early on, the firm used Herter Brothers for some

12   Robert Koch, Louis C. Tiffany, Rebel in Glass (New York, 1966).
13   Koch, Louis C. Tiffany, Rebel in Glass, p. 64.
14   Koch, Louis C. Tiffany, Rebel in Glass, p. 22.

interiors, but also relied on Armstrong, Saint-Gaudens, John Singer Sargent, and Elihu Vedder, to mention just a few. Vedder, like so many painters, designed everything: murals, stained glass, frames, firebacks, tiles, and magazine covers. Stanford White, perhaps the consummate Renaissance man, was an architect, painter, designer of interiors, furniture, frames, magazine covers, and jewelry, and a collector and connoisseur of antiques (Fig. 90). No item was considered too insignificant for serious artistic treatment.

The philosophy of interior decoration during the late 1870s and 1880s was based upon historical precedent, but not in any strict sense. Styles were mixed harmoniously, although this did not imply symmetry or uniformity. *Artistic Houses*, published in 1883, describes Tiffany's apartment "as an exemplification of these two principles of decorative design, the principle of fitness, and the principle of irregular balance."[15] The ideal of harmony meant a unity of decorative elements from the floors, furniture, bric-a-brac, and walls to the ceiling and coordination of various colors and textures. Although each room might be done in a different style, the general feeling was "so unobtrusive and in other respects felicitous, . . . that you step easily and naturally, without shock or importunity, into one of these apartments from any other of them."[16] This new approach brought about the introduction of mosaics and parquet for floors; extensive use of wood paneling, wallpapers, leather or imitation leather (Lincrusta), and tapestries for walls; portieres for doors; stained glass for windows; a renewed interest in the fireplace, which could be antique, a copy of an earlier style, or decorated with tiles in the "newest fashion"; wallpapers, murals, stencil, or raised distemper decoration for ceilings. The robust realism of the mid-century was replaced by flat, stylized patterns that tended to cover all surfaces. Thrown into this potpourri were new, antique, or reproduction pieces of furniture and objets d'art from all countries and cultures. Dealing in antiques became a lucrative business. Americans ransacked Europe for everything from paintings to period rooms. This wide-ranging eclecticism produced some highly personal and inventive interiors.

In its inception, this new taste was dependent upon extreme wealth, although stylistic changes quickly filtered down to the public through books and periodicals. The critic and writer Mary Gay Humphreys commented that "the accumulation of great wealth has rendered it possible to undertake, on a scale hitherto unattempted, certain decorative works, which must be considered to some degree experimental. The result of an experiment of such importance is by no means confined to the satisfaction which a man may get out of his own surroundings, but bears certain relations to art in general, and to American art in particular, of which we have the right to take cognizance."[17]

The first entries in the battle to erect the largest and grandest mansion were three members of the Vanderbilt family. All their houses (long since destroyed) were commissioned about 1878.[18] Until then, only the A.T. Stewart mansion (1864–1869) could be considered a "palace," and in a way it represents "a bridge between early nineteenth century mansions and those built later in the century."[19] With the Vanderbilt houses one feels a sense of

15 *Artistic Houses, Being a Series of Interior Views of a Number of the Most Beautiful and Celebrated Homes in the United States* (New York, 1971; first published New York, 1883), p. 6.
16 *Artistic Houses*, p. 28. This passage refers to the David L. Einstein house, New York City, which had an Early English hall, a Louis XIII library, a Henry IV dining room, an Anglo-Japanese sitting room, a Chinese reception room, and a Louis XVI parlor.
17 Mary Gay Humphreys, "The Cornelius Vanderbilt House," *The Art Amateur* VIII (May 1883), p. 135.
18 H. Barbara Weinberg found that plans for all three structures were filed on December 8, 1879 ("The Vanderbilt Mansions," *New York Times*, December 9, 1879).
19 Jay E. Cantor, "A Monument of Trade, A.T. Stewart and the Rise of the Millionaire's Mansion in New York," *Winterthur Portfolio* 10 (Charlottesville, Va., 1975), p. 171.

family competition in the creation of the largest, most elaborate, and most expensive monument to financial success, social standing, sophistication, knowledge, and taste. William Henry, the father of the other two, commissioned the decorating firm of Herter Brothers to build an Italianate mansion at Fifth Avenue between Fifty-first and Fifty-second streets. His sons, William Kissam and Cornelius II, hired respectively Richard Morris Hunt for a François 1er chateau on the northwest corner of Fifth Avenue and Fifty-second Street and George B. Post for a Henry IV chateau on the west side of Fifth Avenue between Fifty-seventh and Fifty-eighth streets (Figs. 45 and 46). Contemporary accounts commented on their lavishness and grandeur, only disagreeing as to which one was the most successful.

These three palaces serve as excellent examples of the wide range of architectural and decorative styles and how they were employed during the first phase of the American Renaissance. William K. Vanderbilt's house was perhaps the most academic, both on the outside and inside. Hunt controlled most of the interior decoration. Drawings of the main hall, staircase, parlor, dining room, Moorish room, and library were produced in detail in Hunt's office. The execution of the designs was then carried out by different decorating firms; Herter, Marcotte, and Allard were each assigned various rooms.[20] This became a standard practice.

The Cornelius Vanderbilt II house (Fig. 24) was considered by Mary Gay Humphreys in 1883 to be "the most important example of decorative work yet attempted in this country."[21] It brought together some of the most important artists of the day: John La Farge, the Saint-Gaudens brothers, and Associated Artists. They were assisted by Philip Martiny, a French sculptor, Réne de Quélin, and the painter Will H. Low. Again, individual rooms were assigned to different artists, but in this case Post seems to have allowed them relative freedom to develop their own ideas. He seems to have been concerned only that there be an overall harmony from one space to another. The two most spectacular rooms were the dining and watercolor rooms, which were placed under the direction of La Farge with Saint-Gaudens's help. Mary Guy Humphreys said that the dining room "ceiling requires more detailed mention since it is . . . only paralleled in magnificence and in the luxuriousness of its material, by the decorative work of the fifteenth century, with which it agrees in kind."[22] The dining room has been described further:

> The dining room was forty-five feet long. Its walls were paneled part way up in oak. . . . The space above was covered in brown embossed leather which served as a background to the panels which Saint-Gaudens modeled from La Farge's designs [Fig. 128]. The coffered ceiling was divided into twenty panels of which six were filled with La Farge's opalescent glass studded with jewels. The oak beams were inlaid with a double Greek fret in mother of pearl. At the four corners were mahogany panels with scenes of Apollo and dancing cupids in repoussé gilded bronze. Over the doorway was a narrow panel which as one writer pointed out was directly copied from a tomb frieze in the South Kensington [Victoria and Albert] museum attributed to Matteo Civitale. On either side of the door were carved panels representing

20   John Vredenburgh Van Pelt, *A Monograph of the William K. Vanderbilt House* (New York, 1925), pp. 15–17.
21   Humphreys, "The Cornelius Vanderbilt House," p. 135.
22   Humphreys, "The Cornelius Vanderbilt House," p. 135.

"Hospitalitas" and "Amicitia." The background of these figures was of green marble with the heads, drapery and other details in irridescent metal, ivory and mother of pearl. The center of the wall opposite the door was filled by a panel with the date and by two side panels representing the sun and moon, these being derived according to a medieval ivory at Sens.[23]

This description (there are no photographs) gives an excellent idea of the sumptuousness of design and materials and the random eclecticism so popular during the period. The house was enlarged in 1895, and the decorations of the dining room were incorporated into a billiard room, and the watercolor room was converted into a hallway.

A ten-volume work on the W.H. Vanderbilt mansion and its collections was published shortly after the building was completed.[24] The photogravures and descriptions by Edward Strahan portray the scale, rationale, and magnificence of these early millionaires' palaces. Architecturally, this mansion was the most conservative, but the interior represents the fullest development of the new decorative style. In this case, the New York decorating firm of Herter Brothers was responsible for both the external and internal work, with assistance by the architect Charles B. Atwood.

The designs of everything attached to or forming a part of the building, as well as those of most of the furniture, carpets, mosaics and marquetry, etc., however foreign in appearance, were made in America, in the ateliers of the Architects. The external bronze railings were cast by Bureau Brothers and Heaton of Philadelphia. The internal woodcarving, which has received praise for its spirited sculptural touch, was executed by some two hundred and fifty workmen from the designs of Mr. Christian Herter.[25]

In keeping with the popular taste of the day, one room was in the Japanese taste, one in the Italian Renaissance, one in the Louis XIV, and so on, and real antiques were interspersed with reproductions. The overall effect was extremely inventive (Fig. 91). Strahan commented on how he felt older styles should be used to invent something new. In the W.H. Vanderbilt house, the mixture of old and new and the products of many diverse cultures and different centuries worked to create an exciting environment.

The vestibule, which "unites simplicity with enduring dignity," was roofed with colored glass, the walls were of marble, and the floors of mosaics.[26] Standing in the center was a huge malachite vase purchased by Vanderbilt in 1880 from the Demidoff sale. At that time, it was fittingly referred to as the "Medici Vase," but was actually made in 1819. On the south wall was a copy of Ghiberti's doors, *The Gates of Paradise*, cast by Barbedienne and exhibited at the Paris exposition of 1878. Strahan commented: "*The Gates of Paradise* are not only an extraordinary anticipation of all that decorative sculpture has found out since, but they have never been approached in merit in our own time."[27] The atrium extended to the entire height of the building. The columns and huge mantel were of red African marble. The floor was composed of mosaics covered by a giant carpet of Oriental inspiration made

23   Quoted in John H. Dryfhout, "Augustus Saint-Gaudens' 'Actaeon' and the Cornelius Vanderbilt II Mansion," *The J.B. Speed Art Museum Bulletin* XXXI (September 1976), pp. 5–6.
24   Earl Shinn [Edward Strahan], *Mr. Vanderbilt's House and Collection*. Two editions of this work were published: Japan edition (Philadelphia, n.d.); Holland edition (New York, Boston, and Philadelphia, 1883–1884).

25   Shinn, *Mr. Vanderbilt's House and Collection*, Japan edition, p. 7.
26   Shinn, *Mr. Vanderbilt's House and Collection*, Japan edition, p. 13.
27   Shinn, *Mr. Vanderbilt's House and Collection*, Japan edition, p. 17.

in Britain. The fireplace, enriched with a profusion of bronze ornament, was flanked by two bronze reliefs of figures of Pomona, copies of originals done by Germain Pilon in the sixteenth century. The doors leading off the atrium were hung with portieres. Leading up to and on the second landing of the house were stained glass windows by La Farge. Strahan commented that the design of the portieres and the La Farge windows were "unique in the house as a specimen of designing contributed from American soil, in the strict taste of the best renaissance models, but springing from native industry instead of being a trophy gathered from some old centre of foreign art. In such examples does the house justify itself as a sort of educational force, a college for the development of the higher crafts."[28] Tapestries, mainly copies of earlier

FIG. 92
Library table, 1882.
Herter Brothers (after 1865–*circa* 1900) for the William H. Vanderbilt house, New York City.
Rosewood, brass, and marble; 79.3 x 152.4 x 90.8 cm. (31¼ x 60 x 35¾ in.).
COLLECTION: The Metropolitan Museum of Art, New York City, Mrs. Russell Sage Fund by Exchange.

examples, were seen throughout, as well as objects of every medium, style, and age. There was also a large picture gallery, a new prerequisite for any proper palace. Four of the ten volumes on the house were devoted to Vanderbilt's painting collection, most of which was European.

The library, which was made up of panels of rosewood inlaid with pearl and brass, contained a monumental table

fit to go with the architectural mantelpiece as a serious piece of permanent construction [Figs. 92 and 93]. . . . Specimens like this, put together under exceptional advantages, designed before America can be said to have a style in cabinetmaking, but showing the handpointings

28 Shinn, *Mr. Vanderbilt's House and Collection,* Japan edition, p. 24.

123

and tendencies towards a style, likely to be long preserved, and representing the most deliberate work of a period, are just what will be available to the Chippendales and Boules of the future. . . . The legs are connected by a sort of lambrequin of carved and inlaid wood, making the lateral sides of the table almost solid; on this curtain, inlaid in marquetry, is the terrestrial globe, encircled by the stars of the national banner. The festoons of pearl discs surrounding the rim carry out a motive repeated in much of the woodwork of the room.[29]

This Herter table is remarkable for its originality, luxuriousness, and architectural integration.

It is in marked contrast to a more delicate, rectilinear Herter sideboard of about the same time (Fig. 94). This type of ebonized furniture with overall,

FIG. 93 *Facing page:*
Chimneypiece in the library, William H. Vanderbilt house, New York City, 1879–1881.
Herter Brothers (after 1865–circa 1900), assisted by Charles B. Atwood (1848–1895), architects.
From Earl Shinn [Edward Strahan], *Mr. Vanderbilt's House and Collection,* Holland edition (New York, Boston, and Philadelphia, 1883–1884).

29 Shinn, *Mr. Vanderbilt's House and Collection,* Holland edition, p. 43.

FIG. 94 *Above:*
Sideboard, *circa* 1875. Herter Brothers (after 1865–circa 1900), New York City.
Ebonized cherry;
107.7 x 167.7 x 42.5 cm. (42⅜ x 66 x 16¾ in.).
COLLECTION: The Brooklyn Museum, New York, H. Randolph Lever Fund.

FIG. 95
Armchair, *circa* 1875.
Pottier and Stymus
(1858/1859–after 1900), New York City.
Walnut with tapestry upholstery;
131.5 x 71.1 x 63.5 cm. (51¾ x 28 x 25 in.).
COLLECTION: The Metropolitan Museum of
Art, New York City, Gift of
Auguste Pottier, 1888.

tightly controlled inlaid patterns has become synonymous with the work of Herter Brothers, although other firms were certainly producing similar pieces of the same high quality. This style owes much to the new English "art furniture," but the addition of the beautifully painted panels of female figures shows the incorporation of many different decorative techniques. In 1881 *The Art Amateur* discussed the advantages of tiles as decorative devices and how decorative painting on furniture had become more popular than ever.[30]

The interior of the W.H. Vanderbilt house was important as a summation of the concepts of decorative art during the prelude period of the American Renaissance and gave form to the prevailing notion that at last there was an American taste. Strahan perceptively summed up the significance in his introduction: "In these volumes we are permitted to make a revelation of a private home which, better than any other possible selection, may stand as a representative of the new impulse now felt in the national life. Like a more perfect Pompeii, the work will be the vision and the image of a typical American residence, seized at the moment when the nation began to have a taste of its own, an architecture, a conaissseurship [sic], and a choice in the appliances of luxury, society, culture." He goes on to say that permission from Vanderbilt to share his house with the public "comes at the right moment, prompt and opportune, when wealth is first consenting to act the Medicean part in America, to patronize the inventors, to create the arts, and to originate a form of civilization. The country, at this moment, is just beginning to be astonishing. Re-cemented by the fortunate result of a civil war, endowed as with a diploma of rank by the promulgation of its centenary, it has begun to re-invent everything, and especially the house."[31]

The Decorative Arts

The Vanderbilt houses contained objects that symbolized new directions in all of the decorative arts. The prestigious firm of Pottier and Stymus received extraordinary praise at the time of the Centennial. "Even Paris, the capital which seems to monopolize the cabinet-makers' art and cabinet furniture in general, has sent nothing worthy of being compared, in richness of style, with the beautiful things exhibited by Pottier and Stymus. . . . Two carved walnut arm-chairs [Fig. 95], upholstered in Aubrisson [sic] tapestry, in the Henry II style, are remarkable for originality of form."[32] These chairs represent a transition between old and new trends, a continued mixing of historical styles, but with more direct copying of certain details, including the ciphers of Henry II and Diane de Poiters. The tapestry upholstery and fringe look ahead to the increased use of these materials.

Tapestries, which had not played a very important role in interior decoration since the eighteenth century in Europe and had never developed a strong tradition in this country, became very popular in the last decades of the nineteenth century. At first both originals and copies of French tapestries were imported. A more scholarly interest in tapestries developed after the turn of the century, and the first major exhibition of European tapestry was held in 1893 in Boston. Cheaper substitutes for the costly textiles were quickly discovered. In 1881, "an exhibition [of tapestry paintings], the first of

30 "Tiles for Cabinet," *The Art Amateur* VI (December 1881), p. 19.
31 Shinn, *Mr. Vanderbilt's House and Collection,* Japan edition, pp. v and vi.
32 *Golden Book of Celebrated Manufacturers and Merchants in the United States,* Reports of the Grand Centennial Exhibition, Series 20 (New York, 1876), pp. 129–130.

its kind, [was] held . . . at Howell & James, new art gallery, London."[33] By December 1886, the decorator George A. Glaenzer of New York was exhibiting a painted tapestry panel at the annual Architectural League exhibition.[34]

Candace Wheeler invented and patented in 1883 the "American Tapestry" (Fig. 96). "Realizing that the curtain for the Madison Square Theater [1879–1880] had been too realistic, Wheeler wanted to create a tapestry that would be suggestive in a painterly sense, yet distinctive and practical. Because dust and moths would destroy wool, she decided to use silk for the warp and the woof of the canvas. The face of the canvas was covered with embroidery silk, which passed under the slender warp and was actually sewn into the woof. Wheeler called the process 'needle weaving,' as the needle served as the shuttle carrying the threads. Though expensive to produce, well-to-do clients enthusiastically purchased needle-woven tapestries for their homes."[35] Mrs. Wheeler, along with her daughter Dora Wheeler Keith, Rosina Emmett, and Ida Clark, primarily specialized in designs for printed cottons and silk embroideries, as well as wallpapers.[36] These tended to be more in the Aesthetic movement or Art Nouveau style. It should be pointed out at this juncture that during this period women began to take a more active role in the arts, the "household arts" in particular. Many of the books and articles in periodicals were written by women for women.

There were only a few tapestry manufacturers in this country until around the turn of the century. William Baumgarten, a New York decorator, was producing Boucher-inspired tapestries by the late 1890s. In 1908 Albert Herter began the Herter Looms (first called Aubusson Looms) with showrooms in both New York and San Francisco (Fig. 97). Edgewater Looms, established in 1913 in Edgewater, New Jersey, advertised hand-woven tapestries and needlepoint to order—not as "domestic" but as "made in America."[37]

After mural painting, perhaps the most important and inventive development of the new decorative style was stained glass. Many contemporary critics and artists felt that techniques and styles in the art of stained glass were among America's great national contributions to art. According to one authority, "only a decade ago [1881] there were but eighteen makers of stainglass in the United States, and the work which they turned out was of the very worst description."[38] Will Low observed that the new interest in stained glass "came about the Centennial year, the date from which our future Vasari, if we ever deserve one, will trace the first concerted art movement in this country."[39] Roger Riordan, a writer and stained glass designer, noted that "no other material used in any of the fine arts so well repays experiment. . . . As a consequence, not withstanding the immense progress which all the forms of decorative art have made with us in the last few years, it is safe to say that none of them have improved as much as our work in stained glass."[40]

As in other areas of the arts, a conscious effort was made to study ancient glass techniques. From this exploration, two methods became apparent: the medieval way of using different colored glass with very little or no paint to delineate the design and the Renaissance technique of relying on

33 "Tapestry Painting," *The Art Amateur* V (June 1881), p. 12.
34 "Second Annual Exhibition of Architectural Drawings at The Salmagundi Club with the American Black and White Society," *Architectural League Year Book* (New York, 1886–1887), fig. 183.
35 Wilson H. Faude, "Associated Artists and the American Renaissance in the Decorative Arts," *Winterthur Portfolio* 10 (Charlottesville, Va., 1975), p. 128

36 Faude, "Associated Artists," p. 128.
37 I am indebted to Alice Zrebiec, Assistant Curator, European Sculpture and Decorative Arts, Textile Study Room, The Metropolitan Museum of Art, New York City, for her information on tapestry making in this country. She is preparing a Ph.D. dissertation —"The American Tapestry Manufacturers 1893–1933"—at The Institute of Fine Arts.

38 Roger Riordan, "American Stained Glass," *American Art Review* II (First Division, 1881), p. 229.
39 Will H. Low, "Old Glass in New Windows," *Scribner's Magazine* IV (December 1888), p. 680.
40 Riordan, "American Stained Glass," p. 233.

FIG. 96 *Left:*
The Miraculous Draught of Fishes.
Designed by Candace Wheeler (1828–1923);
made by Associated Artists (1883–1907),
New York City.
Needle-woven tapestry.
Illustrated in Candace Wheeler,
The Development of Embroidery in America
(New York and London, 1921).

FIG. 97 *Below:*
The Gothic Tapestry.
Herter Looms (1908–1933/1934), New York
City and San Francisco.
Tapestry; 181.6 x 348.2 cm. (71½ x 137 in.).
COLLECTION: Cranbrook Academy of
Art Museum, Bloomfield Hills, Michigan.

extensive use of paint to portray the image. During the nineteenth century, the English preferred the painterly, pictorial quality of the Renaissance, while in France and Germany, medieval traditions were more closely followed. Of course, Europe had a tradition of stained glass, which America lacked. During the nineteenth century, particularly with the growing use of the Gothic style for church architecture, stained glass was increasingly used

FIG. 98
Peony Window, 1882.
John La Farge (1835–1910).
Stained glass;
160.0 x 113.0 cm. (63 x 44½ in.).
Made for Sir Lawrence Alma-Tadema.
COLLECTION: Museum of Fine Arts, Boston.

in this country. But it was not until the idea of an overall decorative scheme became important that the full range of the artistic possibilities inherent in glass were developed. "Almost from the first day [stained glass designers] abandoned the usage and traditions of the modern European Schools and aimed at brilliant effect rather than design, striving for artistic and harmonious arrangement of diverse colors rather than merely transparent pictures. So far has the American artist carried this feeling that he can no longer be called a painter on glass, but is really a worker in glass mosaic."[41]

John La Farge seems to have been the first person intersted in integrating stained glass into decorative schemes (Fig. 98). This interest eventually led him to a discovery of opal or opalescent glass, for which he applied for a patent in 1879. It was awarded in February 1880. Tiffany began his experiments at about the same time, but was not granted patents for his ideas until February 1881.[42] In a sense, the controversy over who was the first is inconsequential. Both artists created exceptional works of art using different types of glass and other mediums, such as shells or semiprecious stones, in an unprecedented way. The endless decorative possibilities of stained glass fascinated both architect and artist, and soon the medium was to be found not only in churches such as Trinity but in domestic and public structures as well. Major painters such as Francis Millet, Low, Edwin Blashfield, Vedder, Kenyon Cox, and Robert Blum designed windows, but so did many other artists whose names today are almost forgotten: D. Maitland Armstrong, Frederic Crowinshield, Frederick Dielman, Otto Heinigke, Charles Rollison Lamb, Frederick Stymetz Lamb, Francis Lathrop, Joseph Lauber, and William Willet. There were also a number of women who worked in the medium: Helen Maitland Armstrong, Lydia Field Emmett, Ella Conde Lamb, Violet Oakley, Rosina Emmett Sherwood, Mary E. Tillinghast, and Anne Lee Willet.

The relationships among stained glass artists are difficult to unravel. Many designed independently or organized their own companies. The J. and R. Lamb Studios (Fig. 99), founded by Joseph and Richard Lamb in 1857, is the oldest continuing stained glass company in the United States. They specialize in ecclesiastical art. *Religion Enthroned,* a window shown at the 1900 Paris exposition, was considered one of their finest works, winning two gold medals. Other decorating firms, such as Cottier and Company, advertised that they made stained glass, but it is unclear whether they actually produced it themselves or merely imported it.

Debate raged throughout the American Renaissance period as to the most appropriate style for stained glass—abstract pattern (mosaic) or pictorial (Fig. 3). Among the concerns for pictorial representation was whether the space should be flat or volumetric. As is true with decorative art in general after 1890, stained glass became more pictorial and more reliant on historical precedent. The quality of design and materials declined as the popularity of stained glass sifted down to the middle classes. From the 1890s well into the 1920s, stained glass was a common element in houses from New York to San Francisco.[43]

Decorative schemes often included the ancient art of mosaics, either of glass or stone. Their development was similar to that of stained glass in

41 C. Coleman, "Mosaic Glass," *American Art* I (October 1886), p. 13.
42 See Weinberg, *The Decorative Work of John La Farge,* for an excellent discussion of La Farge's development and work.
43 I am indebted to Sarah B. Webster, a doctoral candidate at the Graduate Center, City University of New York, for making her research on American stained glass available.

FIG. 99 *Facing page:*
Interior, J. and R. Lamb Studios,
New York City, *circa* 1900.
PHOTO: J. and R. Lamb Studios, Inc.,
Northvale, New Jersey.

FIG. 100
Vase, 1876.
Karl Mueller (b. 1820), Union Porcelain
Works (1861–*circa* 1908), Green Point, New
York.
Porcelain; 56.5 x 25.4 cm. (22¼ x 10 in.).
Made for and exhibited at the Centennial
Exhibition, Philadelphia.
COLLECTION: The Brooklyn Museum, New
York, Gift of Carll and Franklin Chace in
memory of their mother, Pastora Forest
Smith Chace, daughter of Thomas Carll
Smith.

FIG. 101
Design for wallpaper, *circa* 1880.
Samuel Colman (1832–1920).
Published in Clarence Cook, *What Shall We Do With Our Walls?* (New York, 1881).

terms of popularity, function, and style. They were used initially to create pattern and texture, often in Renaissance motifs, on floors and walls. Increasingly, though, they became more pictorial, with allegorical overtones, and they often replaced murals in public and religious structures.

There was almost no material that was too insignificant for attention by major artists and decorating and manufacturing firms. Warren, Fuller and Company hired Tiffany and Colman to design wall and ceiling papers for a promotional book, *What Shall We Do With Our Walls?* (1881), written by the critic Clarence Cook. In 1886 the company advertised "Wall Papers manufactured and imported by Warren, Fuller and Lange. Now on exhibition, New and artistic patterns by the Associated Artists and Miss Rosina Emmett. Also recent importations of Japanese, French, German and English hangings, and more than 4000 styles of medium and low-priced goods. Sole Manufactures of Messrs. Herter Bros. Patented Papers, in beautiful colorings."[44]

The philosophy of how to treat walls and ceilings was revolutionized from an architectonic use of pale colors and ornamental wood and plaster work to one of overall pattern, which caused the walls to appear structureless. "To be constantly reminded of the wall as a wall, as a solid piece of masonary [sic], is what we must avoid . . . and yet . . . it is quite [as] possible . . . to make the wall beautiful as for the pearl-oyster to spread its shell with opalescent nacre."[45] Walls tended to be divided into horizontal bands. Wallpaper designs (Fig. 101) became more geometric and flat, even if flowered, and for the first time were used on the ceilings. Leather, either plain or embossed, became popular as a paper substitute, and there was even an imitation leather. Often referred to as Lincrusta-Walton, it was invented by an Englishman, Frederick Walton, in 1877. "After first experimenting with linoleum applied to wall surfaces, Walton developed a new material composed primarily of solidified linseed oil that he molded in elaborate designs. He called it 'Lincrusta'—'lin' for 'linium' [flax] and 'crusta' for relief."[46] The new product had many advantages, not the least of which was that it could be washed. It is not clear when it was first made in this country. In February 1882 *The Art Amateur* reported that "a stock company is being formed in this city [New York] for the purpose of acquiring and developing . . . the patents for the application of compounds of solidified oils to the manufacture of wall and other decorations in solid relief. . . . Mr. Le Prince, a Parisian artist of ability and an enterprising business man is to represent the manufacturers in New York."[47] Also popular were leather-papers made in Japan. The London firm of Rottman Strome and Company, who had a New York salesroom, advertised in 1885: "Our Japanese Leathers are now largely used in connection with the Queen Anne style and the Flemish Renaissance, and admired for their harmony in colour and superior finish. . . . The new Papers for Diningrooms, Libraries, Clubs, Theatres, Halls, Staircases. &c. will stand moist walls, and can be cleaned with soap and water."[48] As European antiques became more popular, old leathers were also imported. Yandell and Company exhibited forty-two panels of seventeenth-century Italian leather work in 1887. The price was $5000.[49] The interest in pattern, texture, and rich colors brought about experimentation with a variety of materials. A reaction

44 "First Annual Exhibition of Architectural Drawings at The Salmagundi Club with the American Black and White Society," *Architectural League Year Book* (New York, 1886).
45 Faude, "Associated Artists," p. 127.
46 Phillip H. Curtis, "The Ballantine House: Preserving a Newark Landmark," *The Newark Museum Quarterly* 27 (Fall 1976), p. 15.

47 "Embossed Wall Decoration," *The Art Amateur* VI (February 1882), p. 65.
48 Curtis, "The Ballantine House," p. 15.
49 "Third Annual Exhibition," *Architectural League Year Book* (New York, 1887–1888), fig. 482.

against this abundance of detail developed in the 1890s as a gradual return to an emphasis on architectonic interior space took place.

The ceramic, glass, and silver industries received renewed financial support after the depression of 1873, but they were also infused with a new impulse to produce wares of artistic merit. Obviously, their business depended upon making utilitarian goods, but there developed a conscious attempt to make objects which were to be considered works of art. Potteries hired sculptors to model vases and sculptural pieces. Large presentation works were made for the increasing number of expositions, such as the Union Porcelain Works' Century Vase (Fig. 100) created for the Philadelphia Centennial. Commercial companies such as Union Porcelain Works, Ott and Brewer, and Knowles, Taylor and Knowles have tended to be ignored in favor of the so-called "art potteries" that developed in the 1880s. The art potteries, considered more avant-garde in their search for simplicity, looked mainly to China and Japan for inspiration, while the more commercial firms, though tantalized by exotic forms and decoration, were inspired more by European historical styles (Fig. 104). Similar impulses were at work; only the stimuli were different. Ultimately, even though part of the art pottery idea was the return to handcraftmanship, many of these potteries, like Rookwood, became as commercial as their competitors (Fig. 103).

FIG. 102 *Facing page:*
Vase, 1893–1895.
Designed by Paulding Farnham (chief designer: 1889–*circa* 1904), Tiffany and Company (1853–present), New York City.
Gold studded with pearls and semiprecious stones and enamels; height: 49.5 cm. (19½ in.).
Presented to Edward Dean Adams, Chairman of the Board of the American Cotton Oil Company, by the stockholders and directors.
COLLECTION: The Metropolitan Museum of Art, New York City, Gift of Edward D. Adams.

FIG. 103 *Below, left:*
Fellowship Cup, 1897.
Sculpted by Clement J. Barnhorn (b. 1857); decorated by W.P. McDonald (1865–1931), Rookwood Pottery (1880–1967), Cincinnati, Ohio.
Earthenware;
37.5 x 26.3 cm. (14¾ x 10⅜ in.).
Presented by the Commercial Club of Cincinnati to the Commercial Club of Chicago on the occasion of their visit to Cincinnati.
COLLECTION: The Chicago Historical Society, Illinois.

FIG. 104 *Above:*
Vase, *circa* 1895.
Knowles, Taylor and Knowles (1888–1898), East Liverpool, Ohio.
Porcelain; 24.5 x 10.6 cm. (9⅝ x 3 9/16 in.).
COLLECTION: Greenfield Village and Henry Ford Museum, Dearborn, Michigan.

FIG. 105
Tile, *circa* 1890.
Herman Mueller (1854–1941), American
Encaustic Tile Company (1875–1935),
Zanesville, Ohio.
Earthenware; 30.8 x 45.7 cm. (12⅛ x 18 in.).
COLLECTION: Moses Mesre, Ohio.

Ceramic tiles played a significant decorative role in this country from the end of the 1870s well into the 1920s. The Tile Club, formed in New York, "was composed first of twelve but eventually included as many as thirty young artists, who originally saw in painting tiles a possible means of making money. The social aspect of the club, however, quickly came to dominate. Among Tile Club members were at one time or another J. Alden Weir, John Twachtman, Stanford White, Edwin Austin Abbey, Winslow Homer and Augustus Saint-Gaudens. . . . The Tile Club lasted about ten years, from 1877 to 1887."[50] The initial inspiration for decorative tiles came from English works that were imported to this country. But soon such companies as American Encaustic Tile (founded 1875), United States Encaustic Tile (1877), Low Art Tile (1878), Trent Tile (1882), Providential Tile Works (1886), Beaver Falls Art Tile (1886), and Cambridge Art Tile Works (1886) were producing excellent tiles for every possible decorative use (Fig. 105). They were "found most commonly in an architectural context such as floor pavement or the embellishment of mantels, but these are only two of many uses. Tiles appear on clock cases, inset in furniture (more typically English) or in iron stoves, and simply as individual decorative objects. The tiles are set in the panels, something after the fashion of a picture in a frame . . . [and] they are ornamented with all kinds of designs, comprising such subjects as birds, flowers, foliage, designs from history, Shakespeare, and the Scriptures."[51] As was true with the other decorative arts, a change began to occur during the 1890s. "One is the general replacement of raised relief designs by painted or molded decoration flush to the surface of the tile. Second is the replacement of tinted, translucent glazes by mat glazes or a mat finish as well as by a variety of other glazing techniques. Third is the insistence, real or illusory, by many of the potteries, on hand

50 Storrs, Conn., The William Benton Museum of Art, *American Decorative Tiles, 1870–1930*, 1979, by Thomas P. Bruhn, p. 45.
51 Storrs, Conn., The William Benton Museum of Art, *American Decorative Tiles*, pp. 7–8.
52 Storrs, Conn., The William Benton Museum of Art, *American Decorative Tiles*, p. 9.
53 Toledo: The Toledo Museum of Art, *Art in Glass*, 1969, pp. 109–110.

craftsmanship."[52] By the end of the 1920s, tiles were regarded as more or less utilitarian and lost their decorative appeal.

Deeply cut glass is most closely associated with this period, although many other types were produced, from "art glass" to Tiffany's favrile. The vogue for cut glass began with the Centennial, but did not reach its zenith until after the World's Columbian Exposition. "During the years from 1880 to 1915, cut glass became a symbol of social prestige. Its opulent surfaces were admirably suited to the formal living patterns of the age. The new prosperity . . . created a market sufficient to sustain the high cost of the heavy lead glass and its extensive ornamentation."[53] Marvels like the Libbey Glass Company table of 1902 (Fig. 106), made especially for the 1904 Louisiana Purchase Exposition in Saint Louis, illustrate why the cut glass of this period

FIG. 106
Table, 1902.
Libbey Glass Company (1888–present),
Toledo, Ohio.
Cut glass; 81.3 x 71.1 cm. (32 x 28 in.).
Made for and exhibited at Louisiana
Purchase Exposition, Saint Louis, 1904.
COLLECTION: Toledo Museum of Art, Ohio,
Gift of Owens-Illinois, Inc.

FIG. 107
Vase, *circa* 1885.
New England Glass Company (1818–1888),
Cambridge, Massachusetts.
Amberina glass; height: 19.7 cm. (7¾ in.).
COLLECTION: Toledo Museum of Art, Ohio,
Gift of Marie W. Greenhalgh in memory of
Alice Libbey Walbridge and William S.
Walbridge.

is referred to as "Brilliant." The First World War, with its changing life styles, brought about the demise of this time-consuming and expensive method of producing opulent glass.

As art potters experimented with new shapes and colors, so did "art glass" manufacturers. Great effort went into searching the past for the knowledge of how to produce certain colors and how to gradate them. Each type developed received a name, such as Amberina, Pomona, Burmese, Peach Glow, or Crown Milano. Historical forms were also sought, as can be seen in the New England Glass Company vase in the shape of a drinking horn (Fig. 107). A great source of inspiration was Venetian glass of the sixteenth and seventeenth centuries. Firms famous for their fine work, other than the New England Glass Company, were the Mount Washington Glass Company and Hobbs, Brockunier and Company. Of course, the most fa-

FIG. 108
Cup, *circa* 1885.
Tiffany and Company (1853–present),
New York City.
Silver, enamel, and semiprecious stones;
15.9 x 13.3 cm. (6¼ x 5¼ in.).
COLLECTION: The Brooklyn Museum, New
York, The Alfred T. and Caroline S.
Zoebisch Fund.

mous and original of all the art glass manufacturers of the late nineteenth
century was Tiffany, who combined the iridescent qualities of ancient glass
with the new organic forms of Art Nouveau.

Silver and gold, by their very natures, have always maintained a certain
stature and artistic importance. The introduction of silver and gold plating
made it possible for many more people to enjoy these materials, but they
were still regarded as status symbols. Companies such as Tiffany[54] and
Gorham produced work of high quality in the popular styles of the day.
Again, in the beginning the eclecticism was freely adapted, while later it
became more academic. Imaginative luxuriousness reminiscent of the Renaissance in the use of enamel and semiprecious stones is seen in the Tiffany
and Company footed cup of about 1885 (Fig. 108). Perhaps no object is more
representative of the Gilded Age than the Adams Vase of gold studded with

54 Tiffany and Company was founded in 1837
by Charles Tiffany, the father of Louis Comfort
Tiffany. This firm is not to be confused with
Louis Comfort Tiffany's Associated Artists, Tiffany's Glass and Decorating Company, or Tiffany Studios.

pearls and semiprecious stones made by Tiffany and Company between 1893 and 1895 (Fig. 102). It was designed by Paulding Farnham and presented to Edward Dean Adams, Chairman of the Board of the American Cotton Oil Company. Tiffany and Company published a booklet on the vase, emphasizing the cost, production time, symbolism of the design elements, and the fact that "every piece of material used, and the artist and his principal assistants, are American, which shows an independence that many countries in the old world might be proud of."[55]

During this period of self-congratulation, the vogue for presentation pieces reached its zenith. The ultimate example, the Admiral Dewey Loving Cup (Fig. 109), gives form to the three general characteristics of the American Renaissance—nationalism, cosmopolitanism, and the genteel tradition. The *New York Journal,* in preparation for Admiral Dewey's triumphal return from the Battle of Manila, asked all Americans to send in one silver dime. These

55 New York, The Metropolitan Museum of Art, *19th Century American Furniture and Other Decorative Arts,* fig. 281.

142

FIG. 111 *Above:*
Armchairs, 1882.
Herter Brothers (after 1865–*circa* 1900),
New York City.
Mahogany;
92.7 x 63.5 x 41.3 cm. (36 x 25 x 16½ in.).
COLLECTION: The Brooklyn Museum, New
York, Gift of Mr. and Mrs. William E.S.
Griswold in memory of her father, John
Sloane.

FIG. 112 *Above, right*
Armchair, 1886.
John Quincy Adams Ward (1830–1910).
Oak, originally upholstered in alligator
skin;
151.1 x 70.5 x 64.8 cm.
(59½ x 27¾ x 25½ in.).
COLLECTION: The Brooklyn Museum, New
York, Gift of the Honorable E.J. Dimock.

would be melted down and made into a large vase that would express Americans' esteem for their hero. Within five months, seventy thousand dimes were collected. William Codman of the Gorham Company was hired to design the 8-foot-4-inch memorial. "Crowned by a splendid figure of Victory, the cup is ovoid in shape, with three handles and an ornate base. It stands on a massive silver pedestal, which in turn rests on an oak platform. . . . Its mammoth size mirrors a day when heroes were larger than life and dimes were made of silver. It is confidence and exuberance, opulence and eclecticism, all expressed in hundreds of pounds of sterling."[56]

A marvelous example of imperial eclecticism based on a variety of styles and the particular interest of the patron is a chair designed by the noted sculptor J.Q.A. Ward in 1886 for Anthony W. Dimock (Fig. 112). The crocodile arms celebrate the fact that Dimock was one of the people who established the existence of the crocodile (as distinguished from the alligator) in Florida.

Interior Decoration: Scientific Eclecticism

The desire to have all the appurtenances of the extremely wealthy and to imitate the new styles of decorative art filtered down to all levels of society. In 1882, for the Fifth Avenue brownstone of John Sloane, Herter Brothers designed a mahogany library with a frieze and ceiling decorated in distemper and gold and also the furniture, gas brackets, and portieres (one set

56 Sharon S. Darling, "Admiral Dewey's Loving Cup," *The Magazine Silver* (January–February 1976), pp. 10, 12.
57 Henry-Russell Hitchcock, *Architecture: Nineteenth and Twentieth Centuries*, 2nd ed. (Baltimore, 1963), p. 228.

is almost identical to one in the W.H. Vanderbilt house) for the room (Fig. 110). A pair of armchairs (Fig. 111) designed for the library illustrate the close approximation of Renaissance styles at this early date. To complete the decoration of the room, the Sloanes, either on their own or with Herter's advice, added Japanese bronzes, European pottery and paintings, a tiger skin rug, and a French shelf clock and matching candelabra. Apparent is an interest in overall pattern and a diffuse eclecticism typical of the prelude period.

Beginning some time in the mid-1880s, there was a gradual change in emphasis from a romantic, synthetic use of the past to a more scientific or archaeological electicism. The increasingly dominant role of the architect had a tremendous effect on interior decoration and the decorative arts. The Villard houses (1882–1886; Fig. 43), designed by McKim, Mead and White, mark a turning point. The exterior, modeled closely after the Palazzo Cancelleria (Fig. 42), illustrates the changing architectural emphasis from a loosely eclectic style to one that is more formal and academic. The interior (Fig. 23), although designed according to the ideas of Stanford White, was contracted out to individual artists—La Farge, Augustus and Louis Saint-Gaudens, D. Maitland Armstrong, and Francis Lathrop—who had a certain amount of freedom to do as they wanted with their own projects (Figs. 23 and 44). The increasing emphasis on "close archeological imitation of a style from the past"[57] brought about a new interest in proportion, balance, and symmetry that directly affected interior decoration. Interior space was seen as an organic part of the total structure. Thus a revulsion grew against overall pattern, asymmetry, textures, and contrasting colors, which were felt to detract from architectural integrity.

Everyone had his own ideas as to which historical styles were the best, and decisions about which style to follow depended on the use, patron, architect, and location of the house. In the late 1880s and 1890s, the urban palace was transported to the summer resort of Newport, Rhode Island. William K. Vanderbilt commissioned Richard Morris Hunt to build his summer mansion, Marble House (1885–1892). Hunt, who had designed Vanderbilt's New York City mansion, had always kept tight control of his interiors. The magnificent iron grill (Fig. 113) that screens the entrance was designed by the architect and executed by the John Williams Bronze Foundry of New York. It illustrates that metalwork had become an increasingly important decorative device both on the exterior and in the interior of buildings.

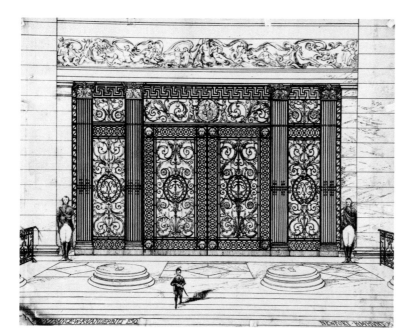

FIG. 113
Design for the entrance grill, William K. Vanderbilt's Marble House, Newport, Rhode Island, 1885–1892.
Richard Morris Hunt (1827–1895), architect.
Ink on paper; 38.1 x 48.2 cm. (15 x 19 in.).
COLLECTION: American Institute of Architects Foundation, Washington, D.C.

FIG. 114
Table, 1909–1911.
Carrère and Hastings.
Oak;
101.6 x 625.2 x 91.4 cm. (40 x 246 x 36 in.).
Designed for The New York Public Library,
New York City.
COLLECTION: The New York Public Library.
PHOTO: Helga Photo Studio
(courtesy of *The Magazine Antiques*).

FIG. 115   *Facing page:*
Dining room, William K. Vanderbilt's
Marble House, Newport, Rhode Island,
1885–1892.
Richard Morris Hunt (1827–1895), architect.
COLLECTION: The Preservation Society of
Newport County.

Hunt had collaborated with Jules Allard et Fils of Paris since 1880 and used them again for the lavish interiors of Marble House (Fig. 115). The French firm opened a New York office in 1885.[58] "Hunt knew that French *décor*—the imperial opulence of Versailles, the ordered classical charm of the Petit Trianon, the subtle grace of the Hermitage of Madame de Pompadour at Fountainebleau—was extremely difficult to replicate correctly and was almost impossible to adapt without great knowledge and greater skill. As the protégé of Lefuel in Paris, he had learned from a master of interpretation, and as the leading palace architect in America, he had gone back to Paris, to Allard, for the high quality of collaboration he required."[59]

Such concern for historical accuracy initiated the wholesale importation of European woodwork. The impetus for the period room seems to have come from the private collector who desired to create a stage set, a fantasy for the symbols of his interests, position, and knowledge. Depending on the person's particular identification, the room could be of any period and from any country. In this regard, it is not surprising to see photographs or paintings of artists' studios (Fig. 122) filled with actual or reproduction Renaissance furniture. As the sentiment that "it is better to repeat some brilliant epigram of the ancients than to utter a brand-new platitude"[60] became more prevalent, architects, designers, and decorators began to collect and rely on architectural and design books of the past. The photograph also became an important tool.

This desire for accuracy of detail and form is seen in the entire decoration of the interior, including the furniture. Allard wrote Stanford White in 1900, illustrating a partial drawing of a Louis XIV table from the Petit Palais, saying: "This table could be executed like that and delivered in New York for about two thousand dollars. We could guarantee that it could not be told from the old, gilding and all."[61] This exact copying of construction and style, whether European or American, presents problems today in determining old from new. Even when "proportions and materials dictated by function and cost" were changed from the original designs, the basic forms and details were fairly accurate (Fig. 114).[62]

The fascination with the American past that became evident in the 1870s was originally sentimental and patriotic in its motivation and did not involve an interest in American aesthetics. Clarence Cook in 1877 recommended Colonial furniture for its simplicity and utility, although he advised against

58 James T. Maher, *The Twilight of Splendor: Chronicles of American Palaces* (Boston, 1975), pp. 51 and 57.
59 Maher, *The Twilight of Splendor*, p. 279.
60 William Francklyn Paris, *Decorative Elements in Architecture: Random Observations on the Eternal Fitness of Things from a Decorative Point of View* (New York, 1917), p. 11.
61 Fernand Allard to Stanford White, August 1, 1900, Collection of Peter White, Saint James, New York.
62 Channing Blake, "Architects as Furniture Designers," *Antiques* CIX (May 1976), p. 1043.

FIG. 116
Side table, 1892.
A.H. Davenport and Company
(1880–present).
Mahogany with satinwood inlay;
71.7 x 99.0 x 45.7 cm. (29¼ x 39 x 18 in.).
COLLECTION: Davenport Memorial
Foundation, Malden, Massachusetts.
PHOTO: Richard Cheek
(courtesy of *The Magazine Antiques*).

FIG. 117
Design for an upstairs bedroom,
Cornelius Vanderbilt II's Breakers,
Newport,
Rhode Island, 1894.
Ogden Codman Jr. (1863–1951).
Watercolor on paper;
35.5 x 61.0 cm. (14 x 24 in.).
COLLECTION: The Metropolitan Museum of
Art, New York City, Gift of the Estate of
Ogden Codman, 1951.

FIG. 118
Living room, Thomas Jefferson Coolidge
house, Manchester, Massachusetts, 1904.
McKim, Mead and White, architects.

exact copies. The term "Colonial Revival" is misleading in that it eventually encompassed everything from late seventeenth-century pieces through Empire styles of the 1830s and 1840s.[63] Although more accurate examples became the norm, there was constant adaptation and confusion of forms and details. The side table (Fig. 116) made by the A.H. Davenport and Company of Boston in 1892 was probably inspired by a Federal card table, but "the inlay on the drawer, in its Adamesque riot of ribbons, swags, and floral motifs, little resembles the restrained decoration on a table of the Federal period."[64] As the century came to a close, interpretation of our past became more archaeological, as can be seen in the Thomas Jefferson Coolidge house (Fig. 118) in Manchester, Massachusetts. Enthusiasm for Colonial Revival styles remained strong well through the 1930s, and in a sense, these styles have never lost their popularity.

The Breakers (Fig. 72), built for Cornelius Vanderbilt II by Hunt, offers striking contrast, not necessarily in method of approach but in style, between its first and second floors. The downstairs, in its grandiose opulence, seems incongruous next to the relative simplicity of Ogden Codman's designs for the upstairs bedrooms (Fig. 117). These rooms are an early example of Codman's philosophy, later summed up in the book *The Decoration of Houses*, which he wrote in collaboration with Edith Wharton in 1897. "The purpose of the book [was] to show how the decoration of rooms should be derived from the harmony of organization of its architectural features. The chapters . . . are devoted to a room by room analysis of what should be done and why. . . . The most important message is that the essence of style lies not in its use of ornament, but in its handling of proportion. Structure conditions ornament, not ornament structure."[65] Codman was one of the first to use painted furniture and encouraged the unification of color, architectural detail, and furniture. *The Decoration of Houses* had a tremendous influence, emphasizing architectural correctness and careful study of previous styles, particularly eighteenth-century French. Elsie de Wolf, author of *The House in Good Taste*, 1913, is given much credit as the first interior decorator and for breaking away from the nineteenth-century approach to interior decoration. However, she owed much to Codman and the whole changing philosophy of the 1890s.

The many refurbishings of The White House offer an excellent illustration of the contrast in attitude that developed between 1876 and 1917. Tiffany and Associated Artists, commissioned by Chester Arthur, radically modernized the first floor hall, the East Room, the State Dining Room, and the Red and Blue rooms. Contemporary accounts particularly praised the "magnificent screen of mosaic glass which shuts off the inner corridor from the public. . . . [It] fills the space between the columns . . . [and] is the most elaborate of the exquisite decorations in glass by Mr. Louis C. Tiffany. . . . Glowing and rich in subdued colors, it is a thoroughly artistic piece of work, exceptional in taste and in perfect harmony with its surroundings."[66] In the East Room, Tiffany painted the ceiling in silver and various ivory tones and had the walls covered with gray painted paper highlighted in gold. In the Blue Room (Fig. 119) "the three-foot high frieze of pale blue and silver blended into the greenish blue wallpaper causing the

63 For further discussion on Colonial Revival see Rodris Roth, "American Art: The Colonial Revival and Centennial Furniture," *The Art Quarterly* 27 (1964), pp. 57–77.
64 Anne Farnam, "A. H. Davenport and Company, Boston Furniture Makers," *Antiques* CIX (May 1976), p. 1055.
65 Pauline C. Metcalf, "Ogden Codman, Jr., Architect-Decorator: Elegance Without Excess" (M. S. thesis, Graduate School of Architecture and Planning, Columbia University, 1978), pp. 46–47.
66 Koch, *Louis C. Tiffany, Rebel in Glass*, p. 21.

FIG. 119 *Right:*
The Blue Room, The White House,
Washington, D.C., 1882.
Louis Comfort Tiffany (1848–1933) and
Associated Artists (1879–1883).
PHOTO: The White House.

FIG. 120 *Facing page, top:*
The Blue Room, The White House,
Washington, D.C., 1902–1903.
McKim, Mead and White, architects.
PHOTO: The White House.

FIG. 121 *Facing page, bottom:*
Desk, *circa* 1910.
Arthur F. Mathews (1860–1945) and
Lucia K. Mathews (1870–1955).
The Furniture Shop (1906–1920), Oakland,
California.
Wood with painted decoration;
149.8 x 121.9 x 50.8 cm. (59 x 48 x 20 in.).
COLLECTION: The Oakland Museum, Gift of
the Concours d'Antiques, Art Guild and
The Oakland Museum Association.

room to be called the 'Robin's Egg Blue Room.' Oval patterns in light bluish-grey and silver gave a silvery tint to the ceilings. Flanking the mantel were sconces with reflectors composed of diamond shaped mosaics encrusted with jewels."[67] The set of gilded furniture dated from 1860.

Theodore Roosevelt hired McKim, Mead and White in 1902 to refurbish all of the main downstairs rooms and some on the second floor. With the Roosevelt administration, the first floor was reserved for more public functions, while the upstairs became the family domain. McKim, Mead and White attempted to restore the house to its original classicism, although they typically relied on a wide range of historical styles in the furnishings.[68] A.H. Davenport and Company, often used by McKim, Mead and White since at least 1890, made the furniture for the State Dining Room. This ranged from eighteenth-century William Kent–type eagle-based serving tables to William and Mary chairs. Colonial Revival was considered appropriate for the family dining room. Davenport again designed the furniture, which ranged from fairly accurate copies of Chippendale to Sheraton. The contrast between Tiffany's Blue Room and McKim, Mead and White's (Fig. 120) clearly demonstrates the dramatic shift towards architectural clarity, a lightening of the palette, and a more scientific eclecticism. The white and gilt chairs made

67 Betty Monkman, "The White House: 1873–1902," *Nineteenth Century* 4 (Spring 1978), p. 81.
68 Charles McKim, the architect in charge, considered his work on the room to be a restoration rather than a simple refurbishing. See: A. Burnley Bibb, "The Restoration of The White House." *House and Garden* 3 (March 1903), pp. 127–139.

by Marcotte and Company of New York present a mixture of styles—Sheraton and French Empire—but they blend and add to the overall classicism.

The popularity of exact reproductions of any style grew during the twentieth century. Although there was a reaction against historicism beginning in the 1890s, as seen in the work of Frank Lloyd Wright, Gustav Stickley, and others, nothing is as clear-cut and definitive as we would like. There exist curious diversions, such as the Lucia and Arthur Mathews desk (Fig. 121), which combines Renaissance form and detail with Arts and Crafts decoration. Furniture manufacturers had no problems with producing Louis XVI chairs along with Mission Oak. The strains of cosmopolitanism, a search for the most beautiful and exotic examples of art from all ages, the genteel tradition, with its moralistic overtones and sense of obligation to raise aesthetic standards, and the growing nationalism, which fostered an interest in America's own past, all contributed to making the decorative arts and interior decoration of the American Renaissance distinct. After the First World War, new motivating forces were at work. The old traditions continued, but the world had changed, and so, eventually, did its surroundings.

8 Painting and Sculpture

A merican artists of the late nineteenth century worked in numerous artistic modes. Some explored the phenomena of perception and the variety of visual effects, while others designed decorative works or sought inspiration from examples drawn from the history of art. Despite their differing approaches to art, however, these artists had a common self-conception. Theirs was a new generation that had completely redirected the course of American art from the minor and provincial "Hudson River School," as they called it,[1] to that of parity with art of nations with much longer traditions. In a time when national "schools" of art were thought of as representing the artistic, even the moral, level of the people, these artists thought of themselves as the creators of a distinctly American School, one that reflected the particular character of the nation. In their view, much colored by a new consciousness of the history of art, American art had experienced its Renaissance and was taking its place in the historical mainstream of art and culture by virtue of their efforts.

Richard N. Murray

The "New Movement" in American Art

The event that seemed to foretell a new era in American art was the Centennial Exposition of 1876 in Philadelphia. Among the vast displays of painting, sculpture, and decorative arts from both familiar and exotic nations was a significant selection of American art, arranged as a historical display that gave many visitors their first opportunity to understand that art had played an important role in the development of American culture. The large exhibition of contemporary American art invited comparisons to contemporary works from other nations. The popularity of the art exhibition was astounding. "No department of the International Exhibition attracted more general attention than that of the Fine Arts,"[2] stated John Weir, and the influential journal *Scribner's Monthly* could predict: "We look forward upon the next quarter of a century to the only general movement in art that our young country has ever known. We are ready for it, and stimulus and direction have come just when we need it."[3]

The Centennial Exposition did stimulate the general public to a new sense of the breadth and variety of art in many nations and constituted a record of the development of art. To younger artists and to critics, however, it also revealed that contemporary American art lacked variety and that American artists rarely had any professional training to speak of. To those who supported the cause of a new American art, the direction suggested by the Exposition was to establish schools for professional training, academies where the traditions of art would be taught and passed on. This idea, so totally different from earlier years, when to be self-taught was thought to be virtuous, came at a time when Europe was experiencing full-scale rebellions against academic restrictions and traditions. But many of the younger generation of American artists were returning from years of training in European academies at the time of the Centennial, and academic training had put them in touch with the traditions of art. Training was the means to overcome

1 For the use of this term see Clarence Cook, "Art in America in 1883," *The Princeton Review* 59 (May 1883), pp. 311–320.
2 John Weir, "Painting and Sculpture," in United States Centennial Commission, International Exhibition, 1876. *Reports and Awards, Group XXVII. Plastic and Graphic Arts* (Philadelphia, 1877), p. 2.
3 Richard Watson Gilder, "American Art," *Scribner's Monthly* 13 (November 1876), pp. 126–127.

FIG. 128 *Right:*
Ceres, 1882.
Augustus Saint-Gaudens (1848–1907).
Pear wood with inlaid mother-of-pearl,
Sienna marble and other marbles, and
repoussé copper;
159.4 x 64.1 cm. (62¾ x 25¼ in.).
COLLECTION: Saint-Gaudens National
Historic Site, Cornish, New Hampshire,
Gift of the Trustees of Saint-Gaudens
Memorial.

FIG. 129 *Facing page:*
Mantelpiece from the
Cornelius Vanderbilt II house.
Augustus Saint-Gaudens (1848–1907) and
John La Farge (1835–1910).
Marble and mosaic;
457.8 x 362.0 cm. (180¼ x 142½ in.).
COLLECTION: The Metropolitan Museum of
Art, New York City, Gift of Mrs. Cornelius
Vanderbilt, Sr., 1925.

FIG. 130
Amor Caritas, 1898.
Augustus Saint-Gaudens (1848–1907).
Gilt bronze relief;
260.3 x 121.9 cm. (102½ x 48 in.).
COLLECTION: The Metropolitan Museum of
Art, New York City, Rogers Fund, 1918.

extent, this interest, too, was a product of training at Parisian schools. Since the 1860s, there had been in France a renewed interest in the art of the Renaissance. The appearance of Paul Dubois's *Florentine Singer* in the Salon of 1865, and its subsequent exhibition in the Universal Exposition of 1867, caused much comment, for it suggested a new set of aesthetic principles in opposition to the lingering conventions of the Grand Style as well as to examples of chaste Christian art. In its many copies it was among the most popular works in France.[21] Too, there was a new emphasis on sensuous modeling, often thought of as "Michelangeloesque," in the work of Dalou and Chapu that paralleled the frankly sensual work of Carpeaux.[22] In painting, Paul Baudry's work exemplified a return to the richly colored Venetian painting of the Renaissance, and Puvis de Chavannes had in his mysterious way succeeded in combining what was thought to be the gravity of the antique and the delicacy of the early Renaissance.[23] These works and many others were studied by American students in Paris, especially those at the École des Beaux-Arts in the 1870s and 1880s, who often worked in the "Chapel," drawing from casts of Renaissance works.[24]

In the United States, perhaps the artist most attracted to the use of Italian Renaissance models was Augustus Saint-Gaudens, who studied at the École des Beaux-Arts with the sculptor François Jouffroy. Through his studies in Paris and during a visit to Rome, Saint-Gaudens developed a very subtle style of delicate modeling using Renaissance ornamental motifs. In cooperation with John La Farge, Saint-Gaudens produced some of the earliest work in the United States to refer to Renaissance art. The reredos of angels in the chancel of Saint Thomas Church in New York City (1877; destroyed) was based directly on Renaissance sculpture, but Saint-Gaudens was much more interested in the techniques of sculpture used by Renaissance artists, especially that of low relief, than he was in using actual Renaissance models. This was exemplified in the mantelpiece (Fig. 129) and two caryatids for the entrance hall of the Cornelius Vanderbilt II house. As Kenyon Cox noted, although the figures are in Greek costume and "serenely beautiful," one does not "feel before them as before Greek sculpture, the awe and admiration of abstract beauty, but rather a kind of tender personal feeling. . . . They are not goddesses but *women*, alike yet different, each, one feels, with her own character, her own virtues, and, perhaps, her own faults. Here then, is the note of the Renaissance, the love of individuality, and its complement in the manner of the execution is equally present. These figures are almost entirely detached, and yet in the *paleness* of the modeling and in the avoidance of deep hollows and dark shadows,—the chisel never quite going into the depths of the form, but leaving as it were, a diaphanous veil between it and our eyes and a mystery for the imagination to penetrate . . .—we find even here the principle of low relief."[25] These figures and those for the Morgan Tomb served as models for one of Saint-Gaudens's best-known works, *Amor Caritas* of 1898 (Fig. 130). The delicate quality of low relief, the suggestive play of light on surfaces, and the use of these two elements in works that have the character of individuals were thought by American artists to be characteristics that belonged particularly to the Italian Renaissance.[26]

21 New York, Sheperd Gallery Associates, Inc., *Western European Bronzes of the Nineteenth Century*, by Robert Kashey and Martin Reymert, 1973, cat. no. 50. See also Philadelphia, The Philadelphia Museum of Art, *The Second Empire, 1852–1870: Art in France under Napoleon III*, 1978, pp. 226–227.
22 William C. Brownell, "Contemporary French Sculpture: Chapu–Dubois," *The Century Magazine* 33 (December 1886), pp. 194–199.
23 See Kenyon Cox, "Puvis de Chavannes" and "Paul Baudry," in *Modern French Painters*, ed. John C. Van Dyke (New York, 1896), pp. 17–28, 61–70.
24 For this and other opportunities for study in Paris see Richard Whiting, "The American Student at the Beaux-Arts," *The Century Magazine* 23 (December 1881), pp. 258–272.
25 Kenyon Cox, "Augustus Saint-Gaudens," *The Century Magazine* 35 (November 1887), pp. 28–37.
26 Kenyon Cox, "Sculptors of the Early Italian Renaissance," *The Century Magazine* 29 (November 1884), pp. 62–66.

Although other artists favored imaginary scenes of the Renaissance (Fig. 40), Abbott Thayer was the painter who most used evocative form and Renaissance compositional elements to refer to the art of the Renaissance. In many ways Thayer's work corresponds to the sculpture of Augustus Saint-Gaudens. Thayer, who studied with Jean Leon Gérôme at the École des Beaux-Arts in Paris, returned to the United States in 1879 and began to paint portraits and landscapes. However, far from being obsessed with strict and highly studied drawing preliminary to painting, he was experimental in his approach to painting, often changing compositions many times before arriving at the final version. He purposely retained the loosely painted surface, with form left unclear and undefined. He used this suggestive technique in the late 1880s in his well-known figures that suggest the highly refined Venetian painting of the Renaissance. *Angel* (*circa* 1889; Fig. 131), with its sumptuous frame composed of Renaissance decorative elements, was followed by what is perhaps Thayer's best known work, *Caritas* of 1895

FIG. 131
Angel, circa 1889.
Abbott Thayer (1849–1921).
Oil on canvas;
92.0 x 71.5 cm. (36¼ x 28⅛ in.).
COLLECTION: National Collection of Fine Arts, Smithsonian Institution, Gift of John Gellatly.

FIG. 132 *Above:*
La Jeunesse, circa 1910.
Herbert Adams (1856–1945).
Polychrome marble and apple wood;
height: 57.1 cm. (22½ in.).
COLLECTION: The Metropolitan Museum of
Art, New York City, Rogers Fund, 1911.

FIG. 133 *Facing page:*
Love Disarmed, 1889.
Will H. Low (1853–1932).
Oil on panel; diameter: 90.2 cm. (35½ in.).
COLLECTION: The Brooklyn Museum, New
York, Gift of Dick S. Ramsay Fund.

164

FIG. 134 *Above:*
Sacred and Profane Love, 1915.
Arthur Frank Mathews (1860–1945).
Oil on canvas;
97.8 x 128.9 cm. (38½ x 50¾ in.).
COLLECTION: The Oakland Museum,
California, Gift of Concours d'Antiques,
Art Guild, and The Oakland Museum
Association.
PHOTO: Herrington Olson.

FIG. 135 *Right:*
Woman with Red Hair, 1894.
Albert Herter (1871–1950).
Oil on canvas;
81.3 x 54.6 cm. (32 x 21½ in.).
COLLECTION: National Collection of Fine
Arts, Smithsonian Institution,
Washington, D.C., Gift of Laura Dreyfus
Barney.

166

(Fig. 37),[27] which invites comparison of technique and subject with Saint-Gaudens's *Amor Caritas*. That Thayer was fascinated with Renaissance art and used such works for inspiration is supported in a letter he sent to Edwin Balshfield: "Tintoretto is bread and wine and air and life to me in four canvasses out of five—Raphael's Madonnas *all* make me tired, but the *other* Raphael, the one that did the Gobelin Cartoons and the Vatican ceilings is among my tippers. Da Vinci I don't really love though I conjure by him from habit—Botticelli's *Birth of Venus* is perhaps my dearest picture in the world and Gozzoli and Pinturicchio I *drink in* to the last drop. Michelangelo I devour hungrily as my God."[28]

The abstract qualities of paintings by artists of the American Renaissance were the products of total design. To many, this was decorative art, and, in fact, the distinctions between decorative art and the representative arts became very unclear. The distinction between artists and decorators actually ceased to exist, for each art elicited similar aesthetic responses. Artists such as Albert Herter, who produced furniture and tapestries, also painted works such as *Woman with Red Hair* of 1894 (Fig. 135) that suggest through pose and decorative devices the rarefied fifteenth century. In California, Arthur Mathews and his wife, Lucia, produced some of the most exquisite designs in furniture, paintings, and frames of the entire period. They would often use paintings as decorative elements within their furniture and painted works such as *Sacred and Profane Love* (Fig. 134), which has as its model the well-known painting by Titian.[29] A most compelling use of polychrome decoration of sculpture was in the work of Herbert Adams. In such work as his *La Jeunesse* (*circa* 1910; Fig. 132) the use of color blurs the distinction between a work of sculpture and a work of decorative art. The objects produced by many artists and architects were often highly refined decorative works with historical ornament and mythological and antique subjects blended together to form works of art that are at the same time paintings and crafted decorative objects, such as Will H. Low's *Love Disarmed* (Fig. 133) of 1889.

Critics such as Mariana Griswold Van Rensselaer, who was portrayed in 1888 by Augustus Saint-Gaudens in a fifteenth-century composition (Fig. 136), argued early for the abolishment of long-standing distinctions between a decorative and representative art. She urged artists to consult painting, sculpture, and decorative art from all historical periods, but particularly from the Italian Renaissance.[30] Russell Sturgis, a former disciple of John Ruskin, argued against his former mentor and said that fidelity to natural fact was the total negation of art; that the impulse towards abstract decoration ran through the entire history of painting and sculpture.[31] This was an entirely different way of looking at art; in fact, an entirely new definition of art. Subject was no longer the predominant concern. Instead, knowledgeable critics and artists searched for a kind of disinterested perfection of design.

The artists of the American Renaissance in no way thought of themselves as imitators of the artists of the past. They were instead establishing a whole new form of American art, one that claimed kinship with art and artists from the broad traditions of art, particularly those of the Renaissance,

FIG. 136
Mrs. Schuyler Van Rensselaer, 1888.
Augustus Saint-Gaudens (1848–1907).
Bronze relief;
51.7 x 19.7 cm. (20⅜ x 7¾ in.).
COLLECTION: The Metropolitan Museum of Art, New York City, Gift of Mrs. Schuyler Van Rensselaer, 1917.

27 On Thayer's development of his figure paintings see Thomas Brumbaugh, "A *Seated Angel* by Abbott Thayer," *Bulletin* (Wadsworth Athenaeum), 6th series, vol. VII (Spring and Fall, 1971), pp. 52–65.

28 Abbott Thayer to Edwin Blashfield, n.d., Edwin Howland Blashfield Papers, Box 3, folder T, The New-York Historical Society, New York City.

29 On the work of Arthur and Lucia Mathews see Oakland, Calif., The Oakland Museum, *Mathews: Masterpieces of the California Decorative Style*, by Harvey L. Jones, 1972.

30 Mariana Griswold Van Rensselaer, "Decorative Art and Its Dogmas," *Lippincott's Magazine* 25 (February–March 1880), pp. 213–220, 342–351.

31 Russell Sturgis, "Fine Art as Decoration," *International Monthly* 1 (May 1900), pp. 463–492. For repudiations of the call to fidelity to natural fact by former followers of John Ruskin see William James Stillman, "The Decay of Art," *New Princeton Review* 2 (July 1886), pp. 21–36; and John La Farge, "Ruskin, Art and Truth," *International Monthly* 2 (November 1900), pp. 510–535.

FIG. 137
Rome or *The Art Idea,* 1894.
Elihu Vedder (1836–1923).
Oil on canvas;
74.9 x 140.9 cm. (29½ x 55½ in.).
COLLECTION: The Brooklyn Museum, New York,
Gift of William T. Evans.

168

a period they saw as being much like their own. But they saw themselves as Renaissance artists. John La Farge said in a lecture at The Metropolitan Museum of Art in New York City: "Not only do we obtain, then, a useful material, but our minds are enlarged by having to fit into spaces larger than we knew before; and the fact that these works of men, which we study or admire, contain, in some mysterious way, the informing principle which shaped them brings us into warm and living contact with the being of their makers. We gain some of their life; we are carried forward by their desires."[32] Many artists recorded each other in commemorative works that suggested that these artists belonged both to the Renaissance of the fifteenth century

and to the new American Renaissance. Such is the portrait by Karl Bitter of Richard Morris Hunt (Fig. 141) in the manner of a fifteenth-century medal. More than any other architect, Hunt was responsible for establishing the professional architect as an arbiter of taste through knowledge of historical style. It was in Hunt's studio and office that many architects began learning the vocabulary of traditional architecture. The portrait of Augustus Saint-

FIG. 138
Augustus Saint-Gaudens, 1908.
Kenyon Cox (1856–1919).
Oil on canvas;
82.5 x 119.0 cm. (32½ x 46⅞ in.).
COLLECTION: The Metropolitan Museum of Art, New York City, Gift of Friends of the Sculptor, 1908.

32 John La Farge, *Considerations on Painting: Lectures Given in the Year 1893 at the Metropolitan Museum of Art* (New York, 1901), pp. 9–10.

Gaudens by Kenyon Cox (Fig. 138) has complex levels of meaning and references.[33] Cox was an ardent admirer of both Saint-Gaudens and William Merritt Chase and wrote articles on them and their work that were among the earliest and most astute to be published in widely circulated magazines.[34] In what is actually a double portrait, Cox portrayed Saint-Gaudens in profile, a pose that Saint-Gaudens often used for his own low-relief portraits, such as that of Chase, which Saint-Gaudens is in the act of creating. In the background is *Femme Inconnue* from the Louvre, a Renaissance sculpture much admired by Cox and Saint-Gaudens.

In the opinion of some critics, however, the American Renaissance produced an elitist art that had little or nothing to do with the history of the United States or the actual life of the majority of citizens of the nation.[35] To be sure, sculpture such as Bessie Potter Vonnoh's *Daydreams* of 1903 (Fig. 139) or paintings such as Willard Metcalf's *May Night* (Fig. 140) portrayed a cultured

FIG. 139
Daydreams, 1903.
Bessie Potter Vonnoh (1872–1955).
Bronze;
26.0 x 54.0 x 27.0 cm. (10½ x 21¼ x 11 in.).
COLLECTION: Corcoran Gallery of Art,
Washington, D.C.

FIG. 140 *Left:*
May Night, 1906.
Willard Metcalf (1858–1925).
Oil on canvas;
100.3 x 92.5 cm. (39½ x 36⅜ in.).
COLLECTION: Corcoran Gallery of Art,
Washington, D.C.

FIG. 141 *Above:*
Portrait Relief of Richard Morris Hunt, circa
1895.
Karl T. Bitter (1867–1915).
Bronze; diameter: 76.2 cm. (30 in.).
COLLECTION: American Institute of
Architects, Washington, D.C., Gift of
Mrs. R. Sharp Smith.

leisure class that lived easily with old and elegant objects not readily available to most people; the Empire sofa and the eighteenth-century Greek Revival house were hardly common objects.

The artists who were returning to the Renaissance and its antecedents were, however, equally interested in investigating and recovering the American Colonial past, in redefining American art in its own terms. This movement, too, was a reference to the Renaissance, for the discovery and settlement of the Americas was, after all, a phenomenon of Renaissance inquisitiveness. American history was tied directly to that of the European Renaissance. Francis Millet painted subjects from the antique and the English as well as the American Colonial period with equal care and attention to costume detail. His studio in East Bridgewater, Connecticut, contained many American Colonial objects and even a Colonial kitchen reconstructed

33 For an excellent analysis of this portrait see the entry for it by Doreen Bolger Burke in the forthcoming catalogue of American paintings at The Metropolitan Museum of Art, New York City.
34 Kenyon Cox, "William Merritt Chase, Painter." *Harper's New Monthly Magazine* 78 (March 1889), pp. 549–557; and "Augustus Saint-Gaudens," *The Century Magazine* 35, n.s. 13 (November 1887), pp. 28–37.

35 An early example of criticism of the movement is that of Francis Marion Crawford, "False Taste in Art," *North American Review* 135 (July 1882), 89–98. See also Aline Gorren, "American Society and the Artist," *Scribner's Magazine* 26 (November 1899), pp. 628–633. For architecture and the decorative arts see W.G. Purcell and G.G. Elmsie, "American Renaissance?" *The Craftsman* 21 (January 1912), pp. 420–435.

FIG. 142
At the Inn, 1886.
Francis Davis Millet (1846–1912).
Oil on canvas; 38.1 x 76.2 cm. (15 x 30 in.).
COLLECTION: Union League Club, New
York City.

with great accuracy. His *At the Inn* (Fig. 142), exhibited in 1886, was intended to evoke a mellow and homey past through its carefully contrived setting. Whether the painting is English or American in subject is ambiguous, for Millet had since 1884 spent much time in the English village of Broadway, a picturesque locale seemingly unaffected by time.[36] Edwin Abbey also lived and worked at Broadway and was also fascinated with recapturing the Renaissance in England and its American colonies. Through his famous illustrations for Shakespeare and Herrick, the past seemed to be dramatically enlivened. Abbey painted many works with themes similar to those of his extraordinary pen drawings. *An Old Song* (Fig. 143) has the same attention to detail of costume and furnishings.[37]

Illustrated articles on American history began to crowd prestigious journals such as *The Century, Harper's Monthly,* and *Atlantic Monthly.* Through these channels, interest in the American past was nurtured by artists highly skilled at catering to the new antiquarian interests of the people. Other, public works of art also recalled the American Colonial past. Two sculptures have nearly attained the status of icons of American Colonial history—Daniel Chester French's *Minute Man* of 1871–1875 (Fig. 25) and Augustus Saint-Gaudens's *The Puritan* (Deacon Samuel Chapin) of 1887 (Fig. 144).

36 Weinberg, "The Career of Francis Davis Millet," p. 8.
37 For Abbey's illustrations and paintings see New Haven, Conn., Yale University Art Gallery, *Edwin Austin Abbey 1852–1911,* by Kathleen Foster and Michael Quick, 1973.

FIG. 143 *Above:*
An Old Song, 1885.
Edwin Austin Abbey (1852–1911).
Watercolor and pencil;
64.8 x 120.7 cm. (25½ x 47½ in.).
COLLECTION: Yale University Art Gallery,
New Haven, Connecticut, Edwin Austin
Abbey Memorial Collection.
PHOTO: Joseph Szaszfai.

FIG. 144 *Left:*
The Puritan, circa 1898, from original of
1887.
Augustus Saint-Gaudens (1848–1907).
Bronze cast; height: 78.7 cm. (31 in.).
COLLECTION: The Metropolitan Museum of
Art, New York City, Bequest of Jacob
Ruppert, 1959.

173

FIG. 145
Robert Gould Shaw Memorial, 1884–1897.
Augustus Saint-Gaudens (1848–1907).
Bronze; 335.3 x 426.7 cm. (132 x 168 in.).
PHOTO: Richard Benson.

174

French's *Minute Man* was among the first works by an American artist to blend the traditions of classical art with the newfound interest in American Colonial history. In preparation for the Centennial Exposition, the sculpture was commissioned by the City of Concord, Massachusetts, as an appropriate symbol of its past. French worked through a first, rather awkward design before settling on the now familiar image of the minute man in an alert yet graceful pose that was based on *Apollo Belvedere*.[38] Saint-Gaudens's *Puritan*, erected in 1881 in Springfield, Massachusetts, does not immediately recall a classical or Renaissance model. As in his other works, it was Saint-Gaudens's technique of modeling and the emphasis on the subject's individuality that gave it the character of a work of the Renaissance. The sculpture had "no conventionalism, neither any romanticism or melodrama," noted Kenyon Cox. "He is not merely a Puritan of the Puritans, he is a man also, a rough-hewn piece of humanity enough, with plenty of an old Adam about him; and one feels that thus and not otherwise must some veritable old Puritan deacon have looked."[39] To Cox, this was a new definition of "ideal portraiture." Rather than conventionalizing the features, Saint-Gaudens had imagined a characteristic Puritan deacon and individualized the features and costume.

A look through the popular magazines also reveals a deep interest in the details and firsthand records of the most stunning historical event in recent American history—the Civil War. Memoirs of the war and detailed maps of campaigns were avidly read by thousands of people for whom the war was a deeply etched memory.

Artists, especially sculptors, responded to interest in this most immediate aspect of American history by creating for the public an instant aura of tradition for the heroes of the war. Such is the monument by Augustus Saint-Gaudens for Colonel Robert Shaw (Fig. 145) and his regiment of black soldiers from Massachusetts. Commissioned in 1884 by the State of Massachusetts, the work was not completed until fourteen years later. It was perhaps Saint-Gaudens's most difficult work, undergoing almost constant change. Ultimately it proved to be the artist's most successful embodiment of the hero in a rarified realm of history. Framed by simple and dignified classical motifs designed by the architect Charles McKim, Saint-Gaudens's work is both an equestrian monument and a relief and recalls both aspects of Renaissance sculpture. The addition of the figure of Victory with the laurel wreath and the poppy of sleep intensifies the sense that these men, portrayed in carefully modeled and highly individualistic portraits, belong not to this world but to that of historical heroes. Saint-Gaudens's other masterfully conceived monument to a Civil War hero, that of General William Tecumseh Sherman in New York City, carried the concept of the hero still further. It sits on a simple yet monumental base designed by Charles F. McKim in a setting by Frederick Law Olmsted, Jr. It is an equestrian monument that in its sense of power, authority, and vitality was praised as the successor of Verrocchio's *Colleoni* and Donatello's *Gattamelata*.[40] Saint-Gaudens again expanded the historical support for the heroic figure by adding the figure of Victory (Fig. 146).[41] This is no adoring allegorical figure, but one that suggests that Sherman is riding into an exalted realm. One

38   New York, The Metropolitan Museum of Art, *Daniel Chester French: An American Sculptor*, by Michael Richman, 1976, pp. 39–47.
39   Cox, "Augustus Saint-Gaudens," p. 30.
40   Royal Cortissoz, *Augustus Saint-Gaudens* (Boston and New York, 1907), p. 63.
41   For the history of this work see Kenyon Cox, "The Sherman Statue," *The Nation* 76 (June 18, 1903), pp. 491–493.

FIG. 146
Victory, for General Sherman Memorial,
New York City, 1912.
Augustus Saint-Gaudens (1848–1907).
Gilded bronze; height: 106.0 cm. (41¾ in.).
COLLECTION: The Metropolitan Museum of
Art, New York City, 1917.

might easily say that the Shaw and Sherman monuments do not simply
memorialize men and events of the past. They propose that the men portrayed were destined for historical greatness even before they performed
their celebrated deeds.

Abraham Lincoln, the greatest hero of the Civil War, was the subject of
many works, both mundane and heroic, and was portrayed in numerous
ways, from the pensive works by Daniel Chester French in Lincoln, Neb-
raska (1909–1912), and Augustus Saint-Gaudens's in Chicago (standing version, 1887; seated version, 1897–1905), to the strange, colossal, and visionary
works by George Gray Barnard. But never was Lincoln represented so

42 For the iconography of the Lincoln Memorial see the articles by Charles Moore, Henry
Bacon, Jules Guerin, and Frank Owen Payne in
Art and Archeology 13 (June 1922), pp. 247–268.
43 Jules Guerin, ''The Mural Decorations in
the Lincoln Memorial,'' *Art and Archeology* 13
(June 1922), p. 259.
44 French's statue of Lincoln is discussed in
Richman, *Daniel Chester French,* pp. 171–186.
45 Quoted in Wayne Craven, *Sculpture in
America* (New York, 1964), p. 429.

totally immersed in symbolism, allegory, and tradition as in the Lincoln Memorial in Washington, D.C. (1911–1922).[42] The Lincoln Memorial (Fig. 50) was created by the combined talents of the architect Henry Bacon, the sculptor Daniel Chester French, and the mural painter Jules Guerin. The building was planned as a classical temple with thirty-six columns symbolizing states of the Union when Lincoln was President and forty-eight festoons symbolizing the states of the Union when the memorial was completed. The murals by Jules Guerin, painted between 1912 and 1919, flank either side of the statue of Lincoln and were to "typify in allegory the principles evident in the life of Lincoln."[43] With forty-eight figures corresponding to the number of states in the Union, the murals represent in allegory Emancipation (over the incised Gettysburg Address) and Reunion (over the incised Second Inaugural Address). The Lincoln by Daniel Chester French is no longer a meditative man, but a hero seated upon a Roman chair with two sets of fasces.[44]

Another American sculptor who specialized in public sculpture of heroes of American history was Paul Wayland Bartlett. Although he lived in France most of his life, he was certainly much aware of the rush to create a tradition of American heroes for the public. He was also aware of how much of this public sculpture memorializing the Civil War was poorly executed or uninspiring: "Every city, every village wished to have its monument to the heroes to the war. . . . thus our country is encumbered more and more with indifferent sculptures and grotesque figures of no artistic value whatever."[45] Bartlett's own work was centered more on heroes that preceded the Civil War, such as *Washington at Valley Forge* (n.d.; cast 1927). His powerful equestrian monument *Lafayette* (1899–1908), which calls to mind Renaissance precedents by Verrocchio and Donatello, was actually never seen in the United States except in its several reduced versions (Fig. 147). It was set up in the Louvre in 1908 as a gift of the American people to the French people in the reciprocation for Bartholdi's *Liberty Enlightening the World.*

FIG. 147
Lafayette on Horseback.
Paul Wayland Bartlett (1865–1925).
Bronze;
41.3 x 39.4 x 24.1 cm. (16¼ x 15½ x 9½).
COLLECTION: Corcoran Gallery of Art, Washington, D.C., Gift of Mrs. Armistead Peter III.

The need to create a heroic past for Americans included not only the past of the Anglo culture. Sculptors were prompted to look anew at the American Indian. Alongside the rough and ready cowboys painted by Charles Russell and Frederic Remington, who were most responsible for mythologizing the West, were the extraordinarily refined portrayals of American Indians by A. Phimister Proctor. His *Indian Warrior* (Fig. 148), presents the Indian in quite a different way than narrative sculpture by others. There is a sense of heroic dignity that, in its way, equals that of heroes of the Revolutionary and Civil wars.

The public monument that extolled American history and culture, often phrased in terms of models from the Renaissance, was an effective way of creating a sense of tradition. The imprinting of allegory and symbol on things constantly used was another way to accomplish the same purpose.

FIG. 148 *Above:*
Indian Warrior, 1898.
Alexander Phimister Proctor (1862–1950).
Bronze; 101.6 x 76.8 x 40.6 cm.
(40 x 30¼ x 16 in.).
COLLECTION: Corcoran Gallery of Art,
Washington, D.C.

FIG. 149 *Above, right:*
One-dollar note, educational bill,
designed by Will H. Low (1853–1932) and
engraved by Charles Schlecht (1843–1932).
Bank note; 8.6 x 19.1 cm. (3⅜ x 7½ in.).
COLLECTION: Division of Numismatics,
National Museum of History and
Technology, Smithsonian Institution,
Washington, D.C.

The well-known series of paper currency designed by Will Low (Fig. 149), Edwin Blashfield, and Walter Shirlaw replaced older, stilted, and often disorganized designs with unified allegorical images of subtle decorative quality. Kenyon Cox's design for the one-hundred–dollar bill of 1912 (Fig. 13) represented Commerce in a highly symbolic composition that is closely related to his mural paintings (such as *The Arts* in The Library of Congress [Fig. 11]). Augustus Saint-Gaudens, Hermon McNeil, and Bela Pratt also designed coinage with new symbolic images to replace the rather worn image of Liberty in her Phrygian cap. Much of this new coinage was an outgrowth of a new interest in medallic art prompted by examples designed for the World's Columbian Exposition. President Theodore Roosevelt took a keen interest in new coinage and currency, for the images suggested a new, powerful, and dignified republic.[46] Magazine covers often carried poetic images that recalled the Renaissance (Fig. 150), and book illustrations such as those by Maxfield Parrish for Edith Wharton's *Italian Villas* (Fig. 151) presented the past in terms of a gratifying dream.

Mural Painting and the Civic Image

By far the most public form of the new art based on the past was architecture, but as one supportive artist and critic noted: "Architecture, supreme as it is

46 The new coinage and medals are discussed in Cornelius Vermeule, *Numismatic Art in America* (Cambridge, Mass., 1971), pp. 86 ff.

178

FIG. 150
Illustration for the cover of *Harper's Magazine,* October 1903.
William C. Rice (1875–1928).
Oil on canvas;
53.5 x 48.5 cm. (21 x 19⅛ in.).
COLLECTION: National Collection of Fine Arts, Washington, D.C., Gift of Mrs. Melvin S. Brotman.

FIG. 151
The Theatre at Villa Gori, illustration for *Italian Villas and Their Gardens,* 1903.
Maxfield Parrish (1870–1966).
Oil on canvas; 45.7 x 30.5 cm. (18 x 12 in.).
COLLECTION: Graham Williford, New York City.

FIG. 152
The Arts of Peace, circa 1892.
Gari Melchers (1860–1932).
Oil on canvas;
135.9 x 265.4 cm. (53½ x 104½ in.).
COLLECTION: Belmont, The Gari Melchers
Memorial Gallery, Falmouth, Virginia.
PHOTO: Barry Fitzgerald.

among the arts, can never reach its highest perfection except in conjunction with its sister arts."[47] For the artists and architects trained at European centers, particularly the École des Beaux-Arts, this seemed quite literally true. Architecture called for murals and sculpture to complete its design; in fact, unity of the arts was necessary to the architectural plan from its outset. Mural paintings in particular again became a major form of art during the years of the American Renaissance, and they were painted in well over four hundred buildings throughout the nation.

Since the beginning of the "new movement" in American art in the late 1870s, mural painting and architectural decoration had been in the forefront of change. As new buildings appeared and announced the "intelligent eclecticism" of professionally trained architects,[48] so did mural paintings as decorative adjuncts. Murals by John La Farge and others at Trinity Church in Boston (1876–1878) and the murals by William Morris Hunt at the New York State Capitol at Albany (1879) were likened to the new easel paintings and sculpture being produced by younger artists in major art centers throughout the nation. These murals were so startlingly new in the use of historic style and meditative allegory that they constituted, said Henry Van Brunt, "a new dispensation for monumental art in the United States."[49] Although murals were often painted during the 1880s, most were for churches, such as *The Ascension* by John La Farge (Fig. 38), or were for private homes and were painted by very few artists.[50] The "new dispensation" was not fulfilled until some twenty years later.

The consolidation of effort by architects, painters, and sculptors that was necessary for the large-scale murals and accompanying architectural sculpture was made possible by the vast coordinated building and decorative program worked out for the World's Columbian Exposition in Chicago, the first American exposition wholly planned by artists and architects of the American Renaissance. Although mural paintings were much less in evidence than is usually supposed—most were placed quite high in cupolas and ceilings—in the artists' and architects' minds, and in that of the public through journal articles, murals became a necessary ingredient for decorative schemes in large and small buildings alike. From the exposition, too, arose a new civic image, a need to allegorize or place in a historical context modern events, technology, and ideas. This was nowhere more evident than at the Columbian Exposition. There in the Manufactures and Liberal Arts Building, Gari Melchers's murals *The Arts of War* and *The Arts of Peace* (Fig. 152) presented the two uses of technology and science in the guise of the antique.[51]

The Exposition also provided the opportunity for numerous artists to paint their first murals, and from this experience there was formed a well-defined group specializing in murals for hundreds of private, civic, state, and federal buildings. In 1895 the National Society of Mural Painters was incorporated and served as an association to establish and regulate the new profession (for mural painters dealt with contracts, fees, and other business matters much as did architects) and to educate the public about murals and civic art, another new movement that followed the planning of the Exposition.

47 Candace Wheeler, "Decorative Art," *Architectural Record* 4 (1895), pp. 409–413.
48 Mariana Griswold Van Rensselaer, "Recent Architecture in America, VII," *The Century Magazine* 32, n.s. 10 (May 1886), pp. 13–20.
49 Henry Van Brunt, "The New Dispensation of Monumental Art," *Atlantic Monthly* XLIII (May 1879), pp. 633–641.
50 A general but incomplete survey of mural painting before the Columbian Exposition is by Pauline King, *American Mural Painting* (Boston,

1902). For La Farge's work in private homes and churches in the 1870s and 1880s see Helene Barbara Weinberg, *The Decorative Work of John La Farge* (New York, 1977).
51 The most recent study of the Columbian Exposition and the role of mural paintings is David Burg, *Chicago's White City of 1893* (Lexington, 1976). See also Will H. Low et al., *Some Artists at the Fair* (New York, 1893).

FIG. 153
Study for ceiling of the Gunn Memorial
Library, Washington, Connecticut, *circa*
1914.
H. Siddons Mowbray (1850–1928).
Oil on canvas;
121.9 x 63.5 cm. (48 x 25 in.).
COLLECTION: Henry D. Ostberg, New York
City.

182

Murals were often worked out in programs that referred to local history or to abstract principles of law or government that had meaning in terms of a broad tradition in history. Libraries, repositories for the essentially bookish concept of Culture proposed by Matthew Arnold, which was a basic tenet of the American Renaissance, were sites for major mural projects (Fig. 153). The two mural programs that had the greatest impact on the public in the years immediately following the Exposition were in libraries. Although commissioned before the Columbian Exposition, the mural paintings for The Boston Public Library by John Singer Sargent (Fig. 154), Edwin Abbey, and Puvis de Chavannes were not set in place until 1895, two years after the Exposition

FIG. 154
Frieze of the Prophets, sketch for a mural in The Boston Public Library.
John Singer Sargent (1856–1925).
Oil on canvas; 55.9 x 71.1 cm. (22 x 28 in.).
COLLECTION: Museum of Fine Arts, Boston, Gift of Mrs. Francis Ormond.

FIG. 155
Great Hall of The Library of Congress,
Washington, D.C.
PHOTO: The Library of Congress.

184

closed. Although they added in great measure to the increasing public interest in murals, these works rarely provided an example that other artists could follow. Abbey's *The Quest of the Holy Grail* (Fig. 17) was essentially a religious and literary work of his own design,[52] and its richness of color and detail and complexity of narrative were not attempted by other artists.[53] Sargent's *History of Religion* was on such a massive scale and so overwhelming in allusions to the historical styles of religious belief, such as the archaic, Byzantine, and Renaissance, that no other artist attempted to examine the same subject.[54] The work of the French muralist Puvis de Chavannes was much admired by many Americans, both for the use of symbols and for the pallid early Renaissance color schemes in his murals on science and philosophy, *The Muses of Inspiration Hail the Spirit, the Harbinger of Light.* The murals, sculpture, lushly decorated mosaic halls, and the Renaissance-inspired architecture of The Boston Public Library prompted one as astute at scholarship and criticism as Ernest Fenollosa to declare that it made Boston the "Assisi of American art."[55]

The second important mural project immediately after the Exposition was that in The Library of Congress in Washington, D.C. The architects General Thomas L. Casey, his son Edward P. Casey, and Bernard Green had been so efficient in their financial expenditure that a fund was set aside in 1895 for the decoration of the building with murals and sculpture. The architects were able to commission some nineteen artists to paint one hundred twelve murals and have this work completed in only two years. During this time, twenty-two sculptors were working on their commissions and seven artists were employed at ornamental painting. This, it seemed, was the spirit of the unity of the arts, of the American Renaissance. One critic was moved to note that "the artists like the workmen, were in overalls, and the atmosphere of the place impregnated with the spirit of art and labor. It was something as it must have been in Florence or Venice in the Renaissance."[56]

When completed, The Library of Congress was the most astounding work of decoration in the nation, overwhelming other buildings by sheer size and density of decoration. There were murals symbolizing the arts, the sciences, themes from Homer, from modern poetry, and on the morality of government, on the history of painting, and even on the family. The vast space of the double-storied Great Hall (Fig. 155) was meant only as a display space, and this in a building designed to be as efficient as modern design could make it.[57] One writer, in fact, called the library "our national monument of art."[58] Among the many murals in the building, that by Edwin Blashfield around the collar of the dome in the main reading room (cover) is the most instructive example of the way Americans were thinking about their role as inheritors of the past. *Evolution of Civilization* begins with Egypt and its contribution of writing, and the series progresses through figures representing each nation's contribution to Western civilization. The last figure, representing the United States, is the inheritor of the entire body of learning and art of the West.[59]

Far more than The Boston Public Library, The Library of Congress was used as a model for later mural projects, although none of them equalled it in

52   For Abbey's literary and artistic sources for his mural cycle see E.H. Spielman, "Edwin Austin Abbey, R.A.," *The Magazine of Art* 23 (1896), pp. 145–150, 193–198, 247–253.
53   An exception was the much less impressive mural on this theme painted by William Andrew McKay for a private residence in Greenwich, Connecticut.
54   For the background and iconography of Sargent's mural see Martha Kingsbury, "Sargent's Murals in the Boston Public Library," *Winterthur Portfolio* 11 (1976), pp. 153–172.

55   Ernest Fenollosa, *Mural Painting in the Boston Public Library* (Boston, 1896), p. 9.
56   William A. Coffin, "Decorations in the New Congressional Library," *The Century Magazine* 53 (March 1897), pp. 694–711.
57   There was lively controversy over the library as a functional and efficient storage and delivery system and the incorporation of nonfunctional works of art. See John Y. Cole, "Smithmeyer and Pelz, Embattled Architects of the Library of Congress," *The Quarterly Journal of the Library of Congress* 29 (October 1972), pp. 282–307.

58   Royal Cortissoz, "Our National Monument of Art: The Congressional Library at Washington," *Harper's Weekly* 39 (December 28, 1895), pp. 1240–1241.
59   For further study of this idea see Lois M. Fink, "Evolutionary Theory and Nineteenth Century American Art," *American Art Review* (January 1978), pp. 75–109.

size and complexity. State capitol buildings, in particular, were often given rich mural decorations, and the subjects of the murals are indicative of artists' and architects' attempts to place local history into a larger, more general history. For his murals at the Iowa Statehouse, Kenyon Cox first thought of depicting the "Resources of the State of Iowa," yet his final work was a series of allegorical panels on the Progress of Civilization, "the subject being universal in its application."[60] For the Minnesota State Capitol, the Board of Commissioners instructed that the subjects of the murals be related directly to the history of their state or to the settlement of the Northwest.[61] Despite this injunction, for his murals in the Supreme Court room of the capitol, John La Farge painted four panels that refer to the broad traditions and history of law: Confucius and the "Recording of Precedents," Moses receiving the "Moral and Divine Law," Socrates discussing "The Relation of the Individual to the State," and Count Raymond of Toulouse and the "Adjustment of Conflicting Interests." Enthusiastically, one commentator noted that the images were "drawn from the universal history of mankind rather than any event or legend of special significance in local or national history."[62]

As murals were commissioned more often, a conflict developed between those artists and critics who called for subjects that related to the history of the site (but not the daily life of the people) and those who saw local history as important only as it related to larger cultural history. Charles M. Shean, President of the National Society of Mural Painters, predicted that "the future great art of this Republic, so far as it is expressed in painting, will find its complete and full development on the walls of our public buildings . . . and it will be primarily a recording art," but added that the subjects should commemorate "the growth of the state from the scattered and struggling colonies of the Atlantic seaboard to the Imperial Republic stretching from ocean to ocean."[63] Some artists, such as Edwin Blashfield, arrived at a formula that would depict local history but place it in the realm of allegory. His *Washington Laying Down His Command at the Feet of Columbia* (Fig. 29), painted for the Baltimore Courthouse in 1902, commemorates an event important in the history of Maryland. Through a mixture of portraits of historical personages and people who were actually present at the ceremony—officers and troops of the Continental Army and allied French forces—with allegorical figures representing, among others, Maryland, History, and War, Blashfield suggested a kind of sanctity for the event. The mural recalls through its composition the many "sacred conversation" paintings of the Italian Renaissance.[64]

Rarely did a mural painter work in the style of a particular Renaissance artist. Compositions and decorative elements were usually sufficient to recall in a general way works of the period. H. Siddons Mowbray, however, was so enthralled by the murals and decorative designs of Pinturicchio that he came rather close to direct imitation. In 1902, at the request of Charles McKim, Mowbray studied the murals by Pinturicchio in the newly reopened Borgia Apartments in the Vatican.[65] He then returned to New York and on commission from McKim painted "Pinturicchioesque" murals in the two buildings by McKim, Mead and White that recall most directly Italian

60 Statement by Kenyon Cox in State of Iowa, *The Capitol of Iowa* (Des Moines, 1954), p. 18.
61 Neil B. Thompson, *Minnesota's State Capitol: The Art and Politics of a Public Building* (Saint Paul, 1974), p. 65.
62 "Mural Painting—An Art for the People and a Record of the Nation's Development," *The Craftsman* 10 (April 1906), pp. 54–56.
63 Charles M. Shean, "Mural Painting from the American Point of View," *The Craftsman* 7 (October 1904), pp. 18–27.

64 For the entire mural program in this building see *Murals in the Baltimore Court House* (Baltimore, 1912).
65 Herbert F. Sherwood, ed., *H. Siddons Mowbray, Mural Painter* (privately printed by Florence Millard Mowbray, 1928), pp. 66–68, 75.

models—the University Club (1904) and the J.P. Morgan Library in New York City (1905–1907). Mowbray succeeded in making the style of Pinturicchio his own and continued to paint in this mode. He painted the ceiling mural in the Gunn Memorial Library in Washington, Connecticut (Fig. 153), in 1914, and for Saint John's Church in that village he painted a series of the stations of the cross with similar stylistic references.

In many different ways, mural painters recalled the Renaissance in their work. References to the Renaissance not only lent the substance of history to the work, but helped blend the mural with its surrounding, generally referential architecture. Of the hundreds of murals in public and private buildings, only one states the philosophical premise of the entire American Renaissance: Elihu Vedder's *Rome*, or *The Art Idea* (Fig. 137), which he painted in 1894 for the Walker Art Building at Bowdoin College in Brunswick, Maine.[66] On the left Vedder painted a group of figures representing the art of Michelangelo and on the right another group representing the art of Raphael. In the center stands the figure of Nature. Vedder said: "Her right hand rests on the trunk and roots of the Tree of Life; her left holds a detached branch with its fruit—an art having reached its culmination never lives again; its fruit, however, contains the seeds of another development."[67] For Vedder and his many colleagues, that development was the American Renaissance.

Through the use of traditional subjects and stylistic references to the art of the antique and the Italian Renaissance, American artists gave substance to their own contemporary art and set their history into that of the entire range of Western civilization. They remained Americans, yet they were part of the broad flow of art, history, and culture. The establishment of the American Academy in Rome in 1894 provided the means to train a second generation of mural painters, sculptors, and architects in the principles of the coordination of the arts and in the use of ancient and Renaissance sources. This generation of artists, which included Allyn Cox, Barry Falkner, and Dean Cornwell, continued to paint easel paintings and to provide murals for private and public buildings. Although somewhat less adamantly "classic" in composition and subject, they carried on the well-established ideas of the American Renaissance.

Until well into this century, the institutions formed in the late nineteenth century to articulate the principles of the American Renaissance continued to be strong and vital, although they are now often seen by historians as the reactionary defenders of a bygone era. In 1906, the National Academy of Design merged with the Society of American Artists and gained new strength, and the National Society of Mural Painters and the National Sculpture Society remained potent forces in American art. However, by the 1920s, these institutions no longer dominated the art world, which had, by the second decade of the twentieth century, begun to form itself into distinct and often antagonistic groups.

Painters and sculptors who produced smaller, less public works continued to find their work much appreciated by the general public as well as

66 The entire mural program for this building, including murals by John La Farge, Kenyon Cox, and Abbott Thayer, is discussed in Richard V. West, *The Walker Art Building Murals*, Occasional Papers I (Brunswick, Me., 1972).
67 Statement by Elihu Vedder, *Catalog of the Tenth Annual Exhibition of the Architectural League of New York* (New York, 1895), pp. 49, no. 75.

FIG. 156
Tradition, 1916.
Kenyon Cox (1856–1919).
Oil on canvas;
106.0 x 165.7 cm. (41¾ x 65¼ in.).
COLLECTION: Cleveland Museum of Art,
Ohio, Gift of J.D. Cox.

by major collectors such as John Gellatly, who in 1929 gave his large collection of paintings and sculpture to the National Gallery of Art (now the National Collection of Fine Arts, Smithsonian Institution) with the intention that it represent the achievements of the American Renaissance. Charles Lang Freer initially collected American art by the artists of the American Renaissance and continued to collect such works even while building his collection of Asian art.

Quite early in the century, however, the principles of the American Renaissance had to be defended against critics and artists who were developing their own ideas of what constituted both modern art and an art that more nearly represented contemporary life in the United States. By 1911, two years before the Armory Show, Kenyon Cox had to state clearly the aims of his generation and to vocally defend them against what he saw as "irrational" ideas of modernism:

> The Classic Spirit is the disinterested search for perfection; it is the love
> of clearness and reasonableness and self-control; it is, above all, the love

of permanence and of continuity. It asks of a work of art, not that it shall be novel or effective, but that it shall be fine and noble. It seeks not merely to express individuality or emotion but to express disciplined emotion and individuality restrained by law. It strives for the essential rather than the accidental, the eternal rather than the momentary. And it loves to steep itself in tradition. It would have each new work connect itself in the mind of him who sees it with all the noble and lovely works of the past, bringing them to his memory and making their beauty and charm part of the beauty and charm of the work before him. It does not deny originality and individuality—they are as welcome as inevitable. It does not consider tradition as immutable or set rigid bounds to invention. But it desires that each new presentation of truth and beauty shall show us the old truth and the old beauty, seen only from a different angle and colored by a different medium. It wishes to add link by link to the chain of tradition, but it does not wish to break the chain.[68]

Cox expressed these ideas visually in his painting of 1916, *Tradition* (Fig. 156). The seated figure at the left represents the art of the past, who has given the light from her torch to the lamp of knowledge in the hand of the figure of Tradition, who will pass it on to the art of the future, represented by two figures in Renaissance costume, one in a vaguely Titianesque costume and pose and the other—Literature—crowned with laurel.

Although the ideas of the American Renaissance were strongly defended by many artists and critics, it was clear to many of them that by the First World War their ideas were becoming less and less respected by a new generation of artists and critics. Many of the younger artists of the early twentieth century were trained in precisely the same European centers as those who had established the American Renaissance, who now found themselves the older generation. A conflict between these two groups developed that resembled in many ways that of the late 1870s. This situation was only too painfully clear to Will H. Low, who, while working on his mural project at the State Education Building in Albany, New York, wrote to his friend Kenyon Cox that Low was at work upon a mural "hopelessly out of touch with art as she is spoke at the present time. . . . we, with one or two others, constitute the *vielle garde*, we who yesterday were the insurgents!"[69]

68   Kenyon Cox, *The Classic Point of View* (New York, 1911), pp. 3–5.
69   Will H. Low to Kenyon Cox, October 8, 1917, Kenyon Cox Papers, Avery Library, Columbia University, New York City.

Index

Collections Represented in the Figures

Figure numbers in bold indicate color illustrations.

Selected Further Reading

The following is a basic beginning reading list. For material on specific topics, consult the individual essays.

Contemporary

Blashfield, Edwin H. *Mural Painting in America*. New York: Charles Scribner's Sons, 1913.

Caffin, Charles H. *The Story of American Painting*. New York: Frederick A. Stokes Co., 1907.

Cook, Clarence C. *The House Beautiful*. New York: Scribner, Armstrong & Co., 1878.

Cox, Kenyon. *The Classic Point of View*. New York: Charles Scribner's Sons, 1911.

Desmond, Harry W., and Croly, Herbert. *Stately Homes in America: From Colonial Times to the Present Day*. New York: D. Appleton & Co., 1903

DeWolfe, Elsie. *The House in Good Taste*. New York: Century Co., 1913.

Hamlin, Talbot F. *The American Spirit in Architecture*. The Pageant of America, edited by Ralph Henry Gabriel, vol. 13. New Haven: Yale University Press, 1926.

Hegemann, Werner, and Peets, Elbert. *The American Vitruvius: An Architect's Handbook of Civic Art*. New York: Architectural Book Publishing Co., 1922.

King, Pauline. *American Mural Painting*. Boston: Noyes, Platt & Co., 1902.

Koehler, Sylvester R. *American Art*. New York: Cassell, 1886.

La Farge, John. *Considerations of Painting*. New York: Macmillan and Co., 1895.

Low, Will H. *A Chronicle of Friendships, 1873–1900*. New York: Charles Scribner's Sons, 1908.

Taft, Lorado. *The History of American Sculpture*. New York: Macmillan Co., 1903.

Wharton, Edith, and Codman, Ogden, Jr. *The Decoration of Houses*. 1897. Reprint. New York: W.W. Norton, 1978.

Retrospective

Burg, David F. *Chicago's White City of 1893*. Lexington: University of Kentucky Press, 1976.

Davidson, Marshall B., ed. *The American Heritage History of Antiques from the Civil War to World War I*. New York: American Heritage Publishing Co., 1969.

Horowitz, Helen Lefkowitz. *Culture and the City: Cultural Philanthropy in Chicago from the 1880s to 1917*. Lexington: University of Kentucky Press, 1976.

Jones, Howard Mumford. *The Age of Energy: Varieties of American Experience, 1865–1915*. New York: Viking Press, 1971.

Maher, James T., *The Twilight of Splendor: Chronicles of the Age of American Palaces*. Boston: Little, Brown & Co., 1975.

Morgan, H. Wayne. *New Muses: Art in American Culture, 1865–1920*. Norman: University of Oklahoma Press, 1978.

Morgan, H. Wayne. *Unity and Culture: The United States, 1877–1900*. Baltimore: Penguin, 1971.

Raleigh, John Henry. *Matthew Arnold and American Culture*. Berkeley and Los Angeles: University of California Press, 1961.

Tomsich, John. *A Genteel Endeavor*. Stanford: Stanford University Press, 1971.

Valentine, Lucia, and Valentine, Alan. *The American Academy in Rome, 1894–1969*. Charlottesville: University Press of Virginia, 1973.

Wiebe, Robert H. *The Search for Order: 1877–1920*. New York: Hill and Wang, 1967.

CATALOGUE
OF THE
EXHIBITION

Note Dimensions (sight throughout) are in centimeters (inches in parentheses); height precedes width, and where applicable, a third figure indicates depth. The collection is given in italics.

Not all works in the exhibition are included in the entire tour.

* indicates works shown at The Brooklyn Museum only.

† indicates works shown at The Brooklyn Museum and the National Collection of Fine Arts only.

‡ indicates works shown at the National Collection of Fine Arts, the M.H. de Young Memorial Museum, and The Denver Art Museum only.

§ indicates works shown at the M.H. de Young Memorial Museum and The Denver Art Museum only.

Architecture, Landscape, and City Planning

1
East Elevation, San Francisco City Hall Competition 1912

Designed by Arthur Brown, Jr. Bakewell and Brown, architects. Ink and wash on paper; 58.0 x 99.0 (22 13/16 x 38 15/16) *Sylvia Brown Jensen, California.*

2
Ground Floor Plan, San Francisco City Hall Competition 1912

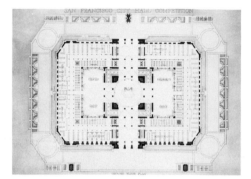

Designed by Arthur Brown, Jr. Bakewell and Brown, architects. Ink and wash on paper; 70.0 x 110.0 (27 9/16 x 43 5/16) *Sylvia Brown Jensen, California.*

3
Third Floor Plan, San Francisco City Hall Competition 1912

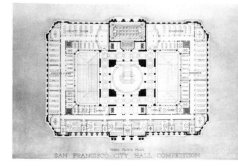

Designed by Arthur Brown, Jr.
Bakewell and Brown, architects.
Ink and wash on paper; 62.0 x 92.0
(24⅜ x 36 ³/₁₆)
Sylvia Brown Jensen, California.

4
Color Study for Lantern of Dome, San Francisco City Hall 1913

Designed by Arthur Brown, Jr.
Bakewell and Brown, architects.
Delineator: Edward L. Frick.
Pencil (?) and watercolor on paper;
96.0 x 46.0 (37 ¹³/₁₆ x 18⅛)
Sylvia Brown Jensen, California.

5
Van Ness Avenue Elevation, San Francisco City Hall 1913
Designed by Arthur Brown, Jr.
Bakewell and Brown, architects.
Ink on linen; 118.0 x 179.0
(46 ⁷/₁₆ x 70½)
Sylvia Brown Jensen, California.
Illustrated on page 74.

6
Details of Rotunda, East and West Elevations, San Francisco City Hall 1914
Designed by Arthur Brown, Jr.
Bakewell and Brown, architects.
Ink on linen; 114.0 x 176.0 (44⅞ x 69¼)
Sylvia Brown Jensen, California.

7
Study for Inspiration Point, Riverside Drive, New York City *circa* 1905
Signed: Arnold Brunner [1857–1925]
and F.L. Olmsted [1870–1957].
Pencil, black ink, yellow wash, and white gouache on gray cardboard;
87.7 x 56.8 (34½ x 22⅜)
Cooper-Hewitt Museum, New York, The Smithsonian Institution's National Museum of Design, Gift of Mrs. Arnold W. Brunner.
Illustrated in color on page 77.

8
View of Courtroom, U.S. Federal Building, Cleveland, Ohio 1917
Arnold W. Brunner (1857–1925), architect.
Pencil on heavy board; 66.5 x 77.1
(26¼ x 30⅜)
Cooper-Hewitt Museum, New York, The Smithsonian Institution's National Museum of Design, Gift of Mrs. Arnold W. Brunner.

9
Ceiling of the Courtroom, U.S. Federal Building, Cleveland, Ohio 1917

Arnold W. Brunner (1857–1925), architect.
Pencil, black ink, and gray wash on white paper; 89.0 x 55.0 (35¹/₁₆ x 21⅝)
Cooper-Hewitt Museum, New York, The Smithsonian Institution's National Museum of Design, Gift of Mrs. Arnold W. Brunner.

10
Facade of a Neoclassic Building in a Plaza. Unknown building for Denver or Cleveland

Arnold W. Brunner (1857–1925), architect.
Pencil and colored chalks on gray-brown paper; 46.3 x 84.0
(18¼ x 33 ¹/₁₆)
Cooper-Hewitt Museum, New York, The Smithsonian Institution's National Museum of Design, Gift of Mrs. Arnold W. Brunner.

11
**Chicago, View Looking West, of the
Proposed Civic Center Plaza and
Buildings, Showing It as the Center of
the System of Arteries of Circulation
and of the Surrounding Country** From
The Plan of Chicago, 1909.
Daniel H. Burnham (1846–1912) and
Edward H. Bennett (1874–1954),
planners.
Rendering by Jules Guerin (1866–1946).
Watercolor on paper; 74.6 x 104.8
(29⅜ x 41¼)
*Burnham Library of Architecture, The Art
Institute of Chicago, Illinois.*
Illustrated on page 20.

12
**Front elevation, 42nd Street Main
Building, The New York Public
Library, New York** 1897–1911
Signed: John M. Carrère and Thomas
Hastings, architects.
Brown ink on white paper mounted on
board; 40.6 x 92.7 (16 x 36½)
*The New York Public Library, Astor, Lenox
and Tilden Foundations.*

13
**Perspective of Bryant Park, N.W.
view, 42nd Street Main Building, The
New York Public Library, New York**
1897–1911

Carrère and Hastings, architects.
Ink on yellow paper; 82.6 x 110.5
(32½ x 43½)
*The New York Public Library, Astor, Lenox
and Tilden Foundations.*

14
**Color Scheme for Temple Israel,
Brooklyn** *circa* 1902

Leon Dabo (1868–1960).
Signed: L. D. and S. Dabo, decorators.
Parfitt Brothers, architects.
Pencil, ink, and watercolor; 75.7 x 55.8
(29 ³/₁₆ x 22)
*Cooper-Hewitt Museum, New York, The
Smithsonian Institution's National
Museum of Design, Gift of Mrs. Leon
Dabo.*

15
**Plan of building group for an urban
square** *circa* 1900
Student drawing made at the École
des Beaux-Arts, Paris, by William A.
Delano (1874–1960).
Black ink and gray wash on paper
(mounted on paper with fragments of
gold border); 92.7 x 73.7 (36½ x 29)
*Avery Library, Columbia University, New
York.*
Illustrated on page 78.

16
**Elevations and sections of building
group for an urban square** *circa* 1900

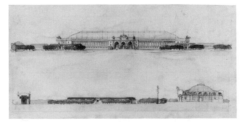

Student drawings made at the École
des Beaux-Arts, Paris, by William A.
Delano (1874–1960).
Pencil and black wash on paper
(mounted on paper with gilt border);
31.4 x 61.9 (12⅜ x 24⅜)
*Avery Library, Columbia University, New
York.*

17
**The Dewey Triumphal Arch and
Colonnade, Madison Square, New
York** 1899
Charles R. Lamb (1860–1942), architect.
Original platinum print; 24.6 x 32.5
(9 ¹¹/₁₆ x 12 ¹³/₁₆)
*Cooper-Hewitt Museum, New York, The
Smithsonian Institution's National
Museum of Design.*

18
U.S. Customs House, New York 1900
Cass Gilbert (1859–1934), architect.
Pen and wash on paper; 62.2 x 86.1
(24½ x 33⅞)
Harold Fredenburgh, New York.

19
**Elevation Art Museum, North Facade,
Expansion Design** 1916
Cass Gilbert (1859–1934), architect.
Graphite and watercolor and
heightening with white; 59.7 x 219.1
(23½ x 86¼)
The Saint Louis Art Museum, Missouri.

20
**Forest Park, St. Louis, Missouri,
Showing Reclamation and
Restoration of World's Fair Grounds
and Museum of Fine Arts** 1916
Drawn by W. P. Foulds.
Cass Gilbert (1859–1934), architect.
Graphite, pen, black and gray ink, and
gray wash; 219.1 x 86.3 (86¼ x 34)
The Saint Louis Art Museum, Missouri.

21
Home of Mutual Life Insurance Co.

Cass Gilbert (1859–1934), architect.
Location of building unknown.
Gouache; 87.0 x 72.4 (34¼ x 28½)
The New-York Historical Society.

22
Washington, D.C.: Bird's-eye view of proposed Union Square (Senate Park Commission's recommendation) *circa* 1902

Rendering by C. Graham.
Watercolor; 75.6 x 130.8 (29¾ x 51½)
U.S. Commission of Fine Arts, Washington, D.C.

23
Rendering of a proposed mausoleum probably intended for the Bliss family, New York City 1901

Hughson Hawley (1850–1936), architect.
Watercolor over pencil on heavy drawing board; 62.8 x 73.4 (24⅝ x 28⅞)
Cooper-Hewitt Museum, New York, The Smithsonian Institution's National Museum of Design, Anonymous Gift.

24
Front elevation of an archives building 1852
Student project by Richard Morris Hunt (1827–1895).
Ink and wash on paper; 64.2 x 96.9 (25¼ x 38⅛)
American Institute of Architects Foundation, Washington, D.C., Prints and Drawings Collection.
Illustrated on page 94.

25
Plan of an archives building 1852
Student project by Richard Morris Hunt (1827–1895)
Pencil, ink, and wash on paper; 98.1 x 66.5 (35⅝ x 26⅛)
American Institute of Architects Foundation, Washington, D.C., Prints and Drawings Collection.
Illustrated on page 95.

26
Section of an archives building 1852
Student project by Richard Morris Hunt (1827–1895).
Ink and watercolor on paper; 61.2 x 99.3 (24 1/16 x 39 1/16)
American Institute of Architects Foundation, Washington, D.C., Prints and Drawings Collection.
Illustrated on page 94.

27
Presentation drawing, front elevation, for William K. Vanderbilt's Marble House, Newport, Rhode Island 1888–1892

Richard Morris Hunt (1827–1895), architect.
Pencil and wash on paper; 24.6 x 46.4 (9 9/16 x 18¼)
American Institute of Architects Foundation, Washington, D.C., Prints and Drawings Collection.

28
Design for the entrance grill, William K. Vanderbilt's Marble House, Newport, Rhode Island 1888–1892
Signed: Richard Morris Hunt [1827–1895], architect.
Ink on paper; 36.9 x 45.3 (14½ x 17½)
American Institute of Architects Foundation, Washington, D.C., Prints and Drawings Collection.
Illustrated on page 145.

29
First Story Plan, William K. Vanderbilt's Marble House, Newport, Rhode Island stamped Jan. 14, 1893

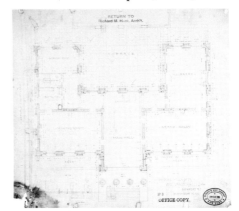

Signed: Richard Morris Hunt [1827–1895], architect.
Pencil, ink, and wash on paper; 42.5 x 47.2 (16¾ x 18 9/16)
American Institute of Architects Foundation, Washington, D.C., Prints and Drawings Collection.

30
Hall section, William K. Vanderbilt's Marble House, Newport, Rhode Island 1888–1892

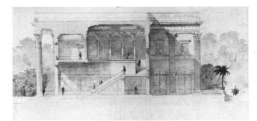

Richard Morris Hunt [1827–1895], architect.
Pencil and wash on paper; 25.2 x 48.7 (9 13/16 x 19 3/16)
American Institute of Architects Foundation, Washington, D.C., Prints and Drawings Collection.

31
Study for the Breakers, Cornelius Vanderbilt II house, Newport, Rhode Island (Venetian version) stamped January 14, 1893
Signed: Richard Morris Hunt [1827–1895], architect, and Jan. 12, 1893
E.L.M. Delineator: E.L. Masqueray.
Pencil and wash on paper; 41.2 x 77.5 (16¼ x 30½)
American Institute of Architects Foundation, Washington, D.C., Prints and Drawings Collection.
Illustrated on page 97.

32
Study for Breakers, Cornelius Vanderbilt II house, Newport, Rhode Island (French Chateau version) stamped Jan. 14, 1893
Signed: Richard Morris Hunt [1827–1895], architect, and December 28, 1892 / E.L.M [E.L.Masqueray].
Pencil and wash on paper; 37.2 x 65.0 (14⅝ x 25⁹/₁₆)
American Institute of Architects Foundation, Washington, D.C., Prints and Drawings Collection.
Illustrated on page 97.

33
Section of Administration Building, World's Columbian Exposition, Chicago, Illinois dated 4/14/91
Signed: Richard Morris Hunt [1827–1895], architect.
Ink and wash on paper; 90.0 x 87.0 (35 ⁷/₁₆ x 34½)
American Institute of Architects Foundation, Washington, D.C., Prints and Drawings Collection.
Illustrated in color on page 104.

34
Police Department of the City of New York, Centre Street elevation 1909

Signed: F.L.V. Hoppin [1867–1941]. Hoppin and Koen, architects.
Ink and pencil on linen; 132.2 x 283.3 (52⅛ x 111½)
Avery Library, Columbia University, New York.

35
Police Department of the City of New York 1909

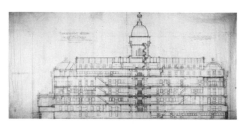

Signed: F.L.V. Hoppin [1867–1941]. Hoppin and Koen, architects.
Black and red ink, gray wash, and pencil on linen; 132.7 x 280.7 (52¼ x 110½)
Avery Library, Columbia University, New York.

36
Washington, D.C.: Bird's-eye view from Arlington (Senate Park Commission's recommendation) 1901
Rendering by Francis L.V. Hoppin (1867–1941).
Watercolor on paper; 86.0 x 181.3 (33⅞ x 71⅜)
U.S. Commission of Fine Arts, Washington, D.C.
Illustrated on page 71.

37
Greek Ionic Order 1896

Signed: M. Katherine Lines [architectural student at Columbia University].
Watercolor on paper mounted on canvas; 85.6 x 59.1 (33½ x 23¼)
Avery Library, Columbia University, New York.

38
Roman Composite Order 1896
Signed: M. Katherine Lines [architectural student at Columbia University].
Watercolor on paper; 52.1 x 71.1 (20½ x 28)
Avery Library, Columbia University, New York.
Illustrated in color on page 93.

39
The Boston Public Library, front elevation *circa* 1888

McKim, Mead and White, architects.
Pencil on paper mounted on cloth; 61.0 x 109.2 (24 x 43)
The New-York Historical Society.

40
Perspective presentation drawing of The Century Club facade 1889

McKim, Mead and White, architects.
Rendering by Francis L.V. Hoppin (1867–1941).
Watercolor and ink; 63.2 x 68.9 (24⅞ x 27⅛)
The Century Association, New York.

41
The Museum of the Brooklyn Institute of Arts and Sciences 1893
McKim, Mead and White, architects.
Rendering by Francis L. V. Hoppin (1867–1941).
Gouache and ink on paper;
62.9 x 166.4 (24¾ x 65½)
The Brooklyn Museum, New York.
Illustrated in color on page 6.

42
Museum Building, Brooklyn Institute of Arts and Sciences, south elevation 1895–1915
McKim, Mead and White, architects.
Ink on linen; 251.8 x 123.2
(138½ x 48½)
The New-York Historical Society.

43
Museum Building, Brooklyn Institute of Arts and Sciences, Section North and South on Axis 1895–1915

McKim, Mead and White, architects.
Ink on linen; 125.7 x 251.8
(49½ x 138½)
The New-York Historical Society.

44
Columns at Plaza Entrance, Prospect Park, Brooklyn, New York 1894
McKim, Mead and White, architects.
Ink on linen; 54.6 x 112.3 (21½ x 44¼)
The New-York Historical Society.

45
Drawing of lamp standard with two globes entitled "Prospect Park [Brooklyn, New York]: Electric Light Standard at Plaza Entrance" 1897
McKim, Mead and White, architects.
Signed: H.D.S [or J].
Ink on linen; 29.2 x 54.6 (11½ x 21½)
The New-York Historical Society.

46
Drawing of lamp standard with single globe entitled "Prospect Park [Brooklyn, New York]: Electric Light Standard at Plaza Entrance" 1897
McKim, Mead and White, architects.
Signed: H.D.S [or J].
Ink on linen; 27.9 x 54.6 (11 x 21½)
The New-York Historical Society.

47
Design for Plaza Entrance, Prospect Park, Brooklyn, New York 1894

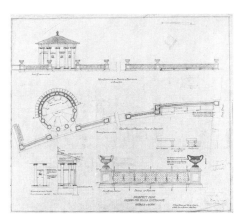

McKim, Mead and White, architects.
Rendering signed: Ives.
Ink on linen; 85.1 x 76.8 (33½ x 30¼)
The New-York Historical Society.

48
Accepted design for the new Rhode Island State Capitol, Providence *circa* 1892
McKim, Mead and White, architects.
Rendering by Hughson Hawley (1850–1936).
Watercolor on paper; 81.3 x 109.2 (32 x 43)
State of Rhode Island and Providence Plantations.
Illustrated on page 53.

49
State Savings Bank, Fort and Shelby Streets, Detroit, Michigan, rendering of front elevation 1898
McKim, Mead and White, architects.
Ink and gouache on paper, linen backed; 54.0 x 33.7 (21¼ x 13¼)
The New-York Historical Society.

50
The Pierpont Morgan Library, New York 1902–1906
McKim, Mead and White, architects.
Watercolor drawing; 78.2 x 119.3 (30 13/16 x 47)
The Pierpont Morgan Library, New York.
Illustrated on page 99.

51
Columbia University, New York 1903
McKim, Mead and White, architects.
Signed: Harry Fenn.
Pen and ink on tracing paper;
41.0 x 60.0 (16⅛ x 23⅝)
Avery Library, Columbia University, New York.

52
Villa Costansi near Rome

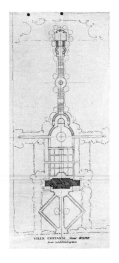

Charles Adams Platt (1861–1933).
Ink and pencil on linen; 52.1 x 23.5 (20½ x 9¼)
Avery Library, Columbia University, New York.

53
Detail of Classical Wall

Charles Adams Platt (1861–1933).
Black chalk (recto only) and colored chalk (recto and verso) on tracing paper; 127.7 x 88.9 (50¼ x 35)
Avery Library, Columbia University, New York.

54
**Untitled view of McCormick house,
Lake Forest, Illinois**
Signed: Charles Adams Platt
[1861–1933], architect.
Drawing by Schell Lewis.
Pencil on tracing paper; 23.5 x 41.2
(9¼ x 16⅛)
*Avery Library, Columbia University, New
York.*

55
**Block Plan of House, Gardens and
Service Buildings, Estate of Harold F.
McCormick, Lake Forest, Illinois,
L19-?** 1912–1913
Signed: Charles Adams Platt
[1861–1933], architect.
Ink and pencil on linen; 130.2 x 89.5
(51¼ x 35¼)
*Avery Library, Columbia University, New
York.*
Illustrated on page 84.

56
**Wrought Iron Entrance Gates, Estate
for H.F. McCormick, Esq., Lake
Forest, Illinois** 1918
Signed: Charles Adams Platt
[1861–1933], architect.
Drawing by Schell Lewis.
Pencil on tracing paper; 40.0 x 73.7
(15¾ x 29)
*Avery Library, Columbia University, New
York.*
Illustrated on page 85.

57
**Presentation elevation of the Bank of
Pittsburgh** 1894
George B. Post and Sons, architects.
Ink and gouache; 73.7 x 106.8 (29 x 42)
The New-York Historical Society.

58 *
**Design for The Library of Congress
Building** 1885
Smithmeyer and Pelz, architects.
Signed: Paul J. Pelz [1841–1918],
delineator.
Colored heliograph with watercolor;
52.0 x 72.0 (20½ x 28⅜)
*The Library of Congress, Washington,
D.C., Architectural Drawings Collection,
Prints and Photographs Division.*
Illustrated on page 105.

59
**View of the Stair Hall, Congressional
Library** 1888

Smithmeyer and Pelz, architects.
Signed: P.J. Pelz [1841–1918],
delineator.
Ink on woven paper backed with linen;
53.1 x 50.3 (20 ¹⁵/₁₆ x 19 ¹³/₁₆)
*The Library of Congress, Washington,
D.C., Architectural Drawings Collection,
Prints and Photographs Division.*

60
**Marble Work, First Story Perspectives
516. The Stair Hall, Building for The
Library of Congress** 1892
Signed: F.C. Sill, delineator. Bernard
R. Green, superintendent and
engineer.
Ink on sized linen; 99.0 x 68.5
(38 ¹⁵/₁₆ x 26 ¹⁵/₁₆)
*The Library of Congress, Washington,
D.C., Central Services Collection.*

61
**Plaster and Stucco Work, Reading
Room and Lantern. No. 615. Elevation
of Reading Room and Dome,
Building for The Library of Congress**
Signed: Bernard R. Green,
superintendent and engineer.
Drawing by E. Schmidt.
Black ink on sized linen; 107.0 x 92.3
(42⅛ x 36 ⁵/₁₆)
*The Library of Congress, Washington,
D.C., Central Services Collection.*
Illustrated on page 100.

62
Copper Gutters, Chateau de Blois 1888

Whitney Warren (1864–1943).
Pencil and watercolor on white paper;
32.0 x 25.0 (12⅝ x 9⅞)
*Cooper-Hewitt Museum, New York, The
Smithsonian Institution's National
Museum of Design, Gift of Mrs. William
Greenough.*

63
**The Loggia del Papa o dei Nobile in
Siena, Italy** 1890
Whitney Warren (1864–1943).
Pencil on white paper; 24.7 x 31.8
(9¾ x 12½)
*Cooper-Hewitt Museum, New York, The
Smithsonian Institution's National
Museum of Design, Gift of Mrs. William
Greenough.*

64
Collage Drawing of Buildings

Warren and Wetmore, architects.
Signed: Vernon Howe Bailey / del.
Black ink, pencil, and gray wash on
paper; 115.6 x 155.6 (45½ x 61¼)
*Avery Library, Columbia University, New
York.*

65
View of the Church of St. Nicholas at Caen, France 1878

Stanford White (1853–1906).
Pencil and watercolor on light cardboard; 30.7 x 42.3 (12⅛ x 16⅝)
Cooper-Hewitt Museum, New York, The Smithsonian Institution's National Museum of Design, Gift of Lawrence Grant White.

66
Untitled drawing. Sketch of house plans
Stanford White (1853–1906).
Pencil (verso) and ink (recto) on paper (stationery of the Grand Union Hotel, New York City); 22.8 x 15.2 (9 x 6)
Avery Library, Columbia University, New York.
Illustrated on page 96.

67
Administration Building Entrance, World's Columbian Exposition, Chicago 1893

Richard Morris Hunt (1827–1895), architect.
Charles Dudley Arnold (b. 1844), photographer.
Platinum print; 47.8 x 41.6
(18 ¹³/₁₆ x 16⅜)
Avery Library, Columbia University, New York.

68
Court of Honor (view from roof), World's Columbian Exposition, Chicago 1893
Charles Dudley Arnold (b. 1844), photographer.
Platinum print; 41.3 x 49.5
(16¼ x 19½)
Avery Library, Columbia University, New York.

69
Court of Honor from Peristyle, World's Columbian Exposition, Chicago 1893
Charles Dudley Arnold (b. 1844), photographer.
Platinum print; 43.2 x 53.8 (17 x 21 ³/₁₆)
Avery Library, Columbia University, New York.

70
Viking Ship and Manufactures Building, World's Columbian Exposition, Chicago 1893
Charles Dudley Arnold (b. 1844), photographer.
Platinum print; 42.1 x 53.3 (16¾ x 21)
Avery Library, Columbia University, New York.
Illustrated on page 14.

71
Columbian Fountain, World's Columbian Exposition, Chicago 1893
Frederick MacMonnies (1863–1937), sculptor.
Charles Dudley Arnold (b. 1844), photographer.
Platinum print; 42.7 x 53.4
(16 ¹³/₁₆ x 21)
Avery Library, Columbia University, New York.
Illustrated page 49.

72
View of Canal with backside of Agricultural and Manufactures Building, World's Columbian Exposition, Chicago 1893
Charles Dudley Arnold (b. 1844), photographer.
Platinum print; 42.2 x 53.1
(16⅝ x 20⅞)
Avery Library, Columbia University, New York.

73
Agricultural Building, World's Columbian Exposition, Chicago 1894
Inscribed: Presented to C.F. McKim, October 25, 1894.
Rendering by Francis L.V. Hoppin (1867–1941).
Gouache on photograph; 33.0 x 75.0
(13 x 29½)
Chateau-sur-Mer, The Preservation Society of Newport County, Rhode Island.

74
The Telephone and the Ticker, study for Manufactures Building, World's Columbian Exposition, Chicago 1891–1892
J. Carroll Beckwith (1852–1917).
Charcoal on white paper; 61.6 x 48.0
(24¼ x 18⅞)
Cooper-Hewitt Museum, New York, The Smithsonian Institution's National Museum of Design, Gift of Carroll Beckwith.

75
Triumphal Bridge, Pan-American Exposition, Buffalo 1901

John M. Carrère, architect.
Charles Dudley Arnold (b. 1844), photographer.
Platinum print mounted on board;
19.1 x 24.5 (7½ x 9⅝)
Avery Library, Columbia University, New York.

76
Graphic Arts Building, Pan-American Exposition, Buffalo 1901
Robert Swaine Peabody (1845–1917), architect.
Charles Dudley Arnold (b. 1844), photographer.
Platinum print; 19.1 x 23.5 (7½ x 9¼)
Avery Library, Columbia University, New York.

77
**Electric Tower at Night,
Pan-American Exposition, Buffalo**
1901

John Galen Howard (1864–1931),
architect.
Charles Dudley Arnold (b. 1844),
photographer.
Platinum print mounted on board;
25.4 x 20.3 (10 x 8)
*Avery Library, Columbia University, New
York.*

78
**The Horticultural Group and The
Temple of Music, Pan-American
Exposition, Buffalo** 1901
Robert Swaine Peabody (1845–1917),
architect. Esenwein and Johnson,
architects.
Charles Dudley Arnold (b. 1844),
photographer.
Platinum print mounted on board;
19.1 x 24.1 (7½ x 9½)
*Avery Library, Columbia University, New
York.*

79
**Interior, The Temple of Music,
Pan-American Exposition, Buffalo**
1901

Signed: Esenwein & Johnson,
architects.
Watercolor on paper; 38.1 x 57.1
(15½ x 22½)
*Buffalo & Erie County Historical Society
Collections, New York.*

80
**Court of Four Seasons,
Panama-Pacific International
Exposition, San Francisco** 1914
McKim, Mead and White, architects.
Rendering by Jules Guerin (1866–1946).
Watercolor; 72.5 x 123.3 (28 ⁹/₁₆ x 48½)
*San Francisco History Room, San
Francisco Public Library, California.*

81
**Arch of the Rising Sun. Rendering of
arch in the Court of the Universe,
Panama-Pacific International
Exposition, San Francisco** 1914
McKim, Mead and White, architects.
Rendering by Jules Guerin (1866–1946).
Watercolor; 106.7 x 91.4 (42 x 36)
*San Francisco History Room, San
Francisco Public Library, California.*
Illustrated in color on page 14.

**Decorative Art: The
Domestic Environment**

Woodwork and Interiors

82 §
Louis XV parlor, G.S. Bowdoin house, New York City
Ogden Codman (1863–1951).
Watercolor on paper; 35.6 x 61.0
(14 x 24)
The Metropolitan Museum of Art, New York, Gift of the Estate of Ogden Codman, 1951.

83 †
Louis XIV bedroom, the Breakers, Cornelius Vanderbilt II house, Newport, Rhode Island 1894
Ogden Codman (1863–1951).
Pencil and watercolor; 35.6 x 61.0
(14 x 24)
The Metropolitan Museum of Art, New York, Gift of the Estate of Ogden Codman, 1951.

84 †
Design for an upstairs bedroom, the Breakers, Cornelius Vanderbilt II house, Newport, Rhode Island 1894
Ogden Codman (1863–1951).
Watercolor on paper; 35.6 x 61.0
(14 x 24)
The Metropolitan Museum of Art, New York, Gift of the Estate of Ogden Codman, 1951.
Illustrated on page 148.

85 †
Bathroom, the Breakers, Cornelius Vanderbilt II house, Newport, Rhode Island 1894
Ogden Codman (1863–1951).
Watercolor on paper; 35.6 x 61.0
(14 x 24)
The Metropolitan Museum of Art, New York, Gift of the Estate of Ogden Codman, 1951.

86 §
Bedroom, the Breakers, Cornelius Vanderbilt II house, Newport, Rhode Island 1894
Ogden Codman (1863–1951).
Watercolor on paper; 35.6 x 61.0
(14 x 24)
The Metropolitan Museum of Art, New York, Gift of the Estate of Ogden Codman, 1951.

87 §
Bathroom, the Breakers, Cornelius Vanderbilt II house, Newport, Rhode Island 1894
Ogden Codman (1863–1951).
Watercolor on paper; 35.6 x 61.0
(14 x 24)
The Metropolitan Museum of Art, New York, Gift of the Estate of Ogden Codman, 1951.

88 †
English Chippendale parlor, possibly F.W. Vanderbilt house, Hyde Park, New York
Ogden Codman (1863–1951).
Watercolor on paper; 35.6 x 61.0
(14 x 24)
The Metropolitan Museum of Art, New York, Gift of the Estate of Ogden Codman, 1951.

89 §
Louis XIV bedroom, F.W. Vanderbilt house, Hyde Park, New York
Ogden Codman (1863–1951).
Watercolor and pencil; 35.6 x 61.0
(14 x 24)
The Metropolitan Museum of Art, New York, Gift of the Estate of Ogden Codman, 1951.

90 †
Parlor, Edgemere, Nathaniel Thayer house, Newport, Rhode Island
Ogden Codman (1863–1951).
Watercolor; 35.6 x 61.0 (14 x 24)
The Metropolitan Museum of Art, New York, Gift of the Estate of Ogden Codman, 1951.

91 †
Interior hall, Edgemere, Nathaniel Thayer house, Newport, Rhode Island
Ogden Codman (1863–1951).
Watercolor; 35.6 x 61.0 (14 x 24)
The Metropolitan Museum of Art, New York, Gift of the Estate of Ogden Codman, 1951.

92 §
North wall of drawing room, Edgemere, Nathaniel Thayer house, Newport, Rhode Island
Ogden Codman (1863–1951).
Watercolor; 35.6 x 61.0 (14 x 24)
The Metropolitan Museum of Art, New York, Gift of the Estate of Ogden Codman, 1951.

93 §
Interior hall, Edgemere, Nathaniel Thayer house, Newport, Rhode Island
Ogden Codman (1863–1951).
Watercolor; 35.6 x 61.0 (14 x 24)
The Metropolitan Museum of Art, New York, Gift of the Estate of Ogden Codman, 1951.

94
Adoration of Saint Joan of Arc 1896

J. William Fosdick (b. 1858).
Wood relief, fire etching; three panels, each 278.8 x 125.7 (109¾ x 49½)
National Collection of Fine Arts, Washington, D.C., Smithsonian Institution, Gift of William T. Evans.

95
Sectional view of the William H. Vanderbilt house, New York City 1879–1881
Herter Brothers (after 1865–*circa* 1900), New York, assisted by Charles B. Atwood (1848–1895), architect.
Illustration from Earl Shinn [Edward Strahan], *Mr. Vanderbilt's House and Collection*, Holland edition (New York, Boston, and Philadelphia, 1883–1884); 24.1 x 32.3 (9½ x 12¾)
The Brooklyn Museum, New York.

96
Staircase, William H. Vanderbilt house, New York City 1879–1881
Herter Brothers (after 1865–*circa* 1900), New York, assisted by Charles B. Atwood (1848–1895), architect.
Illustration from Earl Shinn [Edward Strahan], *Mr. Vanderbilt's House and Collection,* Holland edition (New York, Boston, and Philadelphia, 1883–1884); 29.2 x 22.2 (11½ x 9¼)
The Brooklyn Museum, New York.

97
Drawing room with vista through atrium and picture gallery, William H. Vanderbilt house, New York City 1879–1881
Herter Brothers (after 1865–*circa* 1900), New York, assisted by Charles B. Atwood (1848–1895), architect.
Illustration from Earl Shinn [Edward Strahan], *Mr. Vanderbilt's House and Collection,* Holland edition (New York, Boston, and Philadelphia, 1883–1884); 28.0 x 31.8 (11 x 12½)
The Brooklyn Museum, New York.

98
View in picture gallery, William H. Vanderbilt house, New York City 1879–1881
Herter Brothers (after 1865–*circa* 1900), New York, assisted by Charles B. Atwood (1848–1895), architect.
Illustration from Earl Shinn [Edward Strahan], *Mr. Vanderbilt's House and Collection,* Holland edition (New York, Boston, and Philadelphia, 1883–1884); 27.8 x 33.0 (10¾ x 13)
The Brooklyn Museum, New York.

99
Portion of the conservatory of the William H. Vanderbilt house, New York City 1879–1881
Herter Brothers (after 1865–*circa* 1900), New York, assisted by Charles B. Atwood (1848–1895), architect.
Illustration from Earl Shinn [Edward Strahan], *Mr. Vanderbilt's House and Collection,* Holland edition (New York, Boston, and Philadelphia, 1883–1884); 26.0 x 33.6 (10¼ x 13¼)
The Brooklyn Museum, New York.

100
View in the upper Library, William H. Vanderbilt house, New York City 1879–1881
Herter Brothers (after 1865–*circa* 1900), New York, assisted by Charles B. Atwood (1848–1895), architect.
Illustration from Earl Shinn [Edward Strahan], *Mr. Vanderbilt's House and Collection,* Holland edition (New York, Boston, and Philadelphia, 1883–1884); 28.3 x 22.2 (11⅛ x 8¾)
The Brooklyn Museum, New York.
Illustrated on page 122.

101
Chimneypiece in the library, William H. Vanderbilt house, New York City 1879–1881
Herter Brothers (after 1865–*circa* 1900), New York, assisted by Charles B. Atwood (1848–1895), architect.
Illustration from Earl Shinn [Edward Strahan], *Mr. Vanderbilt's House and Collection,* Holland edition (New York, Boston, and Philadelphia, 1883–1884); 28.5 x 22.5 (11¼ x 8⅞)
The Brooklyn Museum, New York.
Illustrated on page 124.

102
Japanese parlor and lampadaires looking into drawing room, William H. Vanderbilt house, New York City 1879–1881
Herter Brothers (after 1865–*circa* 1900), New York, assisted by Charles B. Atwood (1848–1895), architect.
Illustration from Earl Shinn [Edward Strahan], *Mr. Vanderbilt's House and Collection,* Holland edition (New York, Boston, and Philadelphia, 1883–1884); 23.5 x 28.5 (9¼ x 11¼)
The Brooklyn Museum, New York.

103
Library mantel from John Sloane house, New York City 1882
Herter Brothers (after 1865–*circa* 1900), New York.
Mahogany; 332.7 x 254.6 (131 x 100¼)
The Brooklyn Museum, New York, Gift of Mr. and Mrs. William E.S. Griswold in memory of her father, John Sloane.
Illustrated on page 143.

104
Pair of panels
William Hunt (1842–1931) for Herter Brothers.
Belonged to Frank Hill Smith.
Boxwood; each 102.0 x 10.8 (40⅛ x 4¼)
Museum of Fine Arts, Boston, Massachusetts, Gift of The A.B. Cutter & Co.

105 †
Garland of Flowers and Fruit 1882
Design for decoration on portieres for the Cornelius Vanderbilt II house, New York City.
John La Farge (1835–1910).
Oil, gouache, and wax on paper mounted on canvas; 129.5 x 107.8 (51 x 42 ⁷/₁₆)
The Toledo Museum of Art, Ohio, Gift of Edward Drummond Libbey.

106
Ceres 1883
Augustus Saint-Gaudens (1848–1907).
Holly wood, pear wood, mahogany, mother-of-pearl, copper, and various marbles; 159.4 x 64.2 (62¾ x 25¼)
U.S. Department of the Interior, National Park Service, Saint-Gaudens National Historic Site, Cornish, New Hampshire, Gift of the Trustees, 1979.
Illustrated in color on page 160.

Furniture

107
Dining room armchair from William K. Vanderbilt's Marble House, Newport, Rhode Island *circa* 1890

Jules Allard et Fils.
Gilt bronze, silk, and metallic velvet brocade; 128.3 x 75.6 x 64.8 (50½ x 29¾ x 25½)
Marble House, The Preservation Society of Newport County, Rhode Island.

108
One of a pair of candelabra *circa* 1902

Edward F. Caldwell and Company,
New York.
Marble and gilded brass; height: each
103.9 (40⅞)
The White House, Washington, D.C.

109
Side table 1892
A.H. Davenport and Company
(1880–present), Boston.
Mahogany with satinwood inlay;
71.7 x 99.1 x 45.7 (28¼ x 39 x 18)
*Davenport Memorial Foundation, Malden,
Massachusetts.*
Illustrated on page 148.

110
**Drawing of an upholstered side chair
with the sample of fabric** 1902–1903
A.H. Davenport and Company
(1880–present), Boston, for McKim,
Mead and White.
Ink on paper; 30.5 x 30.2 (12 x 11⅞)
The White House, Washington, D.C.

111
Drawing of a sideboard with eagles
1902–1903
A.H. Davenport and Company
(1880–present), Boston, for McKim,
Mead and White.
Ink on paper; 30.5 x 45.7 (12 x 18)
The White House, Washington, D.C.

112
Colonial Revival mirror 1902

A.H. Davenport and Company
(1880–present), Boston, commissioned
by McKim, Mead and White.
Mahogany veneer and gilded wood;
218.1 x 91.1 (85⅞ x 35⅞)
The White House, Washington, D.C.

113
Sheraton sideboard 1902
A.H. Davenport and Company
(1880–present), Boston, commissioned
by McKim, Mead and White.
Mahogany with satinwood inlay;
142.3 x 246.3 x 71.1 (56¾ x 97 x 28)
The White House, Washington, D.C.

114
Armchair 1902–1903

A.H. Davenport and Company
(1880–present), Boston, commissioned
by McKim, Mead and White.
Oak; 144.2 x 66.0 x 49.2
(56¾ x 26 x 19⅜)
The White House, Washington, D.C.

115
Side chair 1903
A.H. Davenport and Company
(1880–present), Boston, commissioned
by McKim, Mead and White.
Mahogany; 95.3 x 54.6 x 45.4
(37½ x 21½ x 17⅞)
The White House, Washington, D.C.

116
Sideboard *circa* 1875
Herter Brothers (after 1865–*circa* 1900),
New York.
Ebonized cherry; 107.7 x 167.7 x 52.5
(42⅜ x 66 x 16¾)
*The Brooklyn Museum, New York,
H. Randolph Lever Fund.*
Illustrated in color on page 125.

117 †
**Library table from William H.
Vanderbilt house, New York City** 1882
Herter Brothers (after 1865–*circa* 1900),
New York.
Rosewood, brass, and marble;
79.3 x 152.4 x 90.8 (31¼ x 60 x 35¼)
*The Metropolitan Museum of Art, New
York, Mrs. Russell Sage Fund by
Exchange, 1972.*
Illustrated on page 123.

118
**Pair of armchairs from John Sloane
house, New York City** 1882
Herter Brothers (after 1865–*circa* 1900),
New York.
Mahogany; 92.7 x 63.5 x 41.3
(36 x 25 x 16½)
*The Brooklyn Museum, New York, Gift of
Mr. and Mrs. William E.S. Griswold in
memory of her father, John Sloane.*
Illustrated on page 144.

119
Tall clock 1886

E. Howard Watch and Clock
Company, Boston.
Belonged to Grant Goodrich,
Goodrich Steam Service Line, who
was involved in lake shipping. The
firm provided water transport from
Evanston to the World's Columbian
Exposition, Chicago, 1893.
Mahogany; 307.1 x 76.2 x 50.8
(123 x 30 x 20)
*Chicago Historical Society, Illinois, Gift of
the Estate of George D. Goodrich.*

120
Shield-back side chair 1903
L. Marcotte and Company, New York,
commissioned by McKim, Mead and
White.
White wood with gilt;
94.2 x 58.1 x 46.3 (37⅛ x 22⅞ x 18¼)
The White House, Washington, D.C.

121
Armchair 1903

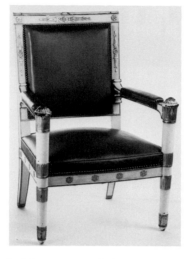

L. Marcotte and Company, New York,
commissioned by McKim, Mead and
White.
White wood with gilt;
107.0 x 74.2 x 58.1 (42⅛ x 29¼ x 22⅞)
The White House, Washington, D.C.

122
Desk *circa* 1910
Designed and decorated by Arthur F.
Mathews (1860–1945) and Lucia K.
Mathews (1870–1955).
The Furniture Shop (1906–1920),
Oakland, California.
Carved and painted wood;
149.8 x 121.9 x 50.8 (59 x 48 x 20)
*The Oakland Museum, California, Gift of
Concours d'Antiques, Art Guild, The
Oakland Museum Association.*
Illustrated on page 151.

123 §
Side chair *circa* 1875
Pottier and Stymus (1858/1859–after
1900), New York.
Walnut with tapestry upholstery;
123.8 x 64.7 x 58.4 (48¾ x 25½ x 23)
*The Metropolitan Museum of Art, New
York, Gift of Auguste Pottier, 1888.*

124 †
Armchair *circa* 1875
Pottier and Stymus (1858/1859–after
1900), New York.
Walnut with tapestry upholstery;
131.5 x 71.1 x 63.5 (51¾ x 28 x 25)
*The Metropolitan Museum of Art, New
York, Gift of Auguste Pottier, 1888.*
Illustrated on page 126.

125
Armchair 1886
John Quincy Adams Ward (1830–1910),
New York.
Oak, originally upholstered in alligator
skin; 151.1 x 70.5 x 64.8
(59½ x 27¾ x 25½)
*The Brooklyn Museum, New York, Gift of
the Honorable E.J. Dimock.*
Illustrated on page 144.

126
Lamp *circa* 1884
Designed by John Williams for
Stanford White.
Presented to Mrs. Grover Cleveland
by Stanford White.
Brass; height: 76.2 (30)
*The White House, Washington, D.C., Gift
of Mrs. T. Dorrington Wadleton.*

127
Armchair *circa 1875*

Possibly New York.
Ebony with marquetry of various
woods, ivory, and mother-of-pearl;
99.1 x 65.7 x 66.5 (39 x 25⅞ x 26⅜)
The Brooklyn Museum, New York,
H. Randolph Lever Fund.

128
Armchair *circa 1875–1876*

Oak and maple; 115.5 x 62.2 x 46.6
(45½ x 24½ x 18⅜)
Museum of Fine Arts, Boston,
Massachusetts, The Arthur Mason Knapp
Fund.

129
Colonial Revival side chair 1889–1891
Oak; 109.5 x 61.9 x 49.5
(43⅛ x 24⅜ x 19½)
The Century Association, New York.

130
Colonial Revival desk from
Kingscote, Newport, Rhode Island
circa 1890

Mahogany with brass;
102.5 x 76.0 x 51.0
(40⅜ x 29 ¹⁵/₁₆ x 20 ¹/₁₆)
Kingscote, The Preservation Society of
Newport County, Rhode Island.

131
Eagle armchair from the Breakers,
Cornelius Vanderbilt II house,
Newport, Rhode Island 1890
Gessoed wood with gilt and paint;
86.0 x 90.0 x 49.0
(33⅞ x 35 ⁷/₁₆ x 19 ⁵/₁₆)
The Breakers, The Preservation Society of
Newport County, Rhode Island.

132
Louis XIV–style armchair from the
Breakers, Cornelius Vanderbilt II
house, Newport, Rhode Island
circa 1895

Gilt and gessoed wood with velvet;
191.0 x 41.0 x 30.0
(75 ³/₁₆ x 16⅛ x 11 ¹³/₁₆)
The Breakers, The Preservation Society of
Newport County, Rhode Island.

133
Armchair from the Harry Harkness
Flagler house, New York City
circa 1905

Maple veneer, birch, and cane;
87.3 x 59.4 x 66.3 (34⅜ x 23⅜ x 26⅛)
Museum of the City of New York, Gift of
Harry Harkness Flagler.

Silver and Gold

134
Six-piece tea and coffee service
circa 1875
J.E. Caldwell and Company
(1839–present), Philadelphia.
Silver; heights: urn with cover, stand,
and fuel lamp: 52.9 (20 3/16); coffee pot:
29.4 (11 11/16); teapot: 28.6 (11¼); waste
bowl: 12.7 (5); sugar with cover: 24.8
(9¾); creamer: 20.6 (8⅛)
The Brooklyn Museum, New York,
H. Randolph Lever Fund.
Urn illustrated on page 116.

135
Loving cup, "Die Meistersinger" 1887
Gorham Manufacturing Company
(1865–present), Providence, Rhode
Island.
Presented to Anton Seidl, conductor of
The Metropolitan Opera, 1885–1891
and 1895–1897, from New York
admirers, February 25, 1887.
Silver; height: 29.2 (11½)
Museum of the City of New York, Gift of
Mrs. Anton Seidl.

136
The Dewey Loving Cup 1898
Designed by William Codman
(working at Gorham from 1891).
Gorham Manufacturing Company
(1865–present), Providence, Rhode
Island.
Presented to Admiral George Dewey
(1837–1917) in commemoration of his
triumphal return from the Battle of
Manila.
Silver on oak base; height: 259.1 (102)
Chicago Historical Society, Illinois, Gift of
George G. Dewey.
Illustrated on page 142.

137
Loving cup with cover 1893
Silver, Howard and Company, New
York.
Presented by the Committee of One
Hundred Citizens of New York to
Daniel Hudson Burnham (1846–1912).
Silver; height: 31.4 (12⅜)
Chicago Historical Society, Illinois, Gift of
the Burnham Family.

138
**Saint-Gaudens Special Medal of
Honor, Pan-American Exposition,
Buffalo** 1901
James Earle Fraser (1876–1953).
Gold; diameter: 8.9 (3½)
U.S. Department of the Interior, National
Park Service, Saint-Gaudens National
Historic Site, Cornish, New Hampshire.

139
**U.S. Twenty-Dollar Coin (Double
Eagle)** 1910
Augustus Saint-Gaudens (1848–1907).
.900 gold; diameter: 3.4 (1⅜)
The Newark Museum, New Jersey, The
Frank I. Liveright Collection.

140
Scepter *circa* 1893

Spaulding and Company, Chicago.
Ivory and gold; height: 34.3 (13½)
Chicago Historical Society, Illinois.

141
Vase *circa* 1874
Tiffany and Company (1853–present),
New York.
Silver-plate; height: 83.8 (33)
The Century Association, New York.

142
Cup *circa* 1885
Tiffany and Company (1853–present),
New York.
Silver, enamel, and semiprecious
stones; height: 15.9 (6¼)
The Brooklyn Museum, New York, The
Alfred T. and Caroline S. Zoebisch Fund.
Illustrated on page 141.

143
Trophy punch bowl 1889

Tiffany and Company (1853–present),
New York.
Inscribed: The Goelet Prize for Sloops
1889. Won by Titania from Bedouin,
Gracie & Katrina.
Sterling silver, gilded inside; height:
30.5 (12)
Museum of the City of New York, Gift of
Mrs. C. Oliver Iselin.

144
Pair of candelabra from dining service
1890
Chrysanthemum pattern patented by
Charles Grosjean, 1880.
Tiffany and Company (1853–present),
New York.
Sterling silver; approximate height:
each 54.6 (21½)
Museum of the City of New York, Gift in
memory of Daisy Beard Brown (Caroline
C. Shults) by her daughters, Bertha Shults
Dougherty and Isabel Shults.

145
Three-handled cup 1899

Tiffany and Company (1853–present), New York.
Presented by President William McKinley to the French Ambassador, M. Jules Cambon, for his services in the negotiation of the Protocol of Peace between the United States and Spain, August 12, 1898.
Silver; height: 34.9 (13¾)
The White House, Washington, D.C.

146
Tray, teapot, creamer, and bowl from a tea, coffee, and chocolate service 1897

Tiffany and Company (1853–present), New York.
Presented to Samuel Sloan, President of the Delaware, Lackawanna and Western Railroad Company, December 25, 1897.
Gold; length of tray: 72.6 (28 7/16); heights: teapot: 19.3 (7⅝); creamer: 12.5 (4 15/16); waste bowl: 10.2 (4)
Museum of the City of New York, Bequest of Katherine Colt Sloan, daughter-in-law of Samuel Sloan.

147
Tray 1904

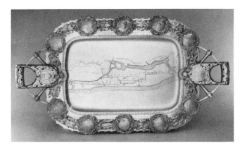

Tiffany and Company (1853–present), New York.
Presented to August Belmont, President of the Rapid Transit Subway Construction Company, by the Rapid Transit Commissioners for the City of New York.
Silver; width: 96.2 (37⅞); depth: 53.7 (21⅛)
Museum of the City of New York, Gift of August Belmont, grandson of August Belmont.

Jewelry

148
Lorgnette *circa* 1905
Cartier, New York.
Platinum and diamonds; 10.3 x 2.5 (4 1/16 x 1)
The Metropolitan Museum of Art, New York, Gift of Miss Susan Dwight Bliss, 1941.

149
Pin pendant *circa* 1900
Florence Koehler (1861–1944)
Sapphires, pearls, emeralds, and enamel on gold; 7.0 x 6.4 (2¾ x 2½)
The Metropolitan Museum of Art, New York, Gift of Emily Crane Chadbourne, 1952.

150
Medal 1889
Designed by Augustus Saint-Gaudens (1848–1907) and modeled by Philip Martiny (1858–1927). Commemorating the centennial of the inauguration of George Washington as the first President of the United States, in New York, April 30, 1789.
Bronze; diameter: 10.6 (4⅜)
The Newark Museum, New Jersey, The J. Ackerman Coles Collection.

151
Medal 1892–1893?
Augustus Saint-Gaudens (1848–1907) and Charles E. Barker (1840–1917). Commemorating the four-hundredth anniversary of the landing of Columbus; issued for the World's Columbian Exposition, Chicago, 1893.
Bronze; diameter: 7.6 (3)
The Newark Museum, New Jersey.

152
Corsage piece 1880–1900
Tiffany and Company (1853–present), New York.
Gold and diamonds; 15.9 x 3.3 (6¼ x 1 3/16)
The Metropolitan Museum of Art, New York, Gift of Miss Susan Dwight Bliss, 1941.

153
Comb *circa* 1910
Tiffany and Company (1853–present), New York.
Tortoiseshell, platinum, and diamonds; 10.0 x 10.3 (4⅛ x 4¼)
The Metropolitan Museum of Art, New York, Gift of Miss Susan Dwight Bliss, 1941.

154 *
Peacock necklace *circa* 1906
Made by Julia Sherman after a design by Louis Comfort Tiffany (1848–1933). Gold with amethysts, opals, sapphires, rubies, pearls, emeralds, demantoids, and topazes; length: 25.3 (10)
The Morse Gallery of Art, Winter Park, Florida.

155 †
Crab necklace 1884
Designed by Stanford White
(1853–1906).
Made by Tiffany and Company
(1853–present), New York.
Designed for Mrs. Stanford White on
the occasion of her marriage, in
Smithtown, New York, February 7,
1884.
Gold with pearl; length: 37.1 (14⅝)
Private Collection.
Illustrated on page 119.

156 §
Bracelet *circa* 1884
Designed by Stanford White
(1853–1906).
Diamonds, rubies, and gold; length:
21.6 (8½)
Private Collection.

157
**Cameo portrait of Jeremiah W. Finch
(1827–1904)**
L. Zoellner.
Cameo with gold frame and diamonds;
5.7 x 4.8 (2¼ x 1⅞)
*The Metropolitan Museum of Art, New
York, Bequest of Helen E. Foulds, 1959.*

158
Brooch *circa* 1910
Diamonds, fresh-water pearls, and
platinum; 6.0 x 2.8 (2⅜ x 1⅛)
*The Metropolitan Museum of Art, New
York, Gift of Miss Susan Dwight Bliss,
1953.*

159
Necklace *circa* 1910
Moonstones, sapphires, and platinum;
length: 68.5 (27)
*The Metropolitan Museum of Art, New
York, Gift of Miss Susan Dwight Bliss,
1953.*

Metalwork

160
Pair of andirons 1903
L. Marcotte and Company, New York.
Gilded brass with cast-iron
reinforcements; each 37.7 x 35.6 x 12.8
(14⅞ x 14 x 4⅞)
The White House, Washington, D.C.

161
Inkwell 1899

E.R. Smith.
Bronze and glass on marble base;
19.1 x 47.9 x 40.6 (7½ x 18⅞ x 16)
*Avery Library, Columbia University, New
York.*

162
Pair of andirons
Possibly designed by Elihu Vedder
(1836–1923).
Iron; each 89.5 x 47.3 x 73.7
(35¼ x 18⅝ x 29)
The Century Association, New York.

163
Lamp post or street lamp late 19th
century

Said to have been designed by
Stanford White (1853–1906).
Stood in front of the house of Abram
S. Hewitt, Mayor of New York,
1887–1888.
Wrought iron and glass with wooden
base; height 388.6 (153)
*Museum of the City of New York, Gift of
Harry Blasof, Inc.*

164
Kiss Tankard *circa* 1899

Enid Yandell (1870–1934).
Bronze; height: 29.6 (11⅝)
*Museum of Art, Rhode Island School of
Design, Providence, Gift of Miss Elizabeth
Hazard.*

165
Pair of wall sconces, from William K. Vanderbilt's Marble House, Newport, Rhode Island *circa* 1890
Gilt bronze; each 41.3 x 24.1 x 15.2 (16¼ x 9½ x 6)
Marble House, The Preservation Society of Newport County, Rhode Island.

166
Gate from the Isaac Vail Brokaw house, New York City 1905
Rose and Stone, architects.
House built *circa* 1887–1888.
Bronze and copper; 181.6 x 110.5 x 3.2 (71½ x 43½ x 1¼)
The Brooklyn Museum, New York, Gift of the Anonymous Arts Recovery Society.

Ceramics

167
Tile before 1893
"Summer" from the Four Seasons Series.
Designed and signed by Herman Mueller (1854–1941).
American Encaustic Tile Company (1875–1935), Zanesville, Ohio.
Earthenware; 30.8 x 45.7 (12⅛ x 18)
New Zanesville Art Center, Ohio.
Illustrated on page 138.

168
Tile before 1893
"Autumn" from the Four Seasons Series.
Designed and signed by Herman Mueller (1854–1941).
American Encaustic Tile Company (1875–1935), Zanesville, Ohio.
Earthenware; 30.5 x 45.7 (12 x 18)
New Zanesville Art Center, Ohio.

169
Vase
Decorated by John G. Low (1835–1907).
Chelsea Keramic Art Works (1872–1889), Chelsea, Massachusetts.
Earthenware; height: 33.3 (13⅛)
Museum of Fine Arts, Boston, Massachusetts, Gift of James Robertson and Sons.

170
Urn *circa* 1904

Empire Pottery, a division of Trenton Potteries Company (1892–1967), Trenton, New Jersey.
Made for the Louisiana Purchase Exposition, Saint Louis, 1904.
Porcelain; 134.6 x 58.4 x 58.4 (53 x 23 x 23)
The Brooklyn Museum, New York, Gift of the Crane Company.

171
Urn in stand *circa* 1890

Hecla Works (1885–1912), Brooklyn, New York.
Ceramic urn, iron stand; overall height: 111.1 (43¾)
The Metropolitan Museum of Art, New York, Edgar J. Kaufmann Charitable Foundation Fund, 1969.

172
Vase *circa* 1895–1900
Knowles, Taylor and Knowles (1888–1898).
East Liverpool, Ohio.
Probably decorated outside factory.
Mark: K. T. K. Co.
Porcelain; height: 24.5 (9⅝)
The Henry Ford Museum, Dearborn, Michigan.
Illustrated on page 137.

173
Fellowship Cup 1897
Sculpted by Clement J. Barnhorn (b. 1857); decorated by W. P. McDonald (1865–1931), Rookwood Pottery (1880–1967), Cincinnati, Ohio.
Presented by the Commercial Club of Cincinnati to the Commercial Club of Chicago on the occasion of their visit to Cincinnati.
Earthenware; height: 37.5 (14¾)
Chicago Historical Society, Illinois.
Illustrated on page 137.

174
Vase 1876
Designed by Karl Mueller (b. 1820), Union Porcelain Works (1861–*circa* 1908), Greenpoint, New York.
Made for and exhibited at the Centennial Exhibition, Philadelphia, 1876.
Porcelain; 56.5 x 25.4 (22¼ x 10)
The Brooklyn Museum, New York, Gift of Carll and Franklin Chace in memory of their mother, Pastora Forest Smith Chace, daughter of Thomas Carll Smith.
Illustrated in color on page 133.

175
Punch bowl with twelve cups, and bronze medal with case from the World's Columbian Exposition, Chicago 1893

Medal awarded to George Leykauf, Detroit, Michigan, for china painting. Porcelain with hand-painted decoration; heights: bowl: 19.8 (7 $^{13}/_{16}$); cups: 6.5 (2 $^9/_{16}$); medal: diameter: 7.1 (3); case: 10.0 x 9.7 (3 $^{15}/_{16}$ x 3 $^{13}/_{16}$)
The Henry Ford Museum, Dearborn, Michigan, Gift of Emma A. Beguhn and Margaret D. Lange.

Glass

176
Compote, "Westward Ho!" (originally "Pioneer") pattern *circa* 1880
James Gillinder and Sons (1861–present), Philadelphia.
Pressed and acid-frosted glass; 29.2 x 22.3 x 14.0 (11½ x 8¾ x 5½)
The Brooklyn Museum, New York.
Illustrated on page 113.

177 †
Punch bowl and six cups 1892
Libbey Glass Company (1888–present), Toledo.
Engraved glass; heights: bowl: 34.3 (13½); cups: 8.6 (3⅜)
The Toledo Museum of Art, Ohio, Gift of the Libbey Glass Company.

178 †
Punch bowl *circa* 1900

Libbey Glass Company (1888–present), Toledo.
Cut glass; height: 32.1 (12⅝)
The Toledo Museum of Art, Ohio, Gift of Mr. and Mrs. Edward G. Kirby, Jr.

179 †
Vase (one of a pair) *circa* 1885

John Liddell, Mount Washington Glassworks (1869–1929), New Bedford, Massachusetts.
Burmese blown glass; height: 37.8 (14⅞)
The Toledo Museum of Art, Ohio, Gift of Alexander K. Liddell and Mrs. Christina Dewar Newth.

180
Vase *circa* 1890–1900

Mount Washington Glassworks (1869–1929), New Bedford, Massachusetts.
Glass; height: 33.6 (13¼)
The Henry Ford Museum, Dearborn, Michigan, Gift of Mrs. Blair T. Alderman.

181 †
Vase *circa* 1883–1888
New England Glass Company (1818–1888), Cambridge, Massachusetts.
Amberina glass; height: 19.7 (7¾)
The Toledo Museum of Art, Ohio, Gift of Marie W. Greenhalgh in memory of Alice Libbey Walbridge and William S. Walbridge.
Illustrated on page 140.

182
Six-piece place setting *circa* 1900

Union Glass Company (1851–1924),
Somerville, Massachusetts.
Glass with gold flecks; heights:
champagne flute: 20.3 (8); stemmed
wine: 15.0 (5⅞); small stemmed wine:
12.7 (5); dessert or champagne: 12.1
(4¾); tumbler: 9.5 (3¾); cordial: 8.5
(3⅜)
*The Henry Ford Museum, Dearborn,
Michigan. Champagne flute given by Mr.
and Mrs. Fotis Takis in memory of Mrs.
Cecil B. Cubbage.*

Stained Glass

183
Lunette-shaped window *circa* 1882

John La Farge (1835–1910).
Stained glass; 76.8 x 160.0 (30¼ x 63)
*The Metropolitan Museum of Art, New
York, Gift of Mrs. Otto Heinigke, 1916.*

184
Infant Bacchus *circa* 1880
John La Farge (1835–1910).
From the Kidder house, Beverly,
Massachusetts.
Stained glass window; 226.5 x 114.0
(89⅛ x 44⅞)
*Museum of Fine Arts, Boston,
Massachusetts, Gift of W. B. Thomas.*
Illustrated in color on page 10.

185
Peony Window 1882
John La Farge (1835–1910).
Made for Sir Lawrence Alma-Tadema.
Stained glass; 160.0 x 113.0 (63 x 44½)
*Museum of Fine Arts, Boston,
Massachusetts.*
Illustrated on page 130.

186
**Project for a stained glass window (for
a Sunday School in Oceanic, New
York)** 1893–1894
Francis L. Lathrop (1849–1909).
Pen and black ink, brown and black
wash, and white gouache on
cardboard; 37.4 x 37.4 (14¾ x 14¾)
*Cooper-Hewitt Museum, New York, The
Smithsonian Institution's National
Museum of Design, Gift of H.A.
Hammond Smith.*

Textiles

187
The Gothic Tapestry 1911
Albert Herter (1871–1950).
Marked: H. L. 1911 Made by Herter
Looms.
Tapestry; 181.6 x 348.2 (71½ x 137 ¹/₁₆)
*Cranbrook Academy of Art Museum,
Michigan.*
Illustrated on page 129.

188 †
Nathan Hale Executed (1776) 1912
Designed by Albert Herter (1871–1950).
Tapestry; 202.0 x 192.3 (84 x 76)
*The Metropolitan Museum of Art, New
York, "A Bicentennial Gift to America
from a Grateful Armenian People," 1978.*

189 §
**Ellsworths New York Fire Zouaves
(1861)** 1912
Designed by Albert Herter (1871–1950).
Tapestry; 202.0 x 144.1 (74 x 60)
*The Metropolitan Museum of Art, New
York, "A Bicentennial Gift to America
from a Grateful Armenian People," 1978.*

190
The Ship *circa* 1913
Albert Herter (1871–1950).
Made by Herter Looms, New York.
Marked: B. R. C.
Made for the Panama-Pacific International
Exposition, San Francisco, 1915.
Tapestry of wool with vertical open
warp design; 297.2 x 148.1 (117 x 58½)
*The Fine Arts Museums of San Francisco,
California, Fine Arts Museums Trustees
Fund.*

191
Embroidered hanging *circa* 1895–1900
Designed by Candace Wheeler
(1828–1923).
Ivory-colored silk woven with raised,
gold-wrapped thread and
embroidered with gold-wrapped
thread and pastel silks; 238.8 x 123.2
(94 x 48½)
*Museum of the City of New York, Gift of
Mrs. George Riggs.*

Wallpaper

Painting

192
Wallpaper fragment from the George T. Bliss house, New York City 1880–1890

Possibly French.
Embossed to simulate leather, backed with muslin; 56.0 x 50.1 (22⅛ x 19⅞)
Cooper-Hewitt Museum, New York, The Smithsonian Institution's National Museum of Design, Gift of Miss Susan Dwight Bliss.

193
Wallpaper fragment 1890–1910
Probably American.
Machine-printed on finely embossed paper; 175.0 x 57.2 (68⅞ x 22)
Cooper-Hewitt Museum, New York, The Smithsonian Institution's National Museum of Design.

194
Boulevard Cafe 1889

Abraham A. Anderson (1847–1940).
Oil on canvas; 94.0 x 128.2 (37 x 50½)
Wadsworth Atheneum, Hartford, Connecticut, Gift of Dr. Eleanor Anderson Campbell.

195
Summer 1890
Frank W. Benson (1862–1951).
Oil on canvas; 127.1 x 101.6 (50 1/16 x 40)
National Collection of Fine Arts, Washington, D.C., Smithsonian Institution, Gift of John Gellatly.

196
The Progress of Civilization: Italy, Germany, and the Middle Ages 1895

Edwin Blashfield (1848–1936).
Oil on canvas: 113.3 x 238.4 (44¼ x 93⅛)
Williams College Museum of Art, Williamstown, Massachusetts.

197
Study for "Washington Laying Down His Command at the Feet of Columbia" 1901–1902
For the Baltimore Courts Building.
Edwin Blashfield (1848–1936).
Oil on canvas; 212.9 x 294.6 (48 x 116)
The Maryland Historical Society, Baltimore, Gift of Mlle A.W.L. Tjarda van Starkenborgh.
Mural illustrated on page 46.

198
**Mural Design for Minnesota State
Capitol, "Peace," or "Abundance"**
circa 1904
Edwin Blashfield (1848–1936).
Oil on canvas; 121.9 x 243.8 (48 x 96)
National Academy of Design, New York.

199
In the Studio *circa* 1880
William Merritt Chase (1849–1916).
Oil on canvas; 71.4 x 101.8
(28⅛ x 40 1/16)
*The Brooklyn Museum, New York, Gift of
Mrs. Carll H. DeSilver in memory of her
husband.*
Illustrated on page 154.

200
**The Bronze Horses of San Marco,
Venice** 1876

Charles Caryl Coleman (1840–1928).
Oil on canvas; 102.0 x 82.5
(40⅛ x 32½)
*The Minneapolis Institute of Arts,
Minnesota, Gift of The Regis Corporation.*

201
Venice 1893

Kenyon Cox (1856–1919).
Oil and pencil on canvas; 77.2 x 153.1
(30⅜ x 60¼)
*Bowdoin College Museum of Art,
Brunswick, Maine.*

202
**Study for frieze "The Common Law,"
the left-hand panel in New York
Appellate Division Courtroom** 1898

Kenyon Cox (1856–1919).
Oil on canvas; 32.0 x 81.5 (12⅝ x 32⅛)
*Cooper-Hewitt Museum, New York, The
Smithsonian Institution's National
Museum of Design, Gift of Allyn Cox.*

203
**Study for frieze "The Statute Law,"
the right-hand panel in the New York
Appellate Division Courtroom** 1898
Kenyon Cox (1856–1919).
Oil on canvas; 31.7 x 81.6 (12½ x 32⅛)
*Cooper-Hewitt Museum, New York, The
Smithsonian Institution's National
Museum of Design, Gift of Allyn Cox.*

204 *
Augustus Saint-Gaudens 1908
Kenyon Cox (1856–1919).
Copy of original destroyed by fire in
1904.
Oil on canvas; 82.5 x 119.0
(33½ x 46⅞)
*The Metropolitan Museum of Art, New
York, Gift of Friends of the Sculptor
(through August F. Jaccai), 1908.*
Illustrated on page 169.

205
On the Heights 1909

Charles C. Curran (1861–1942).
Oil on canvas; 76.5 x 76.5 (30⅛ x 30⅛)
*The Brooklyn Museum, New York, Gift of
George D. Pratt.*

206
Morning 1879
Thomas Dewing (1851–1938).
Oil on canvas; 92.1 x 153.1
(36¼ x 60¼)
Delaware Art Museum, Wilmington.
Illustrated on page 155.

207
The Days 1887
Thomas Dewing (1851–1938).
Oil on canvas; 109.6 x 180.8
(43 3/16 x 72)
*Wadsworth Atheneum, Hartford,
Connecticut, Gift from the Estates of
Louise Cheney and Anne W. Cheney.*
Illustrated on page 47.

208
**William Rush Carving His Allegorical
Figure of the Schuylkill River** 1908

Thomas Eakins (1844–1916).
Oil on canvas; 92.5 x 123.7
(36 7/16 x 48 7/16)
*The Brooklyn Museum, New York, Dick S.
Ramsay Fund.*

209
**Interior of the Artist's Apartment in
Paris**
Walter Gay (1856–1937).
Oil on canvas; 73.0 x 61.0 (28¾ x 24)
*The Pennsylvania Academy of the Fine
Arts, Philadelphia, Presented by Mr. and
Mrs. James P. Magill, 1954.*

210
Woman with Red Hair 1894
Albert Herter (1871–1950).
Oil on canvas; 81.3 x 54.6 (32 x 21½)
National Collection of Fine Arts,
Washington, D.C., Smithsonian
Institution, Gift of Laura Dreyfus Barney.
Illustrated on page 166.

211
Winged Fortune 1878
For mural *Discovery* in the New York
State Capitol, Albany.

William Morris Hunt (1824–1879).
Oil on canvas; 252.7 x 159.4
(99½ x 62¾)
The Cleveland Museum of Art, Ohio, J.H.
Wade Fund.

212
Culebra Cut

Jonas Lie (1880–1940).
Oil on canvas; 127.0 x 152.4 (50 x 60)
The Detroit Institute of Arts, Michigan,
City Purchase.

213
Love Disarmed 1889
Will H. Low (1853–1932).
Oil on panel; 90.2 x 90.2 (35½ x 35½)
The Brooklyn Museum, New York, Dick S.
Ramsay, Graham School of Design, Pratt,
and Smith Funds.
Illustrated in color on page 165.

214
Discovery of the Bay of San Francisco
by Portola 1896
Arthur Frank Mathews (1860–1945).
Oil on canvas; 178.5 x 148.6
(70¼ x 58½)
The Oakland Museum, California,
Collection of John Garzoli.

215
California 1905

Arthur Frank Mathews (1860–1945).
Oil on canvas; 66.0 x 59.7 (26 x 23½)
The Oakland Museum, California, Gift of
Concours d'Antiques, Art Guild, The
Oakland Museum Association.

216 †
May Night 1906
Leonard Metcalf (1858–1925).
Oil on canvas; 100.3 x 92.4
(39½ x 26⅜)
Corcoran Gallery of Art, Washington,
D.C.
Illustrated on page 171.

217
A Handmaid 1886
Francis Davis Millet (1846–1912).
Oil on canvas; 68.7 x 42.2
(27 1/16 x 16⅝)
Graham Williford, New York.
Illustrated on page 158.

218
At the Inn 1886
Francis Davis Millet (1846–1912).
Oil on canvas; 38.1 x 76.2 (15 x 30)
The Union League Club, New York.
Illustrated on page 172.

219
An Autumn Idyll 1892
Francis Davis Millet (1846–1912).
Oil on canvas; 55.7 x 33.6 (21½ x 13¼)
The Brooklyn Museum, New York, Gift of
Michael Friedsam.

220
Study for Ceiling of Gunn Memorial
Library, Washington, Connecticut
circa 1914
Henry Siddons Mowbray (1858–1928).
Oil on canvas; 121.9 x 63.5 (48 x 25)
Henry D. Ostberg, New York.
Illustrated on page 182.

221
Crystal Gazers *circa* 1895
Henry Siddons Mowbray (1858–1928).
Oil on canvas; 35.5 x 15.5 (14 x 6⅛)
Kresge Art Center Gallery, Michigan State
University, East Lansing, Gift of Ransom
Fidelity Co.
Illustrated on page 61.

222
The Theatre at Villa Gori 1903
Illustration for *Italian Villas and Their*
Gardens.
Maxfield Parrish (1870–1966).
Oil on canvas; 43.5 x 29.5 (17⅛ x 11⅝)
Graham Williford, New York.
Illustrated on page 179.

223 †
The New Necklace 1910
William McGregor Paxton (1869–1941).
Oil on canvas; 90.2 x 71.3 (35½ x 28⅛)
Museum of Fine Arts, Boston,
Massachusetts, Zoe Oliver Sherman
Collection.

224
The Attack Upon the Chew House
1898

Howard Pyle (1853–1911).
Oil on canvas; 62.0 x 91.5 (24⅜ x 36)
*Delaware Art Museum, Wilmington,
Howard Pyle Collection.*

225
**Illustration for the cover of "Harper's
Magazine," October 1903**
William C. Rice (1875–1928).
Oil on canvas; 53.5 x 48.5 (28½ x 19⅛)
*National Collection of Fine Arts,
Washington, D.C., Smithsonian
Institution, Gift of Mrs. Melvin S.
Brotman.*
Illustrated on page 179.

226
Edward Robinson 1903
John Singer Sargent (1856–1925).
Oil on canvas; 142.2 x 91.4 (56 x 36)
*The Metropolitan Museum of Art, New
York, Gift of Mrs. Edward S. Robinson,
1931.*
Illustrated on page 31.

227
**Designs in color, "Astarte," for The
Boston Public Library** 1909

John Singer Sargent (1856–1925).
Oil on canvas; 98.0 x 30.5 (38⅝ x 12)
*The Metropolitan Museum of Art, New
York, Gift of Mrs. Francis Ormond, 1950.*

228 †
Angel 1889
Abbott Handerson Thayer (1849–1921).
Oil on canvas; 92.0 x 71.5 (36¼ x 28⅛)
*National Collection of Fine Arts,
Washington, D.C., Smithsonian
Institution, Gift of John Gellatly.*
Illustrated on page 163.

229
The Stevenson Memorial 1903

Abbott Handerson Thayer (1849–1921).
Oil on canvas; 207.2 x 152.6
(81⁹/₁₆ x 60⅛)
*National Collection of Fine Arts,
Washington, D.C., Smithsonian
Institution, Gift of John Gellatly.*

230
La Philtre 1880
Henry O. Walker (1843–1929).
Oil on canvas; 47.0 x 34.9 (18½ x 13¾)
Berry-Hill Galleries, New York.

231
Rome Representative of the Arts or
The Art Idea 1894
Elihu Vedder (1836–1923).
Unfinished study or replica of the large
mural Vedder did for the Walker Art
Gallery, Sculpture Hall, Bowdoin
College, Brunswick, Maine.
Oil on canvas; 74.9 x 140.9
(29½ x 55½)
*The Brooklyn Museum, New York, Gift of
William T. Evans.*
Illustrated in color on page 168.

Sculpture

232
The Singing Boys 1894

Herbert Adams (1856–1945).
Marble relief; 92.1 x 112.3 (36¼ x 44½)
*The Metropolitan Museum of Art, New
York, Bequest of Charles W. Gould, 1932.*

233
La Jeunesse *circa* 1910
Herbert Adams (1856–1945).
Polychrome marble and applewood;
height: 57.1 (22½)
*The Metropolitan Museum of Art, New
York, Rogers Fund, 1911.*
Illustrated in color on page 164.

234
Seated Torso 1881–1895
Paul Bartlett (1865–1925).
Bronze; 33.3 x 12.6 x 17.6 (13⅛ x 5 x 7)
*National Collection of Fine Arts,
Washington, D.C., Smithsonian
Institution, Gift of Mrs. Armistead Peter, Jr.*

235
Lafayette on Horseback
Paul W. Bartlett (1865–1925).
Bronze; 41.2 x 39.4 x 24.1
(16¼ x 15½ x 9½) excluding base
*Corcoran Gallery of Art, Washington,
D.C.*
Illustrated on page 177.

236
Richard Morris Hunt *circa* 1895
Karl T. Bitter (1867–1915).
Marked A.D. 1891 but possibly
executed after Hunt's death in 1895.
Bronze portrait relief; diameter:
61.5 (24¼)
*American Institute of Architects
Foundation, Washington, D.C., Prints
and Drawings Collection.*
Illustrated on page 171.

237
John La Farge
Edith Woodman Burroughs
(1871–1916).
Bronze; height: 41.9 (16½)
The Metropolitan Museum of Art, New York, Rogers Fund, 1910.

238
Arcadia 1888
Thomas Eakins (1844–1916).
Bronze; 30.5 x 63.5 x 5.1 (12 x 25 x 2)
Jamie Wyeth, Pennsylvania.
Painted plaster relief version
illustrated on page 158.

239
The Concord Minute Man of 1775 1889
Daniel Chester French (1850–1931).
Bronze; 83.8 x 36.1 x 48.2
(33 x 14 ³/₁₆ x 18 ¹⁵/₁₆)
*Curator for the Navy, Washington, D.C.
Minute Man* of Concord,
Massachusetts,
illustrated on page 41.

240
Sketch Model of Architecture for Richard Morris Hunt Memorial, Fifth Avenue and 70th Street, New York City 1896–1897
Daniel Chester French (1850–1931).
Plaster; 32.6 x 8.4 x 7.1
(12 ¹³/₁₆ x 3 ⁵/₁₆ x 2 ¹³/₁₆)
*Chesterwood, Stockbridge, Massachusetts,
a property of the National Trust for
Historic Preservation.*

241
Narcissa 1901

Daniel Chester French (1850–1931).
Silver; 32.2 x 13.4 x 9.3
(12 ¹¹/₁₆ x 5¼ x 3 ¹¹/₁₆)
*National Collection of Fine Arts,
Washington, D.C., Smithsonian
Institution, Gift of John Gellatly.*

242
Abraham Lincoln 1912
Daniel Chester French (1850–1931).
Bronze; 95.3 x 31.1 (37½ x 11⅞)
The Newark Museum, New Jersey.

243
"Brooklyn" for Manhattan Bridge 1914
Daniel Chester French (1850–1931).
Plaster; 23.0 x 14.7 x 13.0
(9 ¹/₁₆ x 5 ¹³/₁₆ x 5¹/₈)
*Chesterwood, Stockbridge, Massachusetts,
a property of the National Trust for
Historic Preservation.*

244
Working model for the seated Lincoln for the Lincoln Memorial, Washington, D.C. 1916
Daniel Chester French (1850–1931).
Bronze; height: 82.2 (32⅜)
*The Heckscher Museum, Huntington,
New York.*

245
In Much Wisdom 1902

Charles Allan Grafly (1862–1929).
Bronze; 161.3 x 68.1 x 64.8
(63½ x 27 x 25½) excluding base
*The Pennsylvania Academy of the Fine
Arts, Philadelphia, Gilpin Fund Purchase,
1912.*

246
Elisabeth 1900
William S. Kendall (1869–1938).
Bronze; 38.1 x 26.7 x 20.0
(15 x 10½ x 7⅞)
*National Collection of Fine Arts,
Washington, D.C., Smithsonian
Institution, Gift of Mrs. Pierson
Underwood.*

247
Nathan Hale 1890

Frederick MacMonnies (1863–1937).
Bronze; height: 71.7 (28½)
Princeton University, New Jersey.

248
Pan of Rohallion 1890

Frederick MacMonnies (1863–1937).
Bronze; 76.2 x 20.3 x 20.3 (30 x 8 x 8)
The Newark Museum, New Jersey.

249 *
The Bacchante 1894
Frederick MacMonnies (1863–1937).
Marble; height: 219.7 (86½)
The Brooklyn Museum, New York, Ella C. Woodward Fund.
Illustrated on page 48.

250 ‡
The Bacchante and Infant Faun 1894
Frederick MacMonnies (1863–1937).
Bronze; 86.3 x 27.4 x 36.8
(34 x 10¾ x 14½)
National Collection of Fine Arts, Washington, D.C., Smithsonian Institution, Museum Purchase.

251
The Horse Tamers *circa* 1898

Frederick MacMonnies (1863–1937).
Final sketch model for *The Horse Tamers* at Park Circle Entrance, Prospect Park, Brooklyn, on pedestal by Stanford White.
Bronze; height: 98.0 (38½)
The Art Museum, Princeton University, New Jersey.

252
A Caestus 1883
Charles Henry Niehaus (1855–1935).
Bronze; height: 96.5 (38)
The Metropolitan Museum of Art, New York, Rogers Fund, 1906.

253
Indian Warrior 1898
A. Phimister Proctor
(1862–1950).
Bronze; 101.6 x 76.8 x 40.6
(40 x 30¼ x 16)
Corcoran Gallery of Art, Washington, D.C.
Illustrated on page 178.

254
Panther 1909
Originally modeled 1896–1898.
A. Phimister Proctor (1862–1950).
Reduction from statue standing at Third Street Entrance to Prospect Park, Brooklyn.
Bronze; 29.2 x 9.5 x 31.4
(11½ x 3¾ x 12⅜)
The Brooklyn Museum, New York, Gift of George D. Pratt.

255
Charles F. McKim 1878
Augustus Saint-Gaudens (1848–1907).
Bronze relief; 40.6 x 20.5 (16 x 8 1/16)
The New York Public Library, Astor, Lenox and Tilden Foundations.

256
Actaeon 1881–1882

Augustus Saint-Gaudens (1848–1907).
Painted plaster relief; 160.5 x 64.0 x 9.0
(63¼ x 25 3/16 x 3⅝)
The J.B. Speed Art Museum, Louisville, Kentucky.

257
Kenyon Cox 1888
Augustus Saint-Gaudens (1848–1907).
Bronze relief on original wooden frame; 27.5 x 22.5 x 0.5
(10 13/16 x 8⅞ x 3/16)
Inscribed: Kenyon Cox, painter, in his thirty-third year, Augustus Saint-Gaudens, MDCCCLXXXVIII.
Allyn Cox, Washington, D.C.

258
Mrs. Schuyler Van Rensselaer 1888
Augustus Saint-Gaudens (1848–1907).
Bronze relief; 52.7 x 19.7 (20¾ x 7¾)
The Metropolitan Museum of Art, New York, Gift of Mrs. Schuyler Van Rensselaer, 1917.
Illustrated on page 167.

259
Violet Sargent 1890

Augustus Saint-Gaudens (1848–1907).
Bronze relief; 126.9 x 86.4 x 5.0
(50 x 34 x 2)
National Collection of Fine Arts, Washington, D.C., Smithsonian Institution, Gift of Mrs. John L. Hughes.

260
Four Studies for Negro Soldiers' Heads for Robert Gould Shaw Memorial 1884–1897
Augustus Saint-Gaudens (1848–1907).
Bronze on marble base; overall height: 34.2 (13½)
U.S. Department of the Interior, National Park Service, Saint-Gaudens National Historic Site, Cornish, New Hampshire.
Memorial illustrated on page 174.

261
Diana of the Tower 1899

Augustus Saint-Gaudens (1848–1907).
Bronze; 99.7 x 42.2 (39¼ x 16⅝)
The Cleveland Museum of Art, Ohio, Gift of Mrs. Ralph King, Ralph T. Woods, Charles G. King, and Frances King Schafer.

262
The Puritan 1899
Augustus Saint-Gaudens (1848–1907).
Bronze; height: 77.5 (30½)
U.S. Department of the Interior, National Park Service, Saint-Gaudens National Historic Site, Cornish, New Hampshire.
An illustration of another cast appears on page 173.

263
Model for obverse side of twenty-dollar gold coin, extra high relief version 1907
Augustus Saint-Gaudens (1848–1907).
Plaster; diameter: 30.5 (12)
U.S. Department of the Interior, National Park Service, Saint-Gaudens National Historic Site, Cornish, New Hampshire.

264
Amor Caritas 1898
Augustus Saint-Gaudens (1848–1907).
Gilt bronze relief; 260.3 x 121.9 (102½ x 48)
The Metropolitan Museum of Art, New York, Rogers Fund, 1918.
Illustrated on page 162.

265
"Victory" for General Sherman Memorial, New York 1912
Augustus Saint-Gaudens (1848–1907).
Gilded bronze; height: 102.9 (40½)
U.S. Department of the Interior, National Park Service, Saint-Gaudens National Historic Site, Cornish, New Hampshire.
Version at The Metropolitan Museum of Art illustrated on page 176.

266
Mrs. Stanford White
Augustus Saint-Gaudens (1848–1907).
Bronze relief on oak panel; 49.5 x 26.7 (19½ x 10½)
U.S. Department of the Interior, National Park Service, Saint-Gaudens National Historic Site, Cornish, New Hampshire, Gift of the Trustees.

267
Crucifix, "The Redemption" 1903
John Singer Sargent (1856–1925).
Model for The Boston Public Library.
Bronze; 76.2 x 53.3 (30 x 21)
U.S. Department of the Interior, National Park Service, Saint-Gaudens National Historic Site, Cornish, New Hampshire.

268
George Washington at Valley Forge 1901–1905

Henry Merwin Shrady (1871–1922).
Bronze; height: 65.4 (25¾)
The Metropolitan Museum of Art, New York, Rogers Fund, Charles and Anita Blatt, gift, 1974.

269
Diana 1887
Olin Levi Warner (1844–1896).
Bronze; height: 59.7 (23½)
The Metropolitan Museum of Art, New York, Gift of the National Sculpture Society, 1898.
Illustrated on page 157.

270
Chief Blackbird, Ogalla Sioux
Modeled in 1903, cast in 1907.

Adolph A. Weinman (1870–1952).
Part of a study or an outgrowth of his work *The Destiny of the Red Man* for the Louisiana Purchase Exposition, Saint Louis, 1904.
Bronze; 41.9 x 31.7 x 29.2 (16½ x 12½ x 11½)
The Brooklyn Museum, New York, Gift of George D. Pratt.

271
The Rising Day 1915

Adolph A. Weinman (1870–1952).
Bronze; 144.8 x 135.9 x 43.2 (57 x 53½ x 17)
Corcoran Gallery of Art, Washington, D.C.

272
Descending Night 1915

Adolph A. Weinman (1870–1952).
Bronze; 142.3 x 120.7 x 33.0 (56 x 47½ x 13)
Corcoran Gallery of Art, Washington, D.C.

273
Daydreams 1903
Bessie Potter Vonnoh (1872–1955).
Bronze; 26.7 x 54.0 x 27.9
(10½ x 21¼ x 11)
*Corcoran Gallery of Art, Washington,
D.C.*
Illustrated on page 170.

Works on Paper

274
Merchant of Venice, Act 5, Scene 1
1889
Edwin Austin Abbey (1852–1911).
Pen and ink on paper; 43.9 x 26.1
(17¼ x 10½)
*Yale University Art Gallery, New Haven,
Connecticut, The Edwin Austin Abbey
Memorial Collection.*

275
The Tea Party 1890
Edwin Austin Abbey (1852–1911).
Watercolor and pencil on paper;
38.1 x 73.7 (15 x 29 1/16)
*Yale University Art Gallery, New Haven,
Connecticut, The Edwin Austin Abbey
Memorial Collection.*

276
**Two Figures Study for "Galahad" and
"The Siege Perilous" for the mural
"The Quest for the Holy Grail," The
Boston Public Library** 1892

Edwin Austin Abbey (1852–1911).
Charcoal and chalk on paper;
48.0 x 62.6 (18⅞ x 24⅝)
*Yale University Art Gallery, New Haven,
Connecticut, The Edwin Austin Abbey
Memorial Collection.*

277
**Study for "The Keeper of the Captive
Virtues" for the mural "The Quest for
the Holy Grail," The Boston Public
Library** circa 1895–1900
Edwin Austin Abbey (1852–1911).
Charcoal on bluish gray paper;
61.6 x 48.0 (24¼ x 18⅞)
*Yale University Art Gallery, New Haven,
Connecticut, The Edwin Austin Abbey
Memorial Collection.*

278
**Two studies for girl leaning upon a
pedestal and shown from the back for
the mural "Vintage Festival"**
1895–1898

Robert F. Blum (1857–1903).
Brown and white chalks on gray
paper; 58.0 x 36.7 (23 9/16 x 14 7/16)
*Cooper-Hewitt Museum, New York, The
Smithsonian Institution's National
Museum of Design, Estate of Robert F.
Blum.*

279
**Study for the leader of the procession
for the mural "Vintage Festival"**
1895–1898
Robert F. Blum (1857–1903).
Brown and white chalks on gray
paper; 24.3 x 55.8 (9⅝ x 21 15/16)
*Cooper-Hewitt Museum, New York, The
Smithsonian Institution's National
Museum of Design, Estate of Robert F.
Blum.*

280
**Study for the leader of the procession
for the mural "Vintage
Festival"** 1895–1898
Robert F. Blum (1857–1903).
Crayon on paper; 24.3 x 55.8
(9⅝ x 21 15/16)
*Cooper-Hewitt Museum, New York, The
Smithsonian Institution's National
Museum of Design, Gift of Henrietta
Haller from the Estate of Robert F. Blum.*

281
**Nude study for figure of
"Architecture" for The Library of
Congress Building** 1896
Kenyon Cox (1856–1919).
Graphite on ivory-colored laid paper;
46.0 x 35.0 (18⅛ x 13¾)
*The Library of Congress, Washington,
D.C., Prints and Photographs Division.*

282
**Drapery study for figure of
"Architecture" for The Library of
Congress Building** circa 1896
Kenyon Cox (1856–1919).
Graphite on ivory-colored laid paper,
45.9 x 23.0 (18 1/16 x 9 1/16)
*The Library of Congress, Washington,
D.C., Prints and Photographs Division.*

283
Cathedral at Monreale, Sicily 1902
Cass Gilbert (1859–1934).
Watercolor and pencil on paper;
46.7 x 30.3 (19¾ x 12 15/16)
*National Collection of Fine Arts,
Washington, D.C., Smithsonian
Institution, Bequest of Emily Finch
Gilbert.*

284
**"Anahita," or "The Flight of Night,"
mural for the New York State Capitol,
Albany** 1878
Jane Hunt.
Charcoal on paper on mounting board;
28.0 x 45.0 (11 x 17 11/16)
*The American Institute of Architects
Foundation, Washington, D.C., Prints
and Drawings Collection.*

285
**Design for cover of "The New
Magazine"** 1910–1911
Bancel La Farge (1865–1938).
Pen, blue ink, pencil, blue washes,
and gold paint on paper; 33.8 x 25.6
(13⅜ x 10 1/16)
*Cooper-Hewitt Museum, New York, The
Smithsonian Institution's National
Museum of Design, Gift of L. Bancel
La Farge.*

286
The Ascension 1885–1886
John La Farge (1835–1910).
Sepia on paper; 52.7 x 29.9
(20¾ x 11¾)
Charles Carroll Lee Collection, The
Phillips Library, Mount Saint Mary's
College, Emmitsburg, Maryland.

287
Design for front and spine of
bookbinding for "Spanish Vistas" by
George Parsons Lathrop 1882–1883
Francis L. Lathrop (1849–1909).
Black chalk on paper; 25.0 x 38.6
(10⅞ x 15 ³/₁₆)
Cooper-Hewitt Museum, New York, The
Smithsonian Institution's National
Museum of Design, Gift of H.A.
Hammond Smith.

288
"Renaissance," study for mural at The
Pierpont Morgan Library, New York
City 1904
Henry Siddons Mowbray (1858–1928).
Pencil on paper; 40.8 x 58.5
(16 ¹/₁₆ x 23 ¹/₁₆)
Mrs. Henry S. Mowbray, Connecticut.

289
"The Distribution of the Diplomas of
the Society of the Cincinnati,"
elevation and study for mural in Larz
Anderson house, Washington, D.C.
1909

Henry Siddons Mowbray (1858–1928).
Pencil and watercolor on paper;
29.0 x 49.5 (11 ⁷/₁₆ x 19½)
Mrs. Henry S. Mowbray, Connecticut.

290
The U.S. Fleet Entering Golden Gate,
San Francisco, May 6, 1908
Henry Reuterdahl (1871–1925).
Watercolor on paper; 45.0 x 72.5
(17 ¹¹/₁₆ x 28 ⁹/₁₆)
United States Naval Academy Museum,
Annapolis, Maryland.

291 †
Study for The Boston Public Library
murals, "Ionic Capital"
John Singer Sargent (1856–1925).
Charcoal on paper; 48.0 x 63.0
(18⅞ x 24 ¹³/₁₆)
Museum of Fine Arts, Boston,
Massachusetts, Gift of Miss Emily Sargent
and Mrs. Violet Ormond in memory of
their brother, John Singer Sargent.

292 †
Study for The Boston Public Library
murals, "Sketch for Hell"
John Singer Sargent (1856–1925).
Charcoal on paper; 47.2 x 62.0
(18 ⁹/₁₆ x 24⅜)
Museum of Fine Arts, Boston,
Massachusetts, Gift of Miss Emily Sargent
and Mrs. Violet Ormond in memory of
their brother, John Singer Sargent.

293 §
Study for The Boston Public Library
murals, "Decorative Frieze"
John Singer Sargent (1856–1925).
Charcoal on paper; 61.0 x 40.0
(24 x 15¾).
Museum of Fine Arts, Boston,
Massachusetts, Gift of Miss Emily Sargent
and Mrs. Violet Ormond in memory of
their brother, John Singer Sargent.

294 §
Study for The Boston Public Library
murals, "The Vultures"
John Singer Sargent (1856–1925).
Charcoal on paper; 48.5 x 61.5
(19⅛ x 24 ³/₁₆)
Museum of Fine Arts, Boston,
Massachusetts, Gift of Miss Emily Sargent
and Mrs. Violet Ormond in memory of
their brother, John Singer Sargent.

295
Design for cover of "Scribner's
Magazine," December 1893
Stanford White (1853–1906).
India ink and pencil on yellow paper;
24.8 x 18.1 (9¾ x 7⅛)
Avery Library, Columbia University, New
York.

296
Design for cover of "Scribner's
Magazine," December 1893
Stanford White (1853–1906).
India ink, pencil, and gold paint on
yellow paper; 25.3 x 18.1 (10 x 7⅛)
Avery Library, Columbia University, New
York.

297
The Cathedral of Laon (France)
Stanford White (1853–1906).
Watercolor on paper; 35.6 x 45.7
(14 x 18)
Private Collection.

298
One-Dollar Note
Designed by Will H. Low (1853–1932).
Printed on paper; 18.7 x 8.0 (7⅜ x 3⅛)
The National Numismatic Collections at
the Smithsonian Institution, National
Museum of History and Technology,
Washington, D.C.
Drawing illustrated on page 178.

299
Two-Dollar Note
Designed by Edwin Howland
Blashfield (1848–1936).
Printed on paper; 18.7 x 8.0 (7⅜ x 3⅛)
The National Numismatic Collections at
the Smithsonian Institution, National
Museum of History and Technology,
Washington, D.C.

300
Five-Dollar Note
Designed by Walter Shirlaw
(1838–1909).
Printed on paper; 18.8 x 8.1
(7 ⁷/₁₆ x 3 ³/₁₆)
The National Numismatic Collections at
the Smithsonian Institution, National
Museum of History and Technology,
Washington, D.C.

301
One-Hundred–Dollar Note
Designed by Kenyon Cox (1856–1919).
Printed on paper; 19.0 x 8.0 (7½ x 3⅛)
The National Numismatic Collections at
the Smithsonian Institution, National
Museum of History and Technology,
Washington, D.C.
Drawing illustrated on page 19.

Acknowledgments

To undertake a project of the magnitude and complexity of *The American Renaissance: 1876–1917* requires the support and energy of many people. A special thanks goes to the lenders to the exhibition, without whose cooperation the show would not have been possible. Grateful acknowledgment is also made to Donald C. Peirce, Hope Alswang, Celestina Ucciferri, Eleanor Moretta, and Robert Ferguson of The Brooklyn Museum, who have borne the responsibility of organizing the myriad of details connected with the exhibition and the book, and to the many other staff members of the Museum who have contributed to the project. Finally the authors wish to thank all who have so generously shared their knowledge, time, and encouragement.

For extra time, courtesies, and patience, we thank the following:

Micki Appel *The Henry Ford Museum.*
Trudy Baltz
Barry Baragwanith *Museum of the City of New York.*
Roger M. Berkowitz *The Toledo Museum of Art.*
Sherry Birk *American Institute of Architects Foundation.*
Marilynn Johnson Boardes *The Metropolitan Museum of Art.*
Jeffrey Brown
Doreen Bolger Burke *The Metropolitan Museum of Art.*
Xenia Cage *Cooper-Hewitt Museum.*
Michael Carrigan *The Library of Congress.*
John Cherol *Preservation Society of Newport County.*
Robert Judson Clark *Princeton University.*
Stiles T. Colwill *The Maryland Historical Society.*
Helen Cooper *Yale University.*
Allyn Cox
Phillip Curtis *The Newark Museum.*
Sharon Darling *Chicago Historical Society.*
Joan Darragh
Mark Davis
Elaine Evans Dee *Cooper-Hewitt Museum.*

John Dobkin *National Academy of Design.*
David Donaldson *The Morse Gallery of Art.*
Erin Drake *The New-York Historical Society.*
John H. Dryfhout *Saint-Gaudens National Historic Site.*
Alastair Duncan *Christie, Manson and Woods International, Inc.*
John Gray Faron *Cain, Farrell and Bell.*
Susan Ganelin *American Institute of Architects Foundation.*
John Gerard *Cranbrook Academy of Art Museum.*
Terree Grabenhorst-Randall
James Gregory *The New-York Historical Society.*
Susan Harrison *The University of Virginia.*
Stephen Harvey
Sue Haslett *The Metropolitan Museum of Art.*
James Berry Hill
Ward Hill *The University of Virginia.*
Barbara Hopp *J. and R. Lamb Studios, Inc.*
Cindy Hunt *The Fine Arts Museums of San Francisco.*
William Hutton *The Toledo Museum of Art.*
Mary Ison *The Library of Congress.*
Helena Johnson
Susan Johnson *Museum of Art, Carnegie Institute.*
Harvey Jones *The Oakland Museum.*
Mary Alice Kennedy *The New-York Historical Society.*
David Kiehl *The Metropolitan Museum of Art.*
Margaret Knowland *The Metropolitan Museum of Art.*
Sue Kohler *U.S. Commission of Fine Arts.*
Jack McCullough
Dr. Carol E. Macht *The Cincinnati Art Museum.*
Hugh F. McKean *The Morse Gallery of Art.*
Gail Marciano *The New-York Historical Society.*
James Maroney
Rita Mead
Pauline Metcalf
Christopher Monkhouse *Museum of Art, Rhode Island School of Design.*
Betty C. Monkman *The White House.*

Mrs. Henry S. Mowbray
Pat Murphy *The University of Virginia.*
Christina H. Nelson *The Henry Ford Museum.*
George Neubert *The Oakland Museum.*
Edward Nygren *Corcoran Gallery of Art.*
Janet Parks *Avery Library, Columbia University.*
C. Ford Petris *The Library of Congress.*
Buford L. Pickins *Washington University.*
Dr. Adolf Placzek *Avery Library, Columbia University.*
Geoffrey Platt
Barbara Pollard
Anne-Imelda M. Radice *Office, Architect of the Capitol, Washington, D.C.*
Nancy Rivard *The Detroit Institute of Arts.*
Arthur Rosenblatt *The Metropolitan Museum of Art.*
Guy St. Clair *The Union League Club.*
Donald Samick *J. and R. Lamb Studios, Inc.*
Barea Lamb Seeley
Jan Seidler *Museum of Fine Arts, Boston.*
Wendy Shadwell *The New-York Historical Society.*
Lewis Sharp *The Metropolitan Museum of Art.*
Diane Solomon *The Metropolitan Museum of Art.*
Margaret Stearns *Museum of the City of New York.*
Donald Stover *The Fine Arts Museums of San Francisco.*
Kenneth R. Trapp *The Cincinnati Art Museum.*
William H. Truettner *National Collection of Fine Arts.*
Mr. and Mrs. Vincent Villard
William Voekle *The Pierpont Morgan Library.*
Dr. Katherine J. Watson *Bowdoin College Museum of Art.*
Sarah B. Webster
Barbara Weinberg *City University of New York.*
Heber Wells *Davenport Memorial Foundation.*
Robert White
Graham Williford
Walter Zervas *The New York Public Library.*
John Zukowsky *Burnham Library of Architecture, The Art Institute of Chicago.*

Index to Lenders